COUNTRY
FABRIC
SCRAP CRAFTS

by
Marti Michell

SEDGEWOOD® PRESS
NEW YORK

For Sedgewood® Press:
Director: Elizabeth P. Rice
Editorial Project Manager: Connie Schrader
Project Editor: Bob Oskam
Production Manager: Bill Rose

Photographs by Bread and Butter Studio, Atlanta, Georgia
Photo Stylings by Marti Michell and Mary Frances Hebert
Illustrations by Ann Davis Nunemacher

Copyright © 1990 by Marti Michell

Distributed by Meredith Corporation
ISBN: 0-696-02329-6
Library of Congress Catalog Card Number: 88-062601
Printed in the United States of America
10 9 8 7 6 5 4 3 2 1

Design by Stanley S. Drate, Folio Graphics Company, Inc.
Packaged by Rapid Transcript, a division of March Tenth, Inc.

Contents

Acknowledgments

First, may I thank Sedgewood Press and its entire staff for their confidence in my work and for their encouragement.

While the concept for each design started with me, the projects would not have been completed without the talent and sewing skills of Ann Cookston, Martha Dudley, Ann Nunemacher, and Camellia Pesto. Ann Davis Nunemacher carefully planned and beautifully executed the illustrations. Special thanks to Pat Wilens, who helped me meet one otherwise impossible deadline, and to Pat Van Note, who is always available to cheer me on when I need it most!

After the projects and manuscript were completed, Connie Schrader patiently and efficiently guided me through the continuing steps, and Bob Oskam meticulously edited copy. Mary Frances Hebert dropped everything to help me style the photographs, and Steve Rucker and his assistants kept us moving efficiently at Bread and Butter Studio.

Before this sounds too much like an Oscar acceptance speech, special thanks and love to my Mom and Dad, my husband, Dick, and our children.

Marti Michell

Dear Scrap Crafter:

This book was created for fabric lovers and fabric collectors. Whether you're a beginner or expert sewer, you'll have fun making the projects in Marti Michell's *Country Fabric Scrap Crafts.* These exciting new projects for home-decorating and gift-giving will provide scores of opportunities for using the many fabrics you've collected and treasured over the years.

Brimming with forty-three full-color photographs, scores of line drawings, and many full-size patterns, this book captures Marti Michell's unique talent for combining wonderful patterns and colors into appealing projects. Since 1982, when Sedgewood® Press started its publishing program, we've tried to bring you the best in craft books. We hope we've succeeded, and that *Country Fabric Scrap Crafts* will bring you many hours of crafting enjoyment.

Sincerely yours,
Connie Schrader
Editorial Project Manager

Introduction:
The Many Looks of
Country

"Country" means different things to different people. It is comfortable, simple, not too sophisticated, compatible in the eclectic sense with almost any style, reminiscent, retrospective, from the heart! Perhaps most importantly, it is a tangible link with our past.

Just as beauty is in the eye of the beholder, so too is country. Because it is so subjective, a description of my interpretation should help define this book. There are several kinds of country in decorating circles. In general, this book will delve into what I call "Prairie country" or "turn-of-the-century"—more primitive country feelings. Darker colors are prevalent, simple trims, lots of muslin, smaller prints, etc. Twig furniture, homespun and woven coverlets, stenciling, simple furniture with milk paint colors, baskets, hooked rugs, and folk art items all belong to this look. My favorite kind of country has definite historic references. Many people who decorate in this style enjoy mixing their handmade craft items with actual antiques or, next best, authentic reproductions.

I admit to being greatly influenced by all of the Laura Ingalls Wilder books. When I was in the fourth and fifth grades, my teacher read aloud after lunch each day. She selected the first book, *Little House in the Big Woods,* but we were fascinated and eager to follow as Laura and her family went on to *The Little House on the Prairie* and *The Banks of Plum Creek.* In fact, we wrote letters to Laura Ingalls Wilder, who was then living in Missouri, a neighboring state. Before long, my teacher was corresponding regularly and calling this famous author by her first name. "I got a letter from Laura today," she would say. We were so impressed. Laura, undoubtedly, was a role model before we even knew what that phrase meant.

Many motifs or items have become almost symbolic of country—synonymous symbols you might say. Things like quilts, Americana and patriotic items, sewing accessories, teddy bears, dolls and their accessories, old tools and cooking utensils, baskets and braided rugs, and, of course, hearts. Most of the projects in this book are inspired by them and will probably fit into several of the collections you already have. Forgive my presumption, but every person I know who loves country is also a collector. My favorite explanation of a collection goes like this: "One of something is unique, two is a pair, and three is a collection."

While some of the turn-of-the-century looks of the Victorian Crazy Quilt Period and the heavy fabrics and trims might creep into the country look, it is typically kept in the area called Victorian and not country.

The country look of the 1920s and 1930s moves into a whole new pastel color palette. People talk about "that Depression green," and anyone who has ever seen a Grandmother's Flower Garden quilt knows what color they mean. There are lots of creamy yellows, all shades of lavender, and, of course, blues and pinks. There is more white used with these colors, and more embroidery, more sophisticated trims.

The country look of the 1940s and 1950s is beginning to evolve, if only in the eclectic sense. A few special items from that period have not only been favored with becoming collectible, but are also being reproduced.

Another look that is called country is more what I would describe as romantic country or European country. It is the white wicker and floral chintz look. It is typically more elegant and encompasses the English country, French country, and Gatsby looks.

The country look of the American West and Southwest is very unique, with desert colors and authentic cowboy, Native American, Mexican, and Spanish influences.

A look sometimes called country but that I differentiate as "Li'l Abner country" is epitomized by the use of misspelled words, red bandanas, and denim and is not to be confused with the country look in this book.

There is another type of country that is very popular right now—what I would call "too cute country." It is exemplified by cute sayings and lots of farm animals and is very commercial but has little or no basis in "how it really was." Cute is great, but too cute can be dangerous. Walking the fine line between "sweet cute" and "terminally cute" is one of the objectives of this book.

My personal favorite is "eclectic country," so anything may creep into this book, but the emphasis will be the Prairie country look.

This book emphasizes country fabric crafts. In my opinion, there is a special relationship between fabric and "country." Some of American women's earliest opportunities for self-expression came from the same situation that was one of their burdens, providing clothing and bedding for the family.

"I made quilts as fast as I could to keep my family warm and as pretty as I could to keep my heart from breaking."

—*Pioneer woman's diary*

Collecting, Selecting, and Treating Materials for Country Fabric Scrap Crafting

If you sew, you probably already have many materials you can use in these projects. I know I'm not the only person who has ever moved, and I doubt that I'm the only one to move boxes of fabric. But I may be the only person to admit in writing that I have moved boxes of scraps. If you, too, have moved scraps, then you understand there are few experiences that compare with the great feeling of personal accomplishment when you finally use some of those scraps. It's pleasing to use fabric you've bought speculatively, but it's really exciting to untie and unroll the scraps from cuttings and actually use them.

"How Much Fabric Do I Need?"

This is probably the question most often asked by sewers.

In the spirit that (a) this is a book of projects that really can be made from scraps, (b) scraps often come in odd sizes, and (c) most people don't want to measure odd-shaped scraps, but will instead just lay the pattern on the fabric and "see if there's enough," the only fabric requirements listed are those that require more than ¼ yard to make as shown. Fabric requirements are also listed if the lengthwise measurement is more than 9 inches.

Finished measurements for each project are given. They are good clues to fabric requirements. Of course, looking at the full-size pattern is the best clue as to whether you do or don't have enough fabric.

Necessary notions, including batting and loose fill, are listed even though many of them are also in the scrap category.

Country Fabrics

It takes a little practice to select fabrics that look country. It takes even more to combine prints and textures if you aren't accustomed to doing so. Here are some tips for selecting and using country-looking fabric from your scrap bag or the store.

● Types of fabrics that are associated with country are broadcloth, muslin, denim, corduroy, gingham, plaids, calico and country prints, even dark woolens. Because man-made fibers are a relatively recent addition to our lives, most country fabrics are natural fibers. Occasionally a good imposter can slip through.

● Scale of design is important. While all sizes of fabric designs have always been available, most people think "small prints" when they are thinking country, so it may be easier to project a country look with a good selection of small prints. This is also helpful because many of the projects are small. Don't overdo on tiny. Remember variety. Putting several designs together, especially contrasting designs (geometric versus little floral, for example), is very effective.

● Colors for the typical Prairie look are also thought to be more somber. Also, prints with only two colors per fabric were much more common years ago, and they were often black or another dark color printed on top of a dyed color, an omission of color in the roller to develop a white pattern, or a pattern of two colors printed on a white background.

When trying to reproduce the country look, it is very popular right now to stain and overdye fabrics to make them look old.

● Light, medium, and dark are often more important distinctions than color. Many country fabric craft items develop the special country look because they are made from scraps. When selecting a group of fabrics to work with, good selections of light, medium, and dark are usually more important than matching. If you match too carefully, you will lose the contrast of the fabrics and the scrap look.

● Specific motifs can be meaningful—for example, cows in a print are country; Art Deco motifs typically would be distracting. Substituting an all-over small-heart fabric for a plain polka dot will give a more country look. Teddy bears and duck decoys and watermelon are all motifs that are linked to country.

Country Fabrics That You May Not
Think Of as Country

- *Woven kitchen towels.* Towels for drying dishes were almost always natural fibers. They often were a woven check that could make a nice stuffed toy or pillow background.
- *Chenille bedspreads.* These were prominent in the late 1930s through the early 1960s. My favorite choice for best use of a chenille bedspread is to make a wonderful stuffed rabbit. But I've also seen clothes, pillows, and other animal items that did real justice to chenille.
- *Old neckties.* An obvious use for old neckties is being made into such items as pillows and Christmas stockings for men and boys. But don't forget daughters and granddaughters also cherish items made from a father's or grandfather's neckties. When working with neckties, remember that many are not really washable. Test small pieces and remember to care for the finished items accordingly.
- *Burlap.* Burlap bags say country. They add wonderful texture to the surfaces of many projects. A fringed burlap edge can add just the right detail.
- *Other feed bags.* Bags printed with real names and brand identification were commonly used as quilt linings, curtains for the hired hand, etc. Fabric was fabric and it cost money; if you could substitute something that was free, you did. You can imagine the appeal of feed bags printed with designs suitable for quilts and dresses. Both real and replica feed bags are available.
- *Ticking.* Ticking has been available for many years and was a commonly used fabric.

All of the above are things that were commercially machine-made as opposed to the handmade or hand-decorated items discussed next. They can make wonderful stuffed toys, pillows, basket linings, backgrounds for appliqué, to mention a few. Yet they all accurately convey the mood of the times in which they were originally made.

Fabrics That Probably Aren't Scrap
Crafting Fabrics

There are many obvious fabrics, like those featuring fluorescent colors and surfing prints, that you will not want to include in these projects. You might think gold lamé would never fit into country, but that is not so clear. I have a friend who regularly uses gold and glitter on her country Christmas decorations, and they are stunning! The distinction among fabrics I really want to discuss is more subtle. The fabrics I feel are particularly unsuited to use in country scrap crafts are fabrics that have the added value of handwork.

The Golden Rule of Handwork Preservation

Attractive items made by cutting up antique quilts and other needlework are common in magazines and gift shops and are almost always very appealing. However, most current needleworkers agree that educating people to preserve these handmade items is important. After all, think whose work will be getting cut up one hundred years from now. Generally, if you are a weaver, you are more concerned about preserving hand-woven items than embroidery. Similarly, quilters get most vociferous about quilts. But for *all* handwork items that reflect many hours of a person's life, consider the Golden Rule of Handwork Preservation: *Before cutting into any handmade item, imagine how you would feel if you had made the quilt or lace or done the embroidery and someone else were now cutting it up.* If **you** had made the item and wouldn't want it cut, surely you shouldn't cut it up.

Another rule is that unless you are very knowledgeable, get an opinion from someone who is sufficiently knowledgeable to determine if there is any historic reason to preserve the quilt or other item in its present condition.

Occasionally, it is obvious that a face-lift would be the kindest thing for a quilt or other piece of handwork. For example, you can improve the reputation of the needleworker by using the special parts of a quilt and eliminating badly worn sections, severe stains, or just poor quality. The remaining part becomes a tribute to the maker and a more pleasant piece for you.

It is also important to think of emotional issues. Unless an item is unbelievably unique or valuable, it is probably more important to cut a quilt and make one pillow each for twenty grandchildren than for one child to inherit exclusively. A bit of a lace handkerchief included in a heart pendant for every girl in the family is more meaningful than a handkerchief tucked away in someone's drawer.

So remember, quilts and other handworked or decorated textiles aren't just ordinary fabric. At the risk of editorializing, I believe that most people do handwork as an expression of love and as an extension of themselves. We are caretakers of both the item and the maker's time. It is up to us to make the best decisions we can about end use.

Quilt Tops and Blocks

Old patchwork blocks and completed quilt tops fall somewhere between readily usable and unusable fabric. Each requires separate scrutiny.

Many old quilt tops are still tops and not quilts because they weren't as attractive as the ones our ancestors chose to complete. Sometimes they were poorly made and the original maker was dissatisfied. They were not going to quilt flat, or maybe the colors didn't work. Then, as now, there was a limited time to quilt, so the obvious thing was to quilt the best and easiest. It makes sense that a lesser-quality quilt top might be seen in a better light if someone turns it into a jacket or an elaborate Christmas stocking.

Many of the items can be used decoratively in their incomplete stage. I've seen quilt tops attractively arranged on old expandable clothes-drying racks and stacked on shelves or in a chifforobe near the quilt frame.

Some of my friends are fanatical about preserving quilts or quilt tops exactly as they are found. My position is more moderate. There is no doubt that some quilt tops warrant being preserved exactly as they are, but I also believe that part of the tradition of quilt making is that quilts are passed on in all stages of completion. If you're lucky, you'll inherit fabric, pieced blocks, quilt tops, and quilts—both brand-new and practically "used up." Observations of fabrics in quilts lead us to believe that many antique quilts were pieced at one time and quilted many years later, most likely by subsequent generations of quilters. The process can be compared to sourdough bread—you always keep a bowl of starter for the next batch of bread. Old quilt tops, blocks, and fabrics should, in my opinion, generally be considered starter for the next batch of quilts in the next generation. If in doubt, seek a second opinion. The "Patchwork Projects" chapter incorporates many ideas for using quilt blocks, old or new.

Helping Fabrics Look Old, or "Instant Antiques"

My favorite technique for achieving the quilt look in a finished project without sacrificing a quilt is string quilting. (See **String quilting** in the "Fabric Craft Basics" chapter.) The result is a cross between precise patchwork and Victorian Crazy Quilts. It is especially nice because it's adaptable to almost any shape or object. It is not necessary to select and/or develop an appropriate patchwork pattern.

Making new patchwork is, of course, another logical way to save old quilts. Think before sewing. If you are going to make itsy-bitsy rabbits, itsy-bitsy patchwork pieces will look best. Look back at the charming pictures that started you thinking, and you'll see that very few cut-up items need intricate piecing. Think ahead and take advantage of quick piecing techniques and rather simple patchwork patterns. Don't make more patchwork than you need. In reality you are making yardage, so determine the best layout for the pattern pieces. It is possible that 45-inch-wide fabric would be wasteful and 38-inch-wide would be perfect. You are making the fabric; you can make it 38 inches wide. If you do make more patchwork fabric than you need, learn to make little things like heart sachets and Christmas tree ornaments from the scraps. Sew the scraps back together and make bigger pieces. This patchwork yardage can be made from old fabric, if you are lucky enough to have any, or from new fabric.

In addition to the way the fabrics are selected and sewn, there are physical methods for making fabrics look old. Any of these techniques can be used on yardage or new patchwork.

• *Tea dyeing.* Tea dyeing or staining is very popular right now, and it is exactly what its name states. Many people feel that the faint stain of tea gives fabrics an aged look. In country fabric craft circles, there are recipes for tea dye, instructions for tea dyeing in your microwave, tips on which teas have rose overtones, and methods for spotting and staining with tea. You can use coffee as well as tea to "age" a fabric.

Tea dyeing is not something I particularly recommend, but when necessity calls, I have been known to indulge in the practice. There are several reasons I prefer not to tea dye. In spite of the fact that we call it stained, if the finished project is to be a washable item, the color will lighten with every wash. While most teas don't leave much odor, the instant coffee that I have used to achieve a more golden color leaves a definite aroma. There is some question, too, about the long-term effects of the tea's acids on the fibers. Moreover, if you need very much fabric or if you later need more, consistency is hard to achieve. I do tea dye on occasion when I'm working on something small, because tea dyeing is quick, requires no special equipment, and gives me the effect I need.

So when you must, there are a few obvious pointers: The stronger the tea or coffee, the darker the stain. To a degree, leaving the fabric in longer can get a darker look. Different teas and coffees give different colors—pretest before you do the whole piece. Sprinkling dry instant granules on wet fabric can give some very interesting spotted stains. Likewise, drying slightly wadded fabric in the microwave or bright sun will cause it to stain and spot, if that is the desired look.

• *Real dye—overdyeing prints, etc.* Overdyeing gives more controllable results and has the advantage of making possible a wide range of colors. The best results will be achieved by using cold-water fiber-reactive dyes on 100 percent cotton fabrics. There are many old-looking shades besides the light tan color of tea, and the only way to achieve those colors is with dye. The very readily available all-purpose dye is okay if the end product will not be used much or washed many times or put in a sunny area, but for something you want to keep, the color is not permanent enough.

One of the real advantages of overdyed prints—besides their uniqueness—is that in projects where the fabric's backside shows (braided rag rugs, for instance), the overdye color on the back looks great. (See the Blue Angels Christmas Wreath photograph on page 200 for another example.)

• *Reverse dyeing—bleaching and fading.* Occasionally what you are looking for will be achieved best by bleaching a fabric. Soaking fabric in a high concentration of bleach, washing it several times, or just leaving it in the sunlight for several days may give just the right look. Test small pieces of fabric before doing this.

   • *The used quilt look.* To get a used quilt look, try completing the patchwork and quilting and then age the finished item. Several washings will probably develop a few popped stitches, abrasion on seams, shrinkage, and a change of color—all authentic age marks.

   • *Other abuses.* Abusing fabric by beating, rubbing, and scrubbing will also make it look old before its time. This is especially suitable for more primitive-looking items. A really great abuse is baking or microwaving wet, wrinkled tea-dyed fabric. The fabric will dry very unevenly and you'll get a very realistic stained effect. With fabric abused in this way you can definitely make a doll that looks as if it had been buried with the family treasures when Sherman came through Georgia.

Materials to Collect That Aren't Fabric

   Some of the following items are embellishments to add to your scrap collection for country crafting:
   • Old lace and trims
   • Buttons
   • Ribbons, twine, yarns, and other "tieables"
   • Little wooden hearts and cut-outs

   If you are purchasing ribbons and trims speculatively and aren't sure what to buy, just be logical. Buy the colors you use the most in decorating. Buy the most of what you like the best, providing it is in a reasonable price range. Buy a variety of sizes and colors. Variety will make almost anything more interesting.

   The sample projects photographed for this book were made with readily available materials so that they could be replicated easily. For finished items to be more personal, however, you are encouraged to substitute your inherited or personally collected embellishments and fabrics. Specific instructions are given only for the photographed items. There are many suggestions for project variations. Some are illustrated. My hope is that you'll enjoy putting your own signature on these designs.

Fabric Craft Basics

There are several reasons for putting the Fabric Craft Basics in a separate chapter.

- Some of the instructions would otherwise be duplicated many times, and in the interest of saving space and being able to include more projects, the long version of the necessary "how to" techniques is given here once.

- Some of the techniques may be innovative and new to you, and you might like to use them in other projects. If they were only presented with a specific design and you didn't happen to make that item, you might not see the procedure. This is the best reason for you at least to skim this chapter, get a feeling for the subjects, and look at the illustrations.

- Some of you need little or no instruction and the projects move along much more quickly if the instructions just say, "Make ruffles," instead of giving the full details on how to make ruffles with all the options every time. If you aren't sure about ruffles, however, simply turn to the entry for ruffles here and see the appropriate technique spelled out for you clearly.

Throughout this book, should there be any steps where you feel you need additional help, it will most likely be here. Techniques and definitions are listed alphabetically in this chapter, following the notes on how to use patterns in this book. If you are occasionally inconvenienced by having to look up technique details, I hope you will appreciate the reasons.

Using the Patterns in This Book

Tracing patterns. After deciding on a project, you will need to trace the required patterns from the book. Several projects have pattern pieces that exceed the page size. In order to include full-size pattern pieces, it was necessary to divide those pieces. If any pattern says "part A" or "part B," make sure you find the second piece and match the connecting edge and notches during the tracing process to make one full-size pattern piece.

Grainline designation. Grainline arrows appear on all patterns in this book unless they are to be placed on the fold. Whenever possible, the arrow should go in the same direction as the lengthwise grain (parallel to the selvage).

Sometimes selvages are missing from scrap fabrics. Determine lengthwise grain by pulling on opposite sides of the piece in the same direction as the threads run. The direction that is the firmest is the lengthwise grain. The arrow should point in the same direction as the lengthwise grain. Second choice is for the arrow to be perpendicular to the lengthwise grain and pointing in the same direction as the crosswise grain.

When patterns say "place on fold," it also means that the fold is made on the lengthwise grain.

"Cut 2." In sewing lingo, "Cut 2" on a pattern piece means that you fold one layer of fabric with either the right sides or the wrong sides together, put the pattern piece on top, and cut both layers of fabric at the same time. That process ensures having both a left section and a right section for any pieces that need to be cut in a mirror image, such as blouse fronts.

Should you not have a scrap big enough to fold and find it necessary to make two separate cuttings, put the pattern right side up for one piece and right side down for the other.

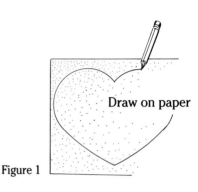

Draw on paper

Figure 1

* * *

APPLIQUÉ TECHNIQUES

Quick and easy fused appliqué. This appliqué technique involves making the design fabric a fusible fabric by ironing a protected fusible web to the back of the fabric. (Brand names are Wonder Under® by Pellon, Transfuse II® by Stacy, and Fine Fuse® from Solar-Kist.) In the past, fused fabrics were synonymous with stiff! Having done it once, lots of people rejected the technique. While these new fusing materials add some stiffness, it is very minimal. So if you haven't tried fusing recently, you might want to now.

Stitch Witchery®, a fusing product that is fine for many things, is *not* suitable for this because it doesn't have the paper-protecting shield.

1. Follow the manufacturer's instructions to fuse web and paper to the back of the fabric. The fusing process converts regular fabric to fusible fabric.

2. The paper backing allows you to draw a design on the paper (Figure 1), but remember, if the design is not symmetrical, it will be reversed. Cut to the shape desired (Figure 2).

3. Remove the protective paper backing (Figure 3), and iron pieces in place (Figure 4).

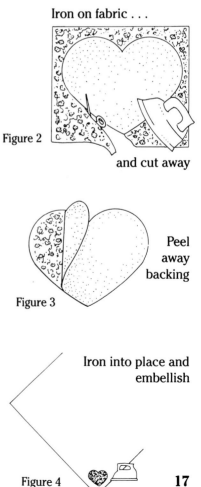

Iron on fabric . . .

Figure 2

and cut away

Peel away backing

Figure 3

Iron into place and embellish

Figure 4

17

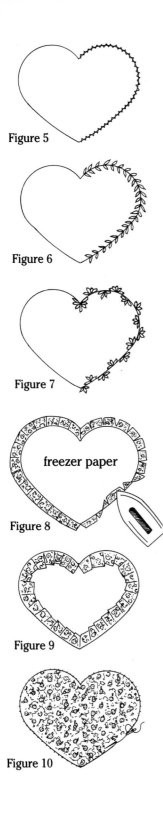

Figure 5

Figure 6

Figure 7

freezer paper

Figure 8

Figure 9

Figure 10

4. It is best to use a narrow, relatively close zigzag stitch with invisible thread on the cut edges (Figure 5). You can, of course, use regular sewing thread, but when the thread is visible, your stitch must be much more carefully done.

A second optional finish would be a decorative stitch from your sewing machine, especially if you are lucky enough to have a machine that does a stitch that looks like a feather stitch or buttonhole stitch (Figure 6). For this, you would switch to a contrasting thread.

A third choice would be a hand embroidery stitch (Figure 7).

Easy but not quick appliqué. This technique incorporates the use of freezer paper for ease and accuracy and is as quick as any hand appliqué.

1. Cut freezer paper the exact size of the design.

2. Rough cut the fabric to approximately the size of the design with a 3/16-inch seam allowance.

3. Position the freezer paper so the nonwaxy surface of the paper is touching the wrong side of the fabric and is centered.

4. With the point of your iron, press the edge of the fabric over the edge of the paper. The fabric will stick slightly to the waxy surface, but it won't make your iron sticky (Figures 8 and 9).

5. Position on the surface fabric and appliqué in place with a hidden stitch that *just* catches the edge of the appliqué (Figure 10).

6. Remove the paper piece as you approach the starting point, or stitch all the way around, then cut away background fabric from behind the appliquéd design and slip the paper piece out.

BATTING

Batting is the soft material that is sandwiched between a quilt top and back to give it dimension and warmth. For most projects in this book, a medium loft, bonded polyester batting is the best choice. If you have a brand you love, great; if not, here are a few sentences on a complex subject.

There are typically three weights of polyester batting. Different brands use different identifying terms. The medium or average batting just mentioned is used for most things. The low loft is used when you want very little "puff," as in garments or place mats. The thick batting is used for comforters.

Fleece is the generic name for a product sold in the interfacing section of fabric stores. I use it as a substitute for low-loft batting. For example, I use it to line pillows I'm not going to quilt but will stuff. It prevents lumps from showing through and gives a nice smooth look to the surface. Thermore® by Hobbs Bonded Fibers and Thermolam® by Stacy are two brand names I can recommend.

There are also battings made from other fibers, but for the items in this book, I would say stick with polyester.

Bias

Bias in fabric is anything that isn't straight across the fabric or parallel to the selvage. True bias goes at a 45-degree angle. (For a more complete discussion, see **Grainline** in this chapter.)

For information on how to cut bias, see Simple Fabric Strip Crafts, page 188.

Binding quilt edges

My favorite way to bind a quilt is with a separate **French fold** binding cut on the straight grain. I machine stitch it to the front of the quilt and then finish on the back by hand. When possible, I cut the bindings on the lengthwise grain because it is more stable than the crosswise grain. I don't cut bias bindings unless I am binding curved edges, because I feel there are more rippling problems with bias-cut bindings.

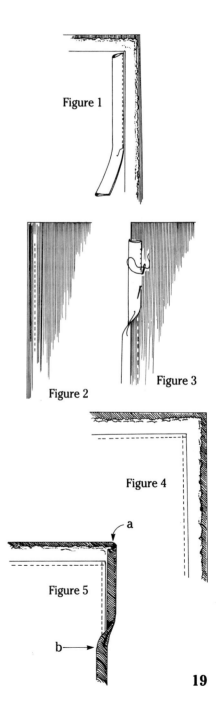

Figure 1

Figure 2

Figure 3

Figure 4

Figure 5

To get the French fold, cut the binding four times as wide as your desired finished width *plus* ½ inch for the two seam allowances and, depending on how thick the batting is, another ⅛- to ½-inch allowance for wrapping around the edge. For example, I like a ⅜-inch visible binding and very thin batting on small doll bed quilts—that means I cut strips 2⅛ inches wide and as long as each edge of the quilt. Press the strips in half lengthwise. Lay the first strip on the top of the trimmed quilt with the raw edges of the quilt and binding matching. Stitch, using a ¼-inch seam allowance (Figure 1).

Trim the batting and backing to "just shorter" than the binding when it is extended away from the quilt (Figure 2). This extra amount of batting will prevent empty, flat-feeling bindings.

Pull the binding up and around the batting so that the folded edge lies right on the stitched line. Catch the fold to the lining with a blind stitch. Do not stitch through to the front (Figure 3).

The easiest way to finish the raw edges of a quilt is to cut the backing fabric and batting larger than the quilt and carefully fold the backing around to the front and hand or machine stitch in place.

When I do this, I cut both the batting and backing between 1¼ inches and 2 inches larger than the finished item. Then I machine stitch ¼ inch from the edge around the entire quilt (Figure 4).

Make the first fold (a) so that the raw edges of the quilt and the backing touch, completely covering the batting. Make the second fold (b) so that the folded edge overlaps the cut edge of the quilt by ¼ inch (Figure 5). When stitching by hand with a blind stitch, I still like to go all the way to the backing fabric and catch a thread or two with every stitch. This helps prevent the edge from rolling.

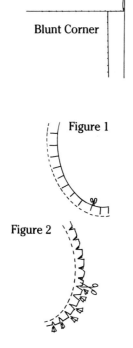

Blunt Corner

Figure 1

Figure 2

BLUNT CORNERS

Where the opposite borders are added to match the size of the interior piece. In essence, one side cuts the other side straight off when added, as opposed to mitered corners.

CLIPPED SEAMS

Clipping is the term used when sharp-pointed scissors are carefully used to cut through the seam allowance so it will spread or overlap without wrinkles when it is turned inside the stitched items. Clipping needs to be done on all curved areas, both inside and outside curves. On inside curves, you *must* clip in order for the seam allowances to spread when turned (Figure 1). On outside curves, notching is best because it prevents the seam allowances from piling up and rippling when turned (Figure 2). The more curved a seam, the more it needs to be clipped. Sharp changes in direction must be clipped.

EMBROIDERY STITCHES

Embroidery can always add interesting detail, but very few stitches are required to finish the projects in this book. They are illustrated here.

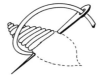

Satin stitch

Outline stitch

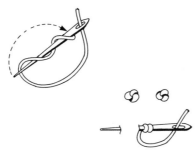

French knot

Lazy Daisy stitch

FLAPPING

This is a wonderful technique that allows you to outline, highlight, and "mat" with an extra color. If you know how to do piping, it's piping without the cord. It is best used when the desired finished width is ¼ inch to ⅜ inch or less.

The reason I like it is that it is easier to be accurate with flapping than with a narrow border that is sewn in position. If you've ever tried to add a border ⅜ inch wide or narrower, you know that if you get off on one seam, you get a wavy effect, and if you get off on both sides, you develop an hourglass effect visible from 30 yards!

Flaps are cut on the lengthwise grain. They are twice as wide as the desired finished width *plus* two ¼-inch seam allowances. They *look* as if they are inserted between a quilt or pillow and its first real border. In fact, you must add the flaps to the edge of the quilt or pillow and then add the borders or binding. Add the opposite sides first. Then sew on the other pair of opposite sides, then the borders in the same order. This is the only way the flaps will cross correctly at the corner. (Flapping is shown on the Broken Dishes Doll Quilt on page 56.)

FRINGE TECHNIQUES

Many of the craft items pictured have taken advantage of the old decorative technique of fringing fabrics on the edges. In most cases, except burlap, the fringe is more attractive if the fabrics are torn and have irregular edges than if they are cut. Burlap must be cut. It is also easier to fringe shorter pieces of fabric when possible. On our Santa Bear (page 210), for example, the muslin was cut into short strips for each section of "fur" before fringing. Pull two or three threads at a time. Keeping a little tension on the strip seems to make the threads pull more easily.

If you are fringing a long edge, you can make the fringing area shorter by clipping perpendicularly across the number of threads you intend to fringe every 12 to 15 inches. Be very careful not to cut into the remaining fabric.

FUSING AND GLUING

Sometimes the best "stitch" means using a hot glue gun or fabric glue. This does *not* mean all-purpose white glue. While that is great for many things, it makes most fabrics very stiff. Check your local fabric store for the relatively new glues specially designed for fabric. You'll be amazed how often you reach for the glue with fabric craft projects. I have even effectively glued the channel in a cafe curtain for the rod.

Gluing and fusing are messier than sewing and, if the adhesives end up in the wrong place, can be very frustrating. Make sure you have a cleared work surface that is properly protected. Have a damp cloth for wiping up drops and spills of water-soluble glues immediately.

For paper-backed fusibles, see the complete description under **Appliqué** (Quick and easy fused appliqué) and the mention under **No-Sewing Patchwork**, both in this chapter. There are cleaning agents for iron surfaces that have met the wrong side of the fusibles, but being careful is easier. Putting scrap fabric across the ironing board when using fusibles saves lots of ironing board covers.

Glue guns can give you stringy hot glue that is messy, frustrating, and worse. They can also be the only solution to joining pieces of fabric—providing the fastest and the most secure bond in some situations.

Glue sticks are another convenient item, most often used for temporarily holding fabric in position. The adhesive washes out but provides basting without the time required for a needle and thread and without the surface distortion of pins.

Grainline

Lengthwise grain refers to threads in woven fabrics that run parallel to the selvage or woven edge. These are the firmest threads.

Crosswise grain refers to the threads that are perpendicular to the selvage. They have considerably more give than lengthwise threads, but nothing like bias.

Bias goes across the threads at any angle, but *true bias* is a 45-degree angle. Cutting at this angle creates very stretchy edges on the fabric. It can stretch in seams and hems and sometimes be a real pest, but then, it can wrap around a curved neckline like nothing else.

Learn the characteristics of the different grainlines and how to use them to your advantage.

Layering

The process of assembling three layers (backing, batting, and surface fabric) for quilting. Safety pin or baste in place.

Backing fabric is the layer that keeps the thread from pulling into the batting and in the process makes the indentation you see in a quilted fabric. In a quilt, it is visible on the back of the quilt. Traditionally, quilt backing was cheap. Muslin was commonly used. Sometimes bleached flour and sugar bags were pieced together. Some of the worst "sale fabric" ever has been spied on the back of quilts. None of those choices are popular today, but it still seems difficult to go out and buy large quantities of fabric to hide on the back of a quilt. Today a new trend is surfacing to piece quilt backs. The backs are generally not as elaborate or as serious as the front, so have become a perfect place to use scraps, especially if your quilt top has medium to dark colors. Pretest backing fabric for shrinking or bleeding.

In quilted pillows, there is a backing fabric that doesn't show and a pillow back fabric that does show. The quilt backing can, again, be any dispensable scrap you have, especially if you are using dark fabrics in the patchwork.

NO-SEWING PAT(

This techniq
background fabri
of the patchwork
that have a very
flexible, and are
the same technic
this case you are
easy fused appli(

Some peopl
time and place f(
useful on some
beginners. It ca
without making
patchwork. It's a

PIECING

A term use(
can be done b
secure threads a

Because I l
piecing. If you
stitches per in(
almost always b

Chain pi
presser foot an(
the directions f(

Perfect pi
Perfect pie
With this techr
cutting. The i
unmanageable
inadvertently st

If this me
triangle sets ar
these directior
nates directior

Making the pe
1. Count
how many squ
grid will be *h(*
two triangle pa
finished squar
2. For th
square. That i

Many designs in this book have carefully detailed shapes. Experience has shown that when working with small detailed shapes, the accuracy of stitching directly on the design line (sewing or seam line) is crucial in determining the final shape. This method, which differs slightly from the normal approach of cutting things out with a ¼-inch seam allowance, gives results well worth a little extra effort. Patterns in this book that don't have added seam allowances are designs in which the technique described here is the recommended method. These shapes are generally cut out *after* they are sewn.

Trace and stitch. Most people can stitch more accurately sewing directly on the drawn seam line rather than trying to stitch in ¼ inch from the cut edge.

1. Trace as many shapes as needed on the *wrong* side of the chosen fabric. Make sure to leave ½ inch between any two lines. Place the drawn fabric and its backing fabric with right sides together.

2. Use a small sewing machine stitch—12 to 14 stitches per inch—on very detailed shapes, and stitch exactly on the line. An open-toed presser foot or clear presser foot also allows you to follow the sewing line more accurately.

3. Leave an opening in the seam for turning the item inside out (Figure 1).

4. Rough cut (see the entry in this chapter). Rough cut prior to step 1 if you are working with large pieces of fabric.

5. Trim and clip (see **Clipped seams** for more details).

6. Turn carefully. When turning inside out, pay careful attention to the detail areas. Use small dull items (chopsticks, crochet hooks, etc.) to prod points to their maximum. Be judicious when pressing. If an item is to be stuffed, pressing is sometimes eliminated, as you might press in unsightly hard lines.

7. Stuffing (see **Stuffing**). If the item is to be stuffed after turning, stuff small amounts into extremities first. Use the same poking tools as above to prod the stuffing into the extremities. Then fill the central areas. When satisfied, close the openings.

8. Close the opening. It is difficult to maintain a design line when you are closing by hand stitching the opening left in the seam for turning. If the item will be exposed on both sides, there is little choice but to use the least conspicuous small stitch to close the opening in the seam securely. However, this problem can be eliminated on items that will not have their backs exposed. Just make an opening in the back piece and stitch all the way around the item, then turn through the opening.

Rough line and turn—suitable for completely covered backs and free spirits. Just slit the back in the center (Figure 2); when turning and stuffing are complete, whipstitch shut if you think it is necessary.

Finished line and turn—suitable for slightly exposed backs and hidden backs made by neatness fanatics. For years I had a smug

Figure 1

Figure 2

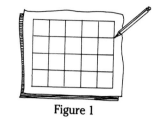

Figure 1

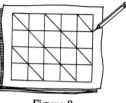

Figure 2

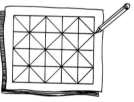

Figure 3

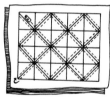

Figure 4

Miter

made with 3⅞-inch squares. Don't throw up your hands about measuring such an odd amount. Today's wide acrylic templates (which you also use with the rotary cutting method) make it accurate and easy. To estimate how much fabric you need, it is easier to round up to the next inch or half inch.

3. Lay the two fabrics you have selected for the triangle sets right sides together, with the lighter color on top. Use your template and a marker to make horizontal lines. Use the same template to make vertical lines perpendicular to the first lines until you have enough squares (Figure 1). It is a good insurance policy to mark a few extra squares.

4. Draw continuous diagonal lines through every other row of squares (Figure 2). Then starting with the first empty square, draw diagonal rows in the opposite direction (Figure 3).

Stitching perfect pieced triangles:

1. Stitch through both layers of fabric on both sides of the diagonal lines. Your seam allowance must be an accurate ¼ inch for the resulting squares to be accurate. Use the edge of your presser foot as a guide if it is ¼ inch (Figure 4).

2. One of the bonuses of marking this way is that you can often stitch the entire grid by just making 90-degree turns at the end of each row. When you have completed one side of the lines, make a 180-degree turn and return on the other side. There are many different grid arrangements, but for the most efficient stitching, look for a corner that has a single diagonal line coming directly into it.

3. Cut the triangles apart on every drawn line. There are two pieced units in every square. Press.

If you need a project to try this method on, try the Bear Paw variations (page 40), Broken Dishes Doll Quilt (page 55), the Ohio Star (page 58), or Attic Window (page 57).

PILLOW FINISHING

Today's good-quality polyester stuffing has eliminated the need to make removable pillow covers, since the better brands of stuffing are washable. Just be sure you're using a washable stuffing. A layer of batting under the top (even if not quilted) will help hide stuffing lumps.

The pillow back should be the same size as the pillow top. Lay the back over the top, right sides together. If there are ruffles or piping, they should already be basted to the top and will lie between top and back. Sew around all sides, leaving a 3- or 4-inch opening to turn the pillow right side out.

Use a dull-pointed object (pencil, crochet hook, etc.) to poke out the corners and to push stuffing in. Stuff the pillow firmly, making it fuller than really seems right, as the stuffing tends to settle and flatten with time.

Close the opening with a tiny, invisible hand stitch.

the cutting surface (remember v
blade. In most cases, a thick a
providing a rigid edge to guide a

Streamline the cutting proc
and using a rotary cutter. Layer
protective mat and cut the strips

You will be more accurate
because most of the cutting is
stopping and starting, as with s

If you do not have a rotary
cut through multiple layers of f
pin the fabrics together and mar
as possible when cutting to pre

RUFFLES

I'm fanatical about ruffles.
with two rows of machine bast
allow ½ inch for edges that are
being sewn to. An alternate wa
stitch over a smooth small strir

Typically, I cut ruffles on
are cut twice as wide as the fi
Cut the length to equal at le
cover—when possible, two an
on bias-cut ruffles. They do tt
gathering the corners a little m
too.

Please use the ruffle widt
line only. When you are wo
pictured, the intensity of color
interrelationships change, so
may also change. Fold the fal
measure and proceed.

Single ruffle. Follow the
Double ruffles. These
widths stacked one on top
ruffles, reduce the fullness to
ter, as the gathered thickness
Mock double ruffle. A
in the pillow seam. Determir
double ruffle. Select the fabr
two seam allowances. Figure
ruffle and subtract the finish
strips together (Figure 3), fc
ruffle. Don't forget you can it
that seam (Figure 4).

PIPING

Piping is an effective fabric-covered trim that adds dimension, a touch of color, and a nice finished look. It can be purchased in limited sizes, colors, and fabrics.

To make your own piping, purchase the desired size of cording and cut bias strips wide enough to wrap around the cord snugly and still have adequate seam allowances. Fold the bias in half, put the cord in the fold, and, using your zipper foot, stitch close to the cord.

PRESSING

Pressing is not an option, it is a very important step in successful projects. It is always best to press a seam before you sew across it again. Sometimes very careful and firm "finger pressing" can postpone that for one step, but use this practice judiciously.

Patchwork seam allowances are almost always pressed in the same direction and toward the darker fabric if there is no overriding reason to do it differently. The importance of accurate pressing in strip piecing techniques cannot be overemphasized.

You will probably want to press both seams in the same direction in craft items that are also going to be stuffed. (Steam irons can be very powerful, so make sure you don't use a hard, distorting action when you press.)

PREWASHING OR PRESHRINKING

For most of the projects in this book, the question of how to prewash or shrink your fabrics has a simple solution. The pieces are small and the fabric is usually wrinkled because you've rolled your scraps for neat storage. Simply run hot water over the fabrics until they are saturated and iron them dry. It is perfect shrinking because it is the heat on the wet fibers that causes shrinking. (This is not to imply that you didn't prewash when you used the fabric the first time, it's just a double-check.)

For larger projects the question looms larger. It is easy for an author or teacher just to say, "Prewash all your fabrics," and drop the subject. I have friends who piously say, "I never walk in the door with fabric without putting it right in the washing machine." Perhaps it is because I have done more than my share of speculative fabric purchases that I take a more realistic approach. Knowing I'm not disciplined enough to prewash every fabric the day I purchase it or to keep fabrics separate in "washed" and "unwashed" closets, I never wash.

I do *test* when I have selected a fabric for a project. Even when fabrics show that they need shrinking, I don't run them through a soaping and three rinses. That just excessively changes the finish and color. It is the heat on the wet fibers that shrinks the fabric, so I put the

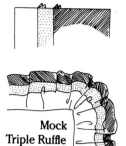

Mock
Triple Ruffle

Figure 5

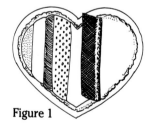

Figure 1

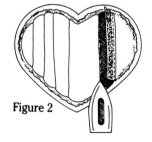

Figure 2

Mock triple ruffle. This is just like the mock double ruffle, except for the obvious—it has a third fabric (Figure 5).

Purchased trims. Some are very lovely, and even though they may seem expensive, if you calculate the time and materials for the ones you would otherwise make, they are usually a good investment.

SEAM ALLOWANCES

If you are accustomed to garment sewing and new to craft and patchwork sewing, a ¼-inch seam allowance may make you feel like you are falling off a cliff. It, rather than ⅝ inch, is the seam allowance of choice for most of our projects and will be what is marked on most of the patterns.

Sometimes there is no seam allowance on the patterns. When the patterns do not include seam allowances, it means the line given is the *sewing* line, not the cutting line. Patterns are given this way when the shaping of the item is very dependent on accurate sewing. It is much easier to sew on a line than to cut something with a ¼-inch seam allowance and then sew a consistent ¼ inch from the cut edge.

The recommended technique for matching pieces is to trace the sewing line onto one piece of fabric with a fade-away fabric marking pen, rough cut it, and place it right sides together with another rough-cut piece of fabric. It is not necessary to trace a pattern piece onto the second piece. Proceed with trimming, clipping, turning, pressing, etc.

See **Line and turn** in this chapter for a more complete explanation of this process when it involves turning in addition to seaming.

STITCH-AND-FLIP TECHNIQUE

This is a process in which fabrics are placed right sides together on a base or background square (often including quilt batting) and stitched together through all layers (Figure 1). Then the top layer is pressed open (Figure 2) and the process is repeated. It most often refers to orderly cut pieces, not scraps.

Quilt-as-you-sew is another name frequently associated with this process, but only if stitching is going through batting and backing fabric at the same time as the pieced fabrics.

String quilting (see below) is a traditional name most often referring to the stitch-and-flip process without batting and backing. It has come to imply using irregular scrap fabrics.

STRING QUILT

As stated above, string quilting means using irregular scraps to make larger pieces of fabric.

It was very common for patchworkers to cut shapes out of newspaper—diamonds, for example—and then stitch and flip irregular scraps on it until it was covered (Figures 1, 2, and 3). They would use the paper as a pattern and trim off the edges and put the diamonds together for a wonderful Eight-Pointed Star (Figure 4).

You can do the same thing with many of the patterns in this book. You can also just sew fabric scraps together until the new piece is big enough to cut out the desired heart (Figure 5) or teddy bear or patchwork pieces.

String quilting is a great loosening up exercise to help people relax about putting odd fabrics together. It's fast, fun, effective, and very "scrap-conducive." Almost any item in the book can be made from string-quilted fabric.

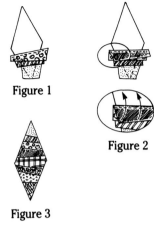

Figure 1

Figure 2

Figure 3

STUFFING

When we refer to the substance used, *stuffing, loose fill,* and *polyester filling* are all words that designate the same thing. While there are other fillings, like cotton or kapok or foam, the only one I recommend for any of the projects in this book is polyester. There are also many different kinds of polyester. Beware of loss-leader fiberfill that lies like a brick in the corner of a pillow. It's not a bargain. Price per ounce or pound or bag is not the determining factor for value. Price per volume filled is the first criterion for judging a good value. The second criterion is the resulting feel of the product. You might call it the "fill and feel" test. Before buying, compare how much volume the different stuffings fill. Think about how it feels through the bag when you squeeze it. What you want is a filling that does not mat down and can be washed in the finished item.

Figure 4

When it comes to the work of stuffing, one of the important considerations is not to try to stuff too much at one time. Many small insertions are usually better than a few large ones. There are also degrees of stuffing, similar to degrees of doneness in cooking meat.

Stuff lightly. When stuffing lightly, you are looking for dimension but are not stuffing in an area that will be expected to get heavy use and tend to pack down. "Lightly" is also the way you stuff if you want to be able to bend the section in question.

Figure 5

Stuff firmly. The amount of stuffing will stand up to wear and will not bend easily. Most pillows are stuffed firmly.

Stuff very firmly. This is the way you stuff something that you don't want to bend at all, like a doll or giraffe neck.

TRAPUNTO

Trapunto is the word used to describe padded or stuffed quilting. For a more complete description of the technique, please see the directions for the Hearts and Roses Trapunto Pillow at the beginning of the "Bears and Other Fun Things" chapter.

Patchwork Projects

Making New Things from Old (or New) Quilt Blocks

When working with old quilt tops and blocks, my preference is to maintain the integrity of the original piece as much as possible. Quilt blocks can look great just layered with batting and backing and assembled in a nice wooden hoop. Do as much quilting as you choose, and leave the quilting needle and thread in position. Add ribbons and a stuffed heart to the hoop to be more decorative, if you desire. You might even paint or stain the hoop. Put it on the wall or with a pretty antique basket and some of your collected sewing paraphernalia.

Country homes are full of arrangements of collected items. They could almost be called still life arrangements. The addition of a piece of work in progress adds the nice touch of anticipation of action.

The most obvious thing to do with old quilt blocks is to make pillows. If the block is a 12-inch to 14-inch square, it's pillow size, with or without ruffles (see Rambler Pillows on page 34). Smaller squares can have lobes added to make heart-shaped pillows. Examples and patterns for these start with the Bow Tie Pillows featured in this chapter. You might make a tote or Pioneer Pocket (see the "Sew a Treat for Yourself" section). Some quilt blocks will make wonderful miniature wall pieces or doll quilts or a small flat quilted piece that sits on a coffee table or shelf protecting the surface and adding decorative appeal to the other items displayed. Tiny little pieces can go in very small hoops for decorative pieces to complement teddy bears or dolls or to set on small chairs.

While many of the items in this chapter are made from old blocks, patterns are given for duplicating those patchwork sections in the event you are starting with new pieces of fabric.

How much fabric? The only items listed with each project under Materials and Notions are notions and those fabrics that require more than ¼ yard to make as shown.

RAMBLER PILLOWS

The Rambler pillows illustrated here were made from old patchwork blocks. The borders and ruffles were made from new fabrics selected to harmonize in color and look old.

To make new squares, cut the following pieces for each pillow:

Twenty-four small triangles from the
    same fabric
Sixteen medium triangles—mix or match
    fabric
Four big triangles
One square

1. Chain piece the smallest triangles to the medium triangles as illustrated (Figure 1). This arrangement is typically called Flying Geese.

2. Assemble two three-piece Flying Geese units and one extra medium triangle into this subunit (Figure 2). Attach a finished Flying Geese subunit to two opposite sides of the center square (Figure 3).

3. Add two big triangles to the opposite sides of the remaining Flying Geese strips (Figure 4).

4. Make the last two seams, sewing one large composite triangular unit to either side of the center strip to complete the patchwork square.

5. Cut and add 1¾-inch strips to the outside of the patchwork square. Sew one strip each to opposite sides. Then sew strips to the remaining two sides. (You see this also in Figure 5). The strips keep the patchwork design from falling over the side when the pillow is stuffed and also make it easy to take a ½-inch seam when you add the ruffles, without disrupting the patchwork design.

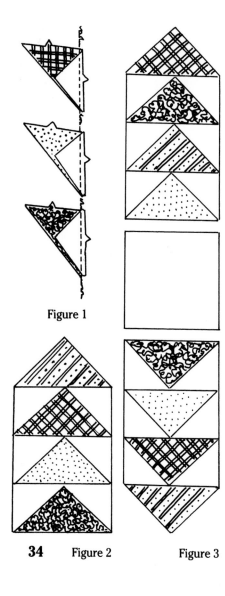

Figure 1

Figure 2   Figure 3

Figure 4

To finish the pillows, layer the pillow top with batting and backing and quilt as desired. Add ruffles.

The ruffles on these pillows are double ruffles, and the top one is a mock double ruffle. On the mock double ruffle, the fabrics were cut 2 inches and 3 inches wide, seamed together, folded in half, and gathered, using a ½-inch seam allowance to gather. The back ruffle was cut 6 inches wide, folded in half, and gathered separately. The two were stacked and seamed to the front of the pillow before the back was added.

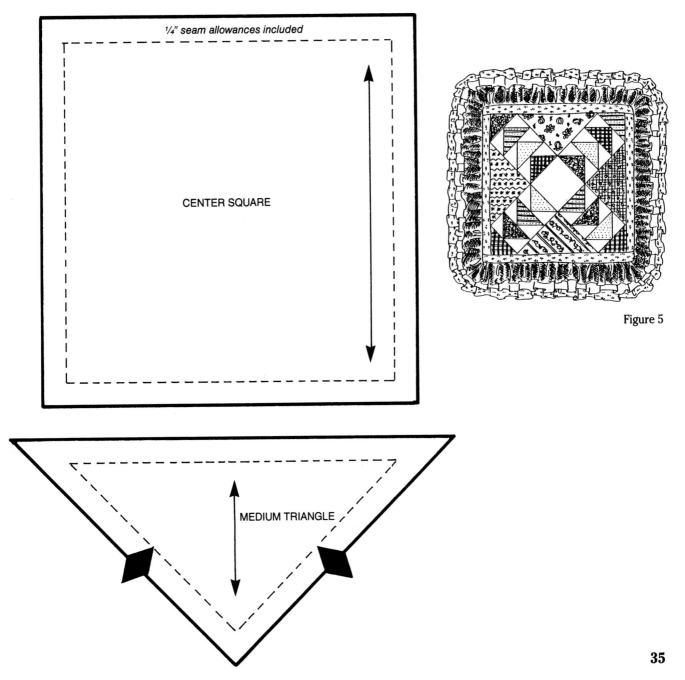

¼" seam allowances included

CENTER SQUARE

MEDIUM TRIANGLE

Figure 5

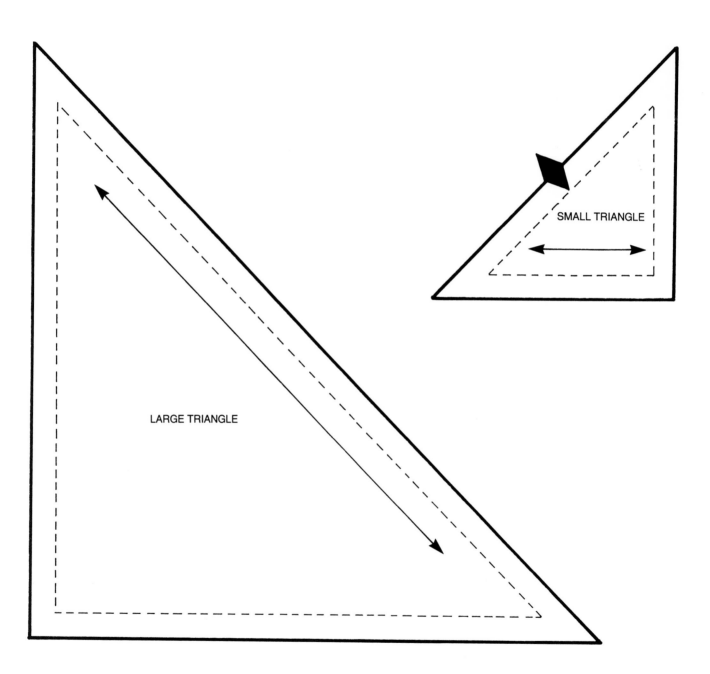

SMALL TRIANGLE

LARGE TRIANGLE

BOW TIE PILLOWS

When you are looking at the items made from the old Bow Tie blocks, it isn't really accurate to say you are looking at silk purses, but it is appropriate to say that we started with sow's ears. "Why?" you might ask. Well, this is why and how I acquired them.

For some years, my husband and I have collected antique quilts. As our collection began to take up more and more space and as prices for quilts began to rise dramatically, I became more interested in quilt tops and sometimes quilt blocks.

Even though the Bow Tie pattern was never one of my favorites esthetically, I was sentimentally attached to the pattern. The first quilt I ever quilted in a frame was a Bow Tie, albeit one of the least appealing Georgia Mountain Bow Tie quilts I had ever seen. (So many Bow Tie quilts have a very primitive look, with stripes and plaids running off grain and blocks haphazardly pieced. Is it because that pattern was often the choice for a teen-age boy's quilt and quilters have always resisted putting lots of work into a quilt for a teen-age boy? Or is it the quilt that little sisters who were still acquiring skills made for a big brother?) At any rate, I seemed to keep adding different Bow Tie quilts to our collection until it was like a sub-collection. The blocks used in these pillows were not very appealing, but it was an unusual arrangement that I didn't have, and "you know how collectors are"—I was sure I could put enough blocks together to make a small wall hanging "or something."

The reason I'm telling all this is that there is a good chance that you have similar things tucked away that you have inherited or bought. First, it's always nice to know that you aren't alone and, second, I hope you will be encouraged to bring them out and enjoy making something and using them. Remember, these ideas can be transferred to almost any appropriate-size blocks.

The colors and fabrics used here are very typical of the turn-of-the-century Prairie fabrics. Take this opportunity to observe the mix of old fabrics with new fabrics that have an old look. Only the fabrics in the small Bow Tie blocks and the white appliqué hearts are authentic turn-of-the-century fabrics. The others were selected because they looked old.

The purchased antique Bow Tie blocks are finished 5-inch squares that have been joined with a stripping and block arrangement to make a 12-inch square. To make these pillows, the larger squares were taken apart to work with the 5½-inch blocks. Pattern pieces included will reproduce the same size.

Pattern Pieces

A. Lopped-off square for Bow Tie
B. Small center square for Bow Tie
C. Alternate appliqué method—patterns would be two squares
D. Alternating solid square, with quilting lines shown for Bow Tie
E. Heart lobe
F. Triangles for Diamond in the Square
G. Strip(s) for edge, Diamond in the Square
H. Squares for border corners
I. Strips for edge, larger pillows
J. Large heart for appliqué
K. Small heart for appliqué
L. Base square for heart appliqué
M. Patterns for Fan (3 pieces)
N. Patterns for Bear Paw (4 pieces)

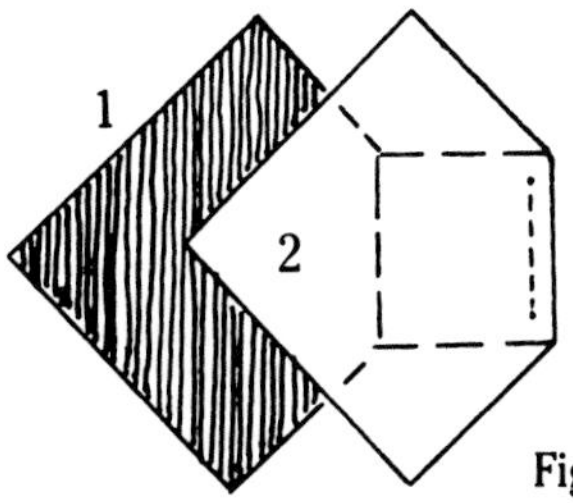

Other options. Additional pillows illustrated beside each set of directions show the optional Fan or Bear Paw variation following the basic Bow Tie arrangement. Simply substitute those or any 5½-inch block.

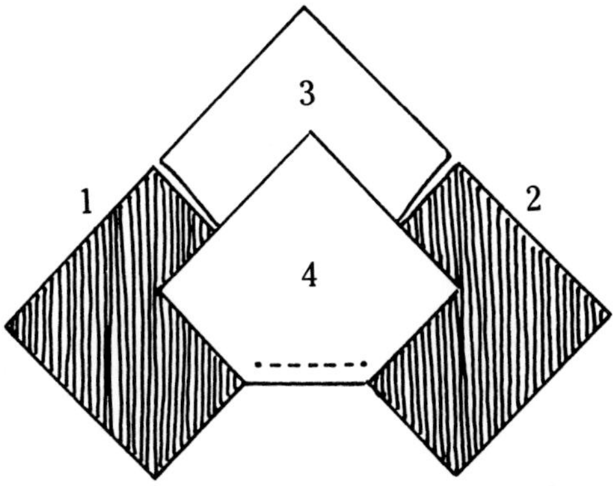

Making the Basic Bow Tie Block

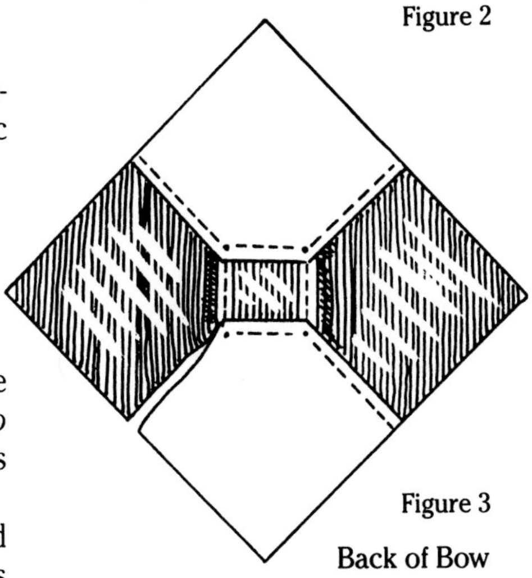

Traditional Patchwork Method

1. Sew one lopped-off square (Pattern A) onto each side of the center square (Pattern B), alternating fabrics as shown in Figure 1. *Do not* stitch into the seam allowance of the square. Press all four seams away from the square.

2. Go around the block, stitching one side seam at a time and being very careful not to catch any of the square in your stitches (Figures 2 and 3). Most people think this technique is easier to control by starting from the center and stitching out.

Faux Patchwork Method

1. Sew four Pattern C squares together, checkerboard style (Figure 4).

2. Turn under all edges of the small center square, position it diagonally across the intersection, and appliqué in place. (If you are machine quilting, this could be added while quilting.)

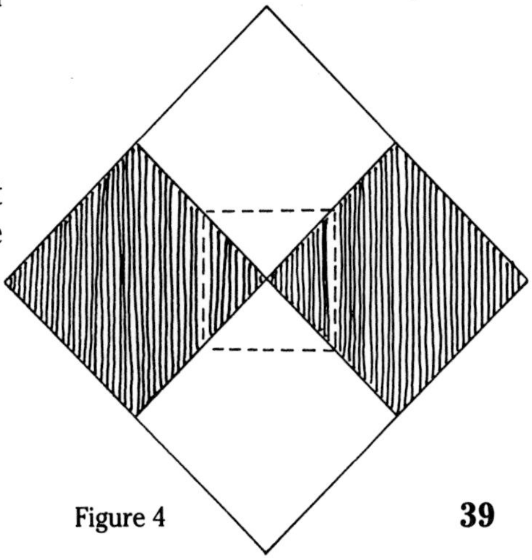

Figure 1

Figure 2

Figure 3

Back of Bow Tie Square

Figure 4

39

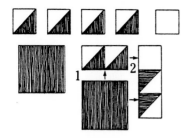

Figure 5

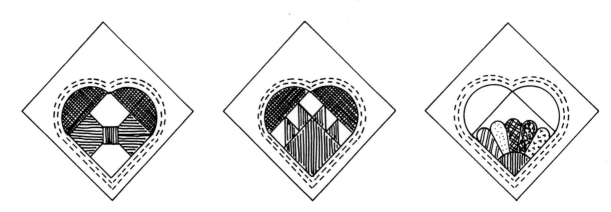

Figure 6

FINISHED SIZE:
9½ inches square plus 3-inch ruffles

MATERIALS:
**Two 10½-inch squares of fabric for pillow
10½-inch squares of batting and backing for quilting
Stuffing**

Bear Paw Pattern

1. For each paw, piece four squares consisting of one light and one dark triangle (N3). Sew into pairs as shown.

2. Sew one pair to larger square (N1) with dark sides touching.

3. Sew small square (N2) to other pair and then the resulting new strip to the large square as shown (Figure 5).

Fan Pattern

1. For each fan, piece five fan pieces (M1).

2. Press the outside curve of the pieced fan under and appliqué it onto the 5½-inch square (Figure 6).

3. Press the curved edge of the center piece (M2) under and appliqué. (When making the version where all fans touch at the center, sew one center circle unless the quarter circles are different colors.)

THE BOW TIE HEART PILLOW

1. Make or purchase 5½-inch square blocks. Pattern included (D) is for 5½-inch unfinished and 5-inch finished Bow Tie and matching lobes (E). (If you want to make the same pillow and have a different size Bow Tie block, make the pattern for the heart lobes by making a circle that has the same diameter as the side of the block. In this case the lobe is half of a 5½-inch circle. Adjust pillow squares to the appropriate size.

2. Add one lobe (E) to each of two adjoining sides of the block. Make sure the Bow Tie is horizontal and that any other block is properly positioned for the heart shape.

When adding lobes, add one at a time. On the first piece, stop ¼ inch from the edge where the lobes will meet. Press away from the block. Lay the second lobe on the adjacent side. Be careful not to stitch across the first lobe.

3. Turn under ¼-inch seam allowance on all edges and appliqué the heart onto a 10½-inch square pillow top. Position so that the block is 1¾ inches from two sides.

4. Add batting and backing; quilt as desired.

5. Add ruffles and back as desired. Ruffles on the red lobed heart are 2 inches and 3 inches finished, but that would be flexible, depending on your fabrics. The back ruffle is a purchased embroidered ruffle. The edge treatment also includes piping made to match the heart lobes. The piping accent was really needed to make these colors interesting, but is optional.

BOW TIE—DIAMOND IN THE SQUARE SET

1. Add triangles (F) to opposite sides of the 5½-inch square. The tips of the triangle corners will extend beyond the square. Press back, then add triangles to the other two opposite sides. Press. Double-check the measurement of the finished block at this point. Cut four border strips (G) 2 inches wide (that allows ½ inch for seam with ruffles) and the length of the block. Add border strips on two opposite sides.

2. Add 2-inch square (H) to both ends of the two remaining border strips and then add the extended strips to the other sides of the square.

3. Add batting and backing. Quilt. Add ruffles and finish as desired. Ruffles shown are actual double ruffles 1½ inches and 2 inches finished.

CIRCLE OF BOW TIES

1. Position four 5½-inch Bow Tie blocks as shown. Add borders (2 inches wide) as for Diamond in the Square.

2. Add batting and backing. Quilt as desired.

3. Add ruffles and finish as desired. The ruffle shown is a mock triple ruffle. In the mock triple ruffle, the actual cut widths were 2¼ inches*, 1 inch, and 4½ inches* (*included ½-inch seam allowance for ruffling and sewing to pillow; all other seams were ¼ inch). Stitch all strips together, fold in half, and treat like a single piece of fabric.

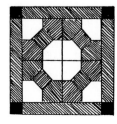

ALTERNATE BOW TIES

1. Piece and position two Bow Tie blocks and two plain blocks (cut 5½ inches or the same size as your finished blocks), as shown.

2. Add 2-inch borders. Add batting and backing; quilt and finish as desired. The ruffle shown is the same as for the Bow Tie Heart pillow.

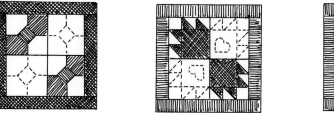

ALTERNATE BOW TIE WITH HEART APPLIQUÉS

Made in the same way as above, except you appliqué hearts on alternate blocks, as shown. Stitch and turn; stuff the smaller heart lightly. The ruffle shown is a mock triple ruffle. Strips were cut 1¾ inches, 1 inch, and 4¼ inches wide.

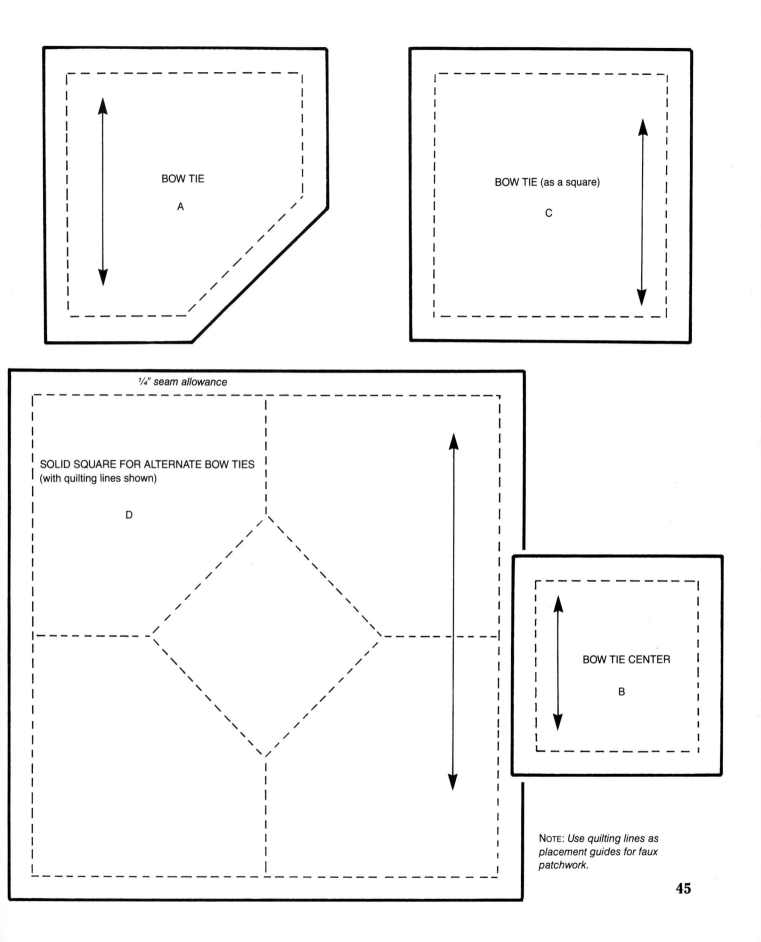

BOW TIE

A

BOW TIE (as a square)

C

¼" seam allowance

SOLID SQUARE FOR ALTERNATE BOW TIES
(with quilting lines shown)

D

BOW TIE CENTER

B

NOTE: *Use quilting lines as placement guides for faux patchwork.*

45

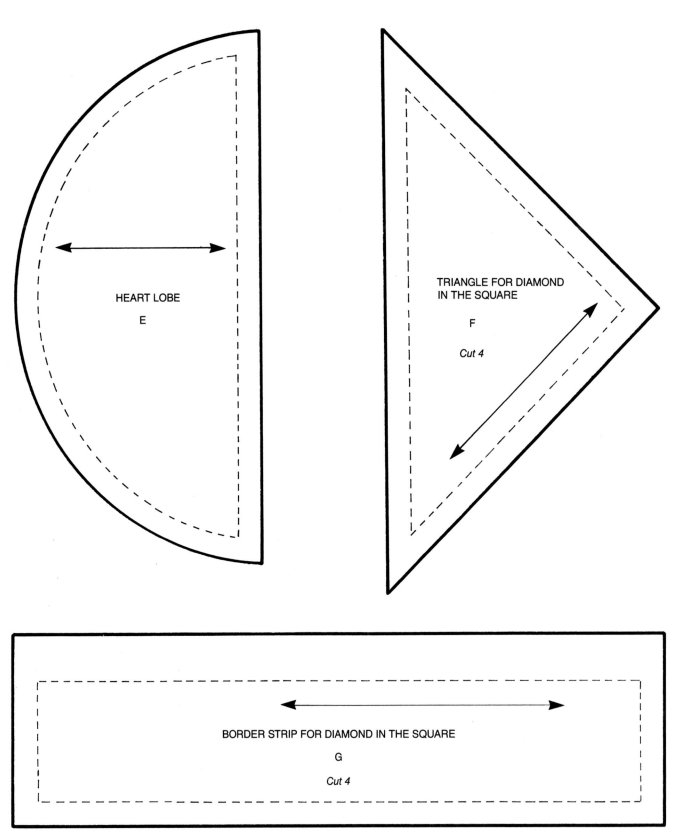

HEART LOBE

E

TRIANGLE FOR DIAMOND
IN THE SQUARE

F

Cut 4

BORDER STRIP FOR DIAMOND IN THE SQUARE

G

Cut 4

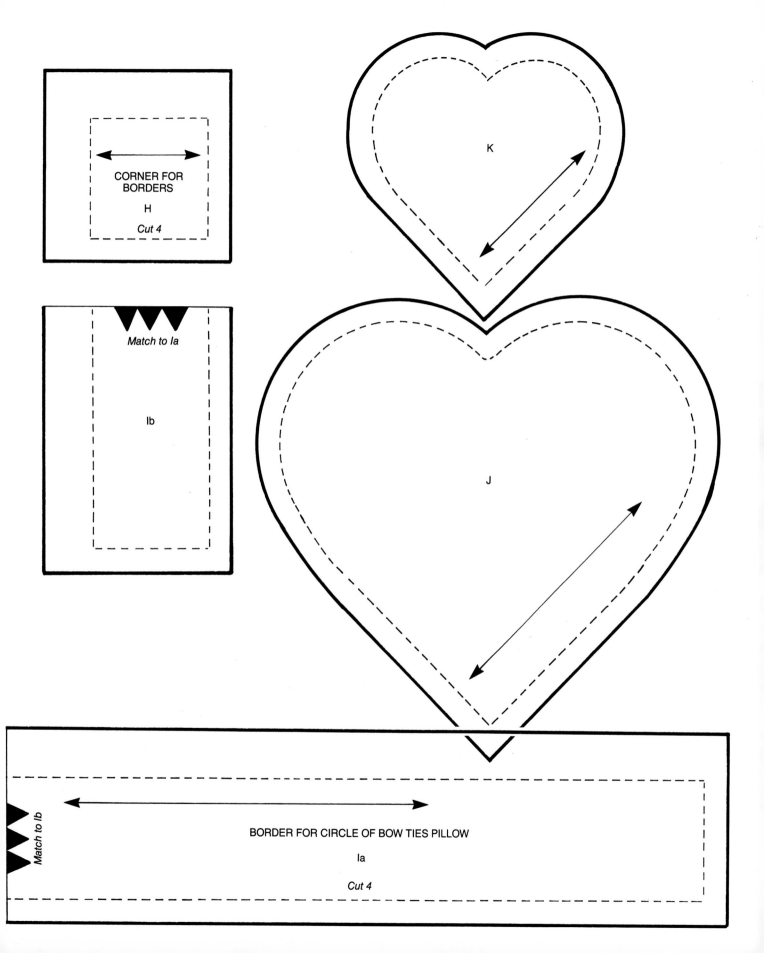

CORNER FOR
BORDERS

H

Cut 4

Match to Ia

Ib

K

J

Match to Ib

BORDER FOR CIRCLE OF BOW TIES PILLOW

Ia

Cut 4

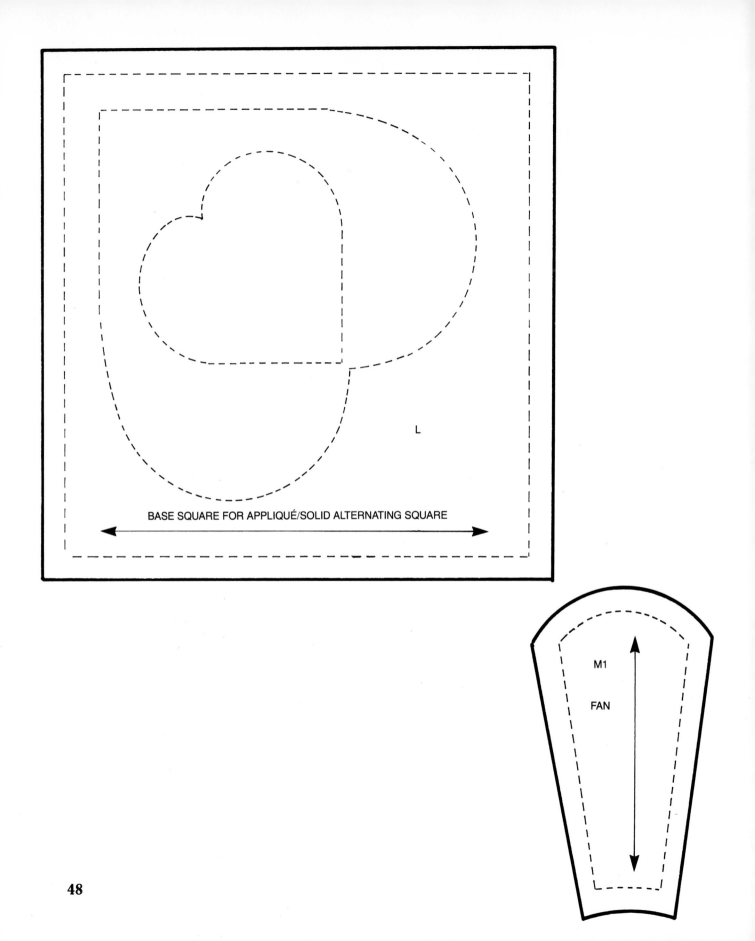

BASE SQUARE FOR APPLIQUÉ/SOLID ALTERNATING SQUARE

L

M1

FAN

48

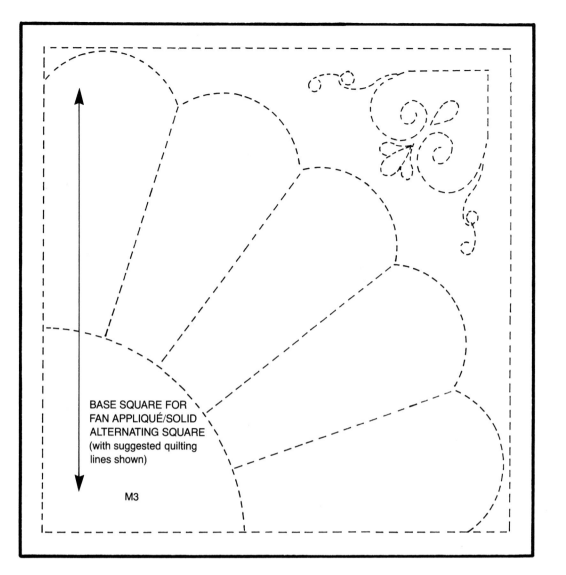

BASE SQUARE FOR
FAN APPLIQUÉ/SOLID
ALTERNATING SQUARE
(with suggested quilting
lines shown)

M3

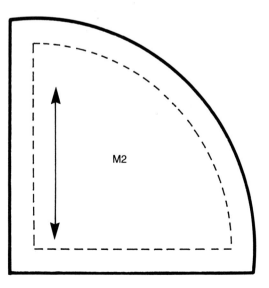

M2

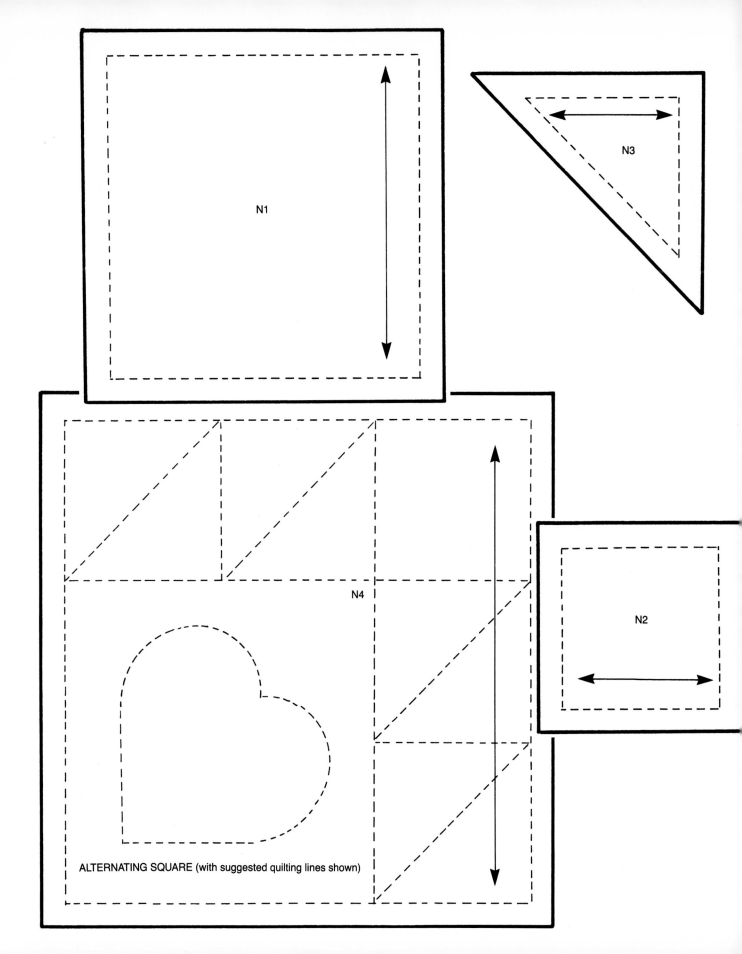

N1

N3

N4

N2

ALTERNATING SQUARE (with suggested quilting lines shown)

GRANDMOTHER'S FLOWER GARDEN

Of all the possible quilt designs available, Grandmother's Flower Garden was probably the all-time rage of the 1920s and 1930s, especially in middle America. It's hard to imagine a family that doesn't have a few blocks of this design in a cedar chest. Start looking—they make wonderful little pillows. Just appliqué the block onto a background surface and add ruffles. The background pattern includes cutting lines for either a circular or hexagonal background, depending on your preference.

If you are making your own Flower Garden blocks, use the small hexagon pattern and cut one, six, and twelve pieces each of the appropriate fabrics. Traditionally, yellow was used for the center, a solid color for the first circle, and a printed fabric for the second circle. Another traditional concept particularly suitable to the hexagon is special positioning of the pattern on the fabric before cutting. Centering the same rose in every hexagon or positioning directionally on a stripe can give wonderful special effects.

While most old Flower Garden blocks were pieced by hand, the block can be pieced by machine if you are careful. When piecing the hexagon by machine, the crucial thing is to avoid stitching into the seam allowances. If you have any difficulty, it's worth it to *mark* the seam lines on each hexagon. Make a plastic or cardboard template from the inside hexagon of the pattern and lightly trace seam allowances on the wrong side of the fabric hexagons.

1. The first step is to add the six pieces of the second ring to the center hexagon. Begin by laying one second-row hexagon face-down on the center piece. Stitch one seam. Repeat with all five other pieces of the second row. Press seam allowances toward the center.

2. Now join the side seams of the pieces of the second row. Press seams open. This is one of the few places in patchwork where pressing seams open is recommended.

FINISHED SIZE:
9 inches across plus 2½-inch ruffles

MATERIALS NEEDED:
Approximately 12-inch square pieces of:
Background fabric
Quilt backing material
Batting
Pillow back fabric
Fabric for ruffles—minimum 10 inches × 36 inches
Stuffing

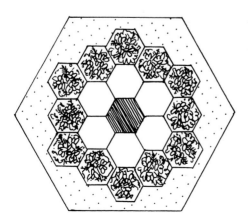

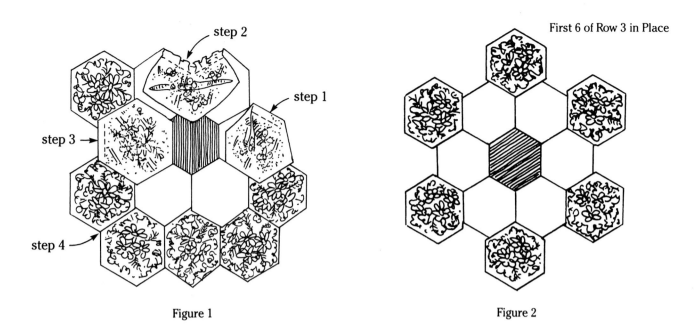

Figure 1

Figure 2

3. The hexagons of the third row are added alternately. That is, add a hexagon, skip a space, and then add the next hexagon, and so on (Figure 1). To add the first six hexagons on the third row, lay one third-row hexagon on the selected second-row piece. Begin with one of the inside angles. Starting on a side edge, stitch toward the inside corner. At that corner, with the needle through the fabric, pivot the top hexagon so that it is lying on the adjoining second-row hexagon and stitch that edge seam (Figure 1, steps 1 and 2). Repeat five times in alternate positions.

Figure 2 illustrates the block's configuration after steps 1 and 2 are completed.

4. Stitch the rest of the third-ring hexagons to the empty straight edges of row two (Figure 1, step 3). Pivot at the corner and sew the second side, or come back and do all adjoining sides like the second row.

5. Turn under and press the seam allowance on the outside edge and appliqué the patchwork to your background fabric. Layer and quilt as desired. Cut in hexagon shape, leaving at least 1 inch around the patchwork.

6. Add desired ruffles. The ones pictured finish at 2 inches and 2½ inches. Add the back. Turn and stuff.

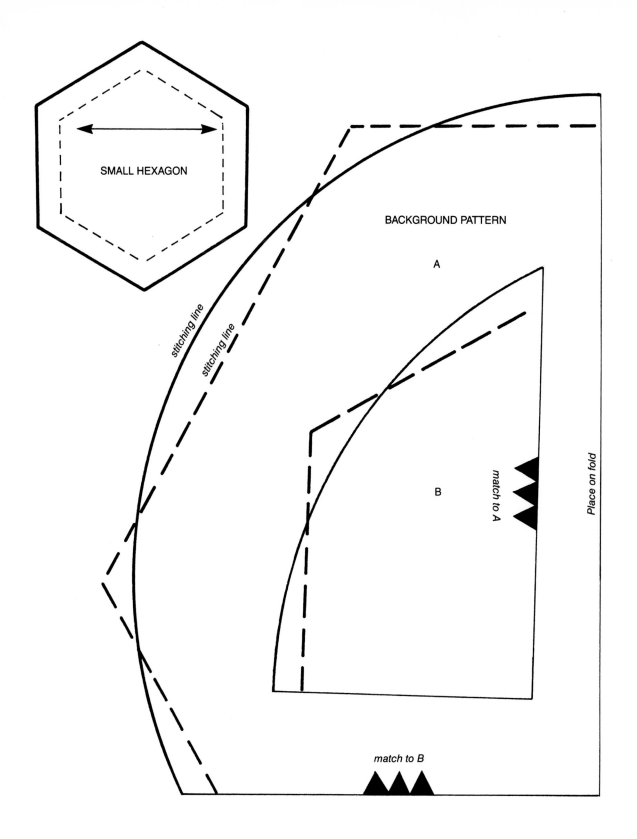

SMALL HEXAGON

BACKGROUND PATTERN

A

stitching line

stitching line

B

match to A

Place on fold

match to B

DOLL QUILTS AND WALL HANGINGS

Quilts don't have to be bed-size, arduous projects. They can be scaled down for dolls and teddy bears to become quick, easy patchwork projects. Even wall hanging and table-size quilts are small enough to finish quite easily. A doll-size quilt is ideal for a little girl's first quilt— or a grown-up's, too—since it will give the beginner a goal easily obtained in a relatively short time.

BROKEN DISHES DOLL QUILT

The small wall hanging or doll quilt was also made from old quilt blocks, but they were rearranged. It is quite a different story from the other old blocks. The original patchwork pieces had a small pieced unit block (see the pull-out on the illustration) alternating with a small white block. I wanted legitimate old white fabric—aged with time, not dye—for a small project, and bought the blocks to take apart and salvage the white fabric. To eliminate guilt about taking them apart, I bought the ugliest blocks I could find. It didn't work. I felt I could appease my guilt by doing something positive with the remaining blocks, including a few white ones. They are quite charming reassembled into a doll quilt.

The small border is new fabric selected because it looked old and picked up the color in some of the fabrics. The actual French fold binding is ⅜ inch finished and accented by a 1⁄16-inch flap—a perfect scale for a doll quilt.

When making the Broken Dishes, make unit blocks of four squares as shown in the illustration. This small doll quilt has thirty-one unit blocks and four plain blocks the same size.

This pattern can be made using a variety of fabrics and put together in any arranged pattern. It would be every bit as pretty using just two fabrics throughout, or delightful as a scrap quilt where the only order needed is a light triangle and a dark triangle in each square arranged in the Broken Dishes pattern. A slightly more orderly arrangement would be at least four blocks of each fabric combination sewn together as shown. Even more orderly is the quilt in the photo, which has multiple fabrics, but arranged in a color pattern.

FINISHED SIZE:
15¾ × 21¾ inches

MATERIALS:
18 × 24-inch batting
18 × 24-inch backing fabric

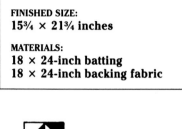

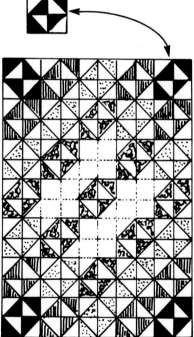

ATTIC WINDOW

The interplay of light, medium, and dark fabrics creates the window effect. Whatever fabrics or color scheme you choose, be sure to keep the darkest fabric at the bottom of the design square. To hide joining seams, it is best to use small prints for the window stripping.

Cut the following pieces:

Twelve of square A from light fabric
Twelve each of strip D/E from medium
      and dark fabrics

FINISHED SIZE:
13 × 10½ inches

ADDITIONAL MATERIALS:
Batting 14 × 11 inches
Backing fabric 15½ × 12
  inches

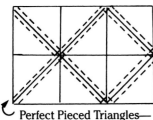

Figure 1

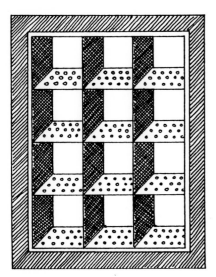

Perfect Pieced Triangles—
layout for stitching, cutting

Perfect Pieced Triangles

1. On the back of a piece of the medium fabric, draw out a grid of six $1\frac{7}{8}$-inch squares for perfect pieced triangles (see "Fabric Craft Basics") as shown in Figure 1. Lay it on top of the dark fabric, right sides together. By following the direction of the arrow, you can stitch all twelve triangle squares without ever taking the fabric out of the machine, pivoting at each corner.

2. Clip the triangles apart on the drawn diagonal lines. Press seam allowances toward the darker fabric.

Making the Design Blocks

1. Sew one dark strip (D) to one side of the square (A). Press seam toward the dark fabric.

2. Sew one triangle-square to one end of the medium strip. Press seam allowance away from the triangle. Join the units as shown in Figure 2. Press seam toward outside of the block. Make twelve design blocks.

3. Join the blocks into three rows of four blocks each, matching seam lines carefully. Join the rows.

Figure 2

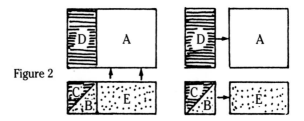

Adding Borders, Quilt-as-You-Sew

1. Lay the backing fabric flat, wrong side up. Lay batting on top of it. Center the pieced unit on top of the batting.

2. Cut two border strips, ¾ inch by 12 inches. With right sides and raw edges together, add these borders to the long sides, sewing through all three layers (see **Stitch-and-flip technique** in "Fabric Craft Basics"). Trim borders even with the patchwork.

3. Cut two border strips ¾ inch by 10 inches and sew to top and bottom in the same way. Trim even with the patchwork.

4. Refer to "Fabric Craft Basics" for tips on bringing the backing fabric over the quilt edges to bind them. Add hand or machine quilting as desired.

OHIO STAR

This little doll quilt is made using the quilt-as-you-sew method—that is, major seams are stitched through all three layers of fabric, batting, and backing.

FINISHED SIZE:
10¾ × 13¾ inches

ADDITIONAL MATERIALS:
Batting 11 × 14 inches
Backing fabric 11 × 14 inches

Making the Quilt Center

1. Begin by piecing the star section. From the appropriate light and dark fabrics as illustrated, cut five of square A (four of one fabric, and one contrasting) and sixteen of triangle B (eight of one fabric and eight of a contrasting fabric). First, sew together pairs of light and dark triangles. Press seams toward the dark fabric. Then join pairs to form squares and press the seam to one side.

2. You now have nine squares of equal size—five plain and four pieced. Arrange them in order as illustrated. Join squares into three rows of three squares each, then join rows into one star block. Press all seams to one side, toward the darker fabric whenever possible.

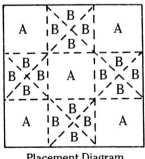

Placement Diagram

3. Lay backing fabric flat, wrong side up. Place batting on top. Secure together with a few pins at corners and edges.

4. Fold your batting in half, then in half again, marking each center point with a pin. Lay batting/backing flat again and position the star unit on it, aligning the block corners with the marked centers. Center a large triangle (C) on one side of the block, matching right sides and raw edges. Stitch through all layers. Repeat on the opposite side of the block. Press triangles very lightly (you don't want to flatten the batting). Add triangles to opposite sides in the same manner.

5. Cut strips of light fabric 1 inch wide and as long as the width of the pieced unit (approximately 7½ inches). Sewing through all layers, add to top and bottom. Repeat at sides (approximately 8½ inches). Add a second strip, the same width and length, to the sides.

Chain Piecing the Checkerboard

In any patchwork that has two squares of fabric side by side repeatedly, the more efficient procedure is to sew before you cut. If you have all the time in the world, of course, you may feel free to cut out thirty-six individual squares and laboriously sew them together. Most of us, though, will want to sew together two strips from which we can cut already joined units.

1. Cut strips of light and dark fabrics 1½ inches wide by 28 inches long. (If your scraps aren't large enough for this, you can work with two pieces 14 inches long or three pieces 10 inches long.) Seam the strips together with a ¼-inch seam allowance; press seam toward the darker fabric.

2. Carefully measure and cut eighteen segments as shown, all 1½ inches wide.

3. Arrange nine segments into a checkerboard and stitch together. Press the seams to one side.

4. Stitch the checkerboard units to the top and bottom of the quilt, sewing through all layers. Complete the quilt by cutting 1-inch-wide strips of light fabric and adding them first at the top and bottom, then the sides of quilt.

5. See "Fabric Craft Basics" for tips on binding.

NOTE: To enlarge the mini quilt to place-mat size, just add 1½-inch-wide borders of the darker fabric to the outside edge before binding.

PINWHEEL MINI QUILT

The Pinwheel Mini Quilt is different from the Attic Window and Ohio Star in that it features repeated blocks set together with strips called sashing.

Cut, then sew

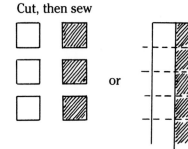

or

Sew, then cut

FINISHED SIZE:
13 × 17¼ inches

ADDITIONAL MATERIALS:
Batting 14 × 18 inches
Backing fabric 15 × 19¼ inches

Making the Pinwheel Block

The Pinwheel is made of four joined squares, each square being made from three pieced triangles. The effect of the design will depend on the placement of light, medium, and dark fabrics.

1. From the lightest and darkest fabrics, cut twenty-four of triangle A. Seam them together into twenty-four pairs, matching shorter sides. Press seams toward the darker fabric.

2. Cut twenty-four of triangle B from the medium fabric. Sew one to each pair of light/dark triangles to make a little square. Press seam allowance toward the large triangle.

3. Arrange four squares into a Pinwheel block as illustrated. Sew adjacent squares together, pressing seams toward the dark fabric. Sew pairs together to complete block. Make six blocks.

Adding Sashing

1. From contrasting fabric, cut seven strips 1⅜ inches and 3¾ inches long. Join the Pinwheel blocks into three rows by putting one sashing strip between each pair.

2. Sew a contrasting square (C) between each pair of remaining strips. Complete the center quilt section by joining rows with sashing between each row. Match seams carefully.

3. Cut sashing strips 1⅜ inches wide and as long as the width of the joined Pinwheels (approximately 8 inches). Sew to top and bottom edges. Repeat at the sides (approximately 14 inches). If your scraps aren't large enough to cut pieces in one length, you can piece together smaller scraps until you have a piece the right size. Using a very small nondirectional print fabric will camouflage joining seams.

Adding Borders and Finishing

1. From the medium fabric, cut borders to match all four sides of the quilt, cutting each strip 2⅛ inches wide.

2. Sew strips to top and bottom. Sew a square (D) onto each end of the side strips, pressing seam toward the dark fabric. Sew side strips onto the quilt, matching corner seams carefully.

3. Layer backing fabric, batting, and quilt top. Quilt as desired by hand or machine.

4. When quilting is finished, turn the extra backing fabric over to the front to bind the quilt edges. (See **Binding quilt edges** in "Fabric Craft Basics.")

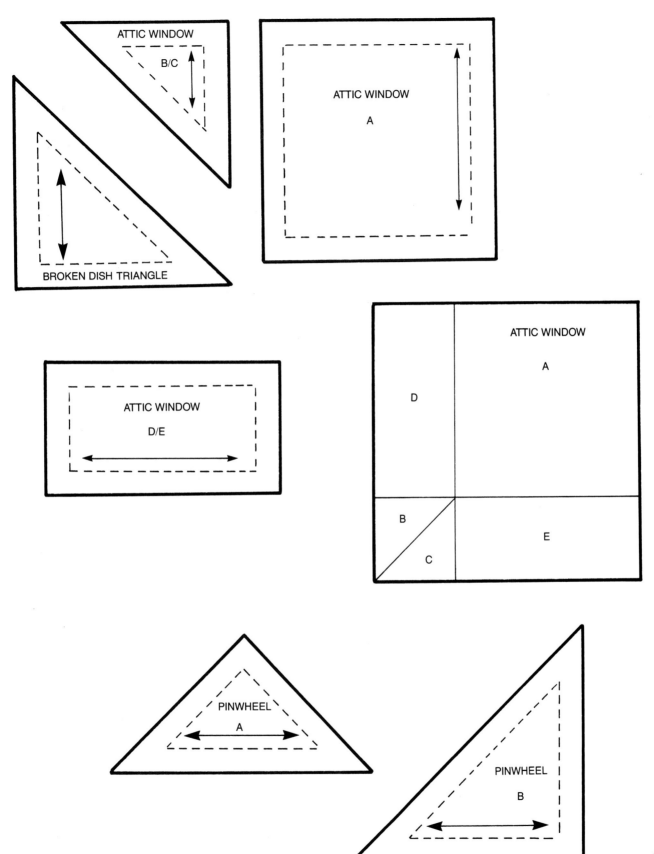

ATTIC WINDOW

B/C

ATTIC WINDOW

A

BROKEN DISH TRIANGLE

ATTIC WINDOW

D/E

ATTIC WINDOW

A

D

B

C

E

PINWHEEL

A

PINWHEEL

B

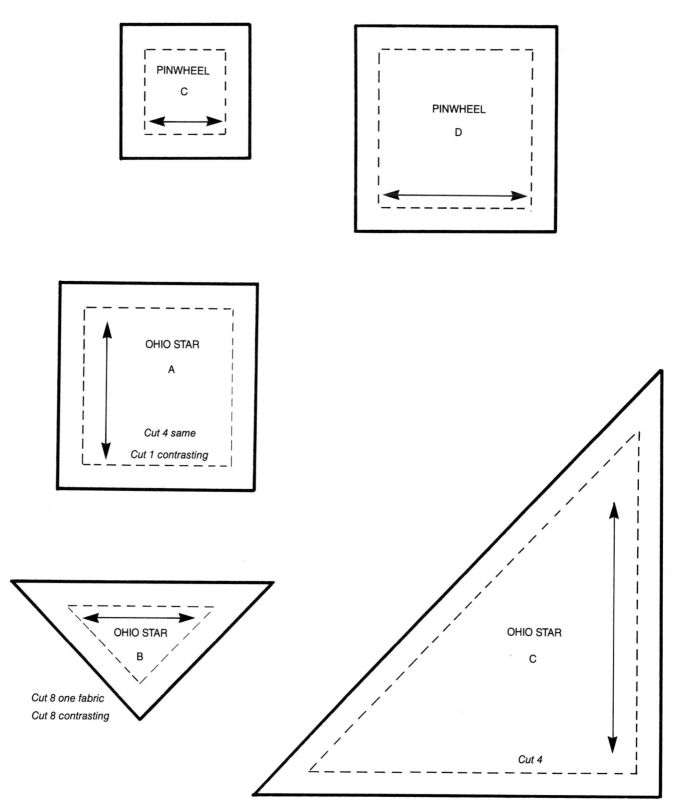

PINWHEEL
C

PINWHEEL
D

OHIO STAR

A

Cut 4 same

Cut 1 contrasting

OHIO STAR

B

Cut 8 one fabric

Cut 8 contrasting

OHIO STAR

C

Cut 4

Things That Look Great on Hooks and Pegs

It's the extra details that make country decorating so warm and interesting. From the simplest twine bow with stuffed heart decoration to the little Prairie Doll in a Swing, fun things to put on hooks and pegs can always find a home.

BABY SUNBONNET

1. Cut two brims from fabric and either one from the stiffest interfacing available or two from lighter weight interfacing. Layer and stitch together on the curved edge. Leave the straight edge open, but press the seam allowance inward when clipping, turning, and pressing the brim.

2. Cut two sunbonnet bodies. The second layer nicely finishes the neck edge, and the double thickness helps prevent bonnet limpness. With right sides together, stitch from dot to dot at the bottom of the "keyhole." (The second dot will be on the opposite side of the pattern piece when it is unfolded.) Turn inside out and press.

3. Topstitch bias tape (the elastic casing) on the lining side as marked on the pattern.

4. Run gathering stitches around the curved (upper) edge from dot to dot through both layers of fabric. Gather to fit the straight edge of the brim.

5. Tuck the gathered sunbonnet into the brim, and topstitch in place.

6. Finish by inserting elastic in the bias tape casing and securing at both ends. Make a "bow" by folding a 4½-inch square in half and stitching the three open sides. Leave an opening for turning. Turn and press and wrap a folded strip (2 inches by 2½ inches) around the center to make a knot.

7. Make streamers from four 2¾-inch by 17¼-inch pieces. Secure in place.

If you are only hanging it decoratively, you may want to fill the sunbonnet top with wadded nylon net to define a perky shape without adding much weight.

FINISHED SIZE:
approximately 10 inches long, plus streamers
(⅝-inch seam allowances included)

MATERIALS:
½ yard of any suitable fabric
10 × 18 inches of heavy interfacing for brim *or* cut two from 20 × 18 inches of lighter weight interfacing
6½ inches of ¼-inch-wide elastic

How much fabric? The only items listed with each project under Materials and Notions are notions and those fabrics that require more than ¼ yard to make as shown.

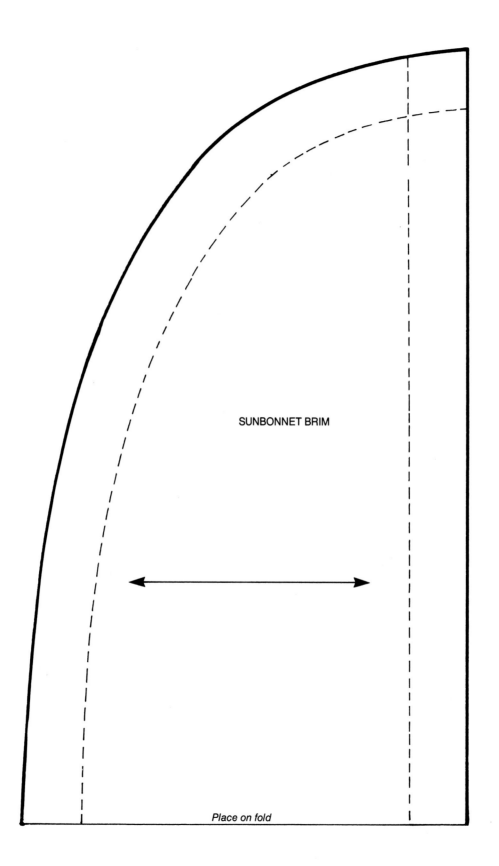

SUNBONNET BRIM

Place on fold

67

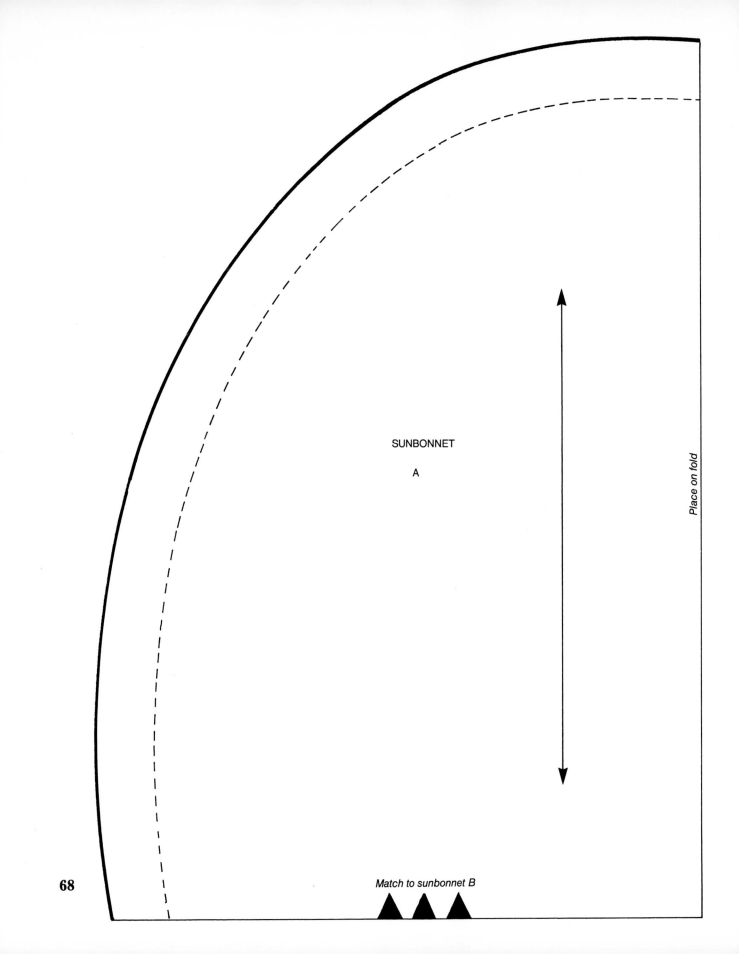

SUNBONNET

A

Place on fold

68

Match to sunbonnet B

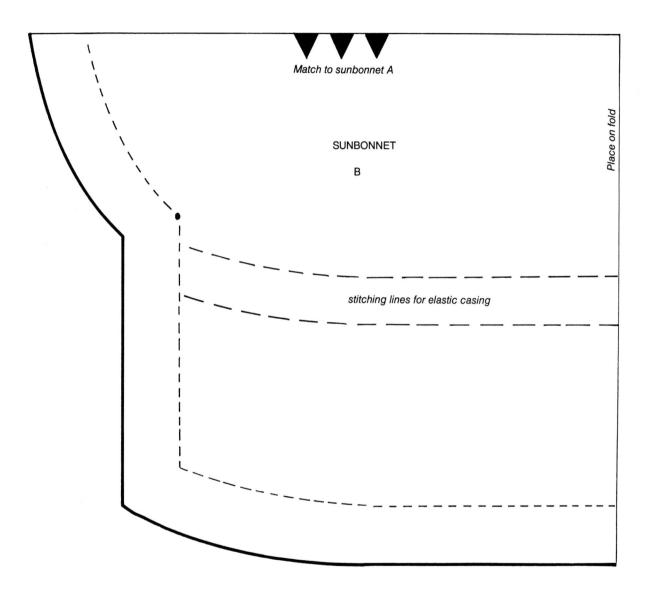

Match to sunbonnet A

SUNBONNET

B

Place on fold

stitching lines for elastic casing

69

HEARTS, HEARTS, AND MORE HEARTS

The possibilities for adding a little color, a good smell (as in hearts filled with potpourri), or a soft touch are never-ending with these Basic Hearts. All sizes, all quantities, and all combinations of hearts and hearts on strings are possible. Anything from a single little heart looped over a hanger to a dozen hearts cascading in one arrangement will add a pleasing accent. The heart strings may be twine or rattail or ribbons or cords. For brevity's sake, they will all be referred to as string.

These are great carry-along projects. Stitch a lot of hearts in one sitting at the sewing machine. Clip and turn, stuff and close anywhere. Having them ready to carry along is an easy way to make extras. They are the perfect thing to have on hand for the unexpected. Stick one on a present, give sets of six or twelve single hearts on bows as Christmas tree ornaments. Have sets of Cascading Hearts made for someone special. Patterns are included for six Basic Hearts and six Basic Folk Hearts.

MATERIALS NEEDED:
Twine
Stuffing

HEART ON A TWINE BOW

One of the simplest decorations that can be used over and over is the heart "knot" on a twine bow. You can use it alone on the Christmas tree, stitched on top of other hearts, or positioned anywhere you might put a ribbon bow. Twine is my favorite string for this item, but if that is too coarse for your decor, it can also be made with ribbon or rattail trim.

1. Use the smallest heart from the Basic Heart patterns.

2. Make a twine bow. (Notice how the "knots" a few inches from the end give the tails a more finished look.)

3. Stitch the bow in position behind the heart.

A SINGLE HANGING HEART

To make a single hanging heart, insert both ends of a short string at the center top of the heart when lining. Hang hearts over doorknobs, alone on small hooks, or fill with sachet for hangers. It is so simple, but so sweet.

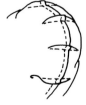

EDGE-TRIMMED DIMENSIONAL HEART

To make a more dimensional heart, work with a pattern one size larger than the finished size you would typically select.

1. Stitch around the heart, then, after clipping but before turning, make double-ended darts perpendicular to and across the seam in at least four places. The darts should extend approximately ½ inch into the heart.

2. Turn and stuff firmly. Close the opening. Measure the circumference to determine the amount of trim needed.

3. Attach trim around the newly created side of the heart. One possibility is a trim that is flat in the center with a ruffle on either side.

BOTTLED LOVE

This is a perfect gift for anyone you would like to constantly remind of your affection. Bottles of all sizes and shapes can be used. A canning jar with calico fabric in the cover, the very attractive commercially available storage jars, or even pickle or mustard jars that incorporate an inside joke to the recipient are all suitable containers.

Add baby's breath, artificial flora, sand and shells, soap balls, or potpourri to the jar to enhance the hearts and complete the story.

A nice addition to the Bottled Love is labels. I've included some labels you can use for starters. Copy with indelible pen on fabric, type them on adhesive labels, or cross-stitch the label, but make sure people know what they are getting. This is not just a couple of stuffed hearts in a jar, this is Bottled Love!

Love is something if you give it away, you keep on getting MORE!

Love is something if you give it away, you keep on getting more...

Love makes the world go 'round

Love makes the world go 'round

Bottled Love ...pass it on!

72

BOTTLED LOVE
Vintage 1990

BUNDLES OF LOVE

Bundles of Love serve the same purpose as Bottled Love. They can be made from any three of the basic hearts, either shape, stacked and tied. The stuffed bow (see "Home for the Holidays," page 202) is the perfect accent. The bundles can also be labeled.

CASCADING HEARTS

Selecting Fabrics

This project is a good one for expanding your ideas about what scraps can and do go together. The biggest piece needed for a single heart is 6 inches by 15 inches. Go through your scraps and look for a large assortment of colors, textures, and designs that are in some way complementary. For example, start with a large floral print that has many colors in it. As you sort, discard any fabric that doesn't look good with that one print. Or pick a plaid and find prints that carry out that color scheme.

This is a perfect example to demonstrate that nearly any project in the book can be adapted to your individual color scheme and decorating mood. It is the fabrication, not the item, that sets the mood and really makes it "read" romantic or patriotic or feminine.

Making the Cascading Hearts

There are six heart patterns each for regular and folk hearts in each set. There are twelve hearts on the ends of six strings, but there are really more than twelve hearts needed when you count the embellishments. When using six strings, select the sizes of hearts so that the largest and smallest are on opposite ends of the same string, the next largest and next smallest, the medium size and medium size, etc. Generally, selecting darker fabrics for the larger hearts and lighter fabrics for the smaller hearts provides a pleasing balance.

1. Cut strings 57 inches long. The strings are all the same length, but are staggered after the hearts are added and before the top bow is tied.

2. Rough cut the fabric pieces. Use the line-and-turn method for all sizes of hearts. When stitching the hearts, insert the string between the fabric pieces so that the short end comes out at the center top, and pull to one side where the opening for turning will be (Figure 1). Do not stitch across the string a second time, but pull it through the opening.

If you know you are going to appliqué additional hearts to one of the hearts on the end of a string, you can use the rough line-and-turn method and insert the string through the slit and to the center top and completely stitch around the heart (Figure 2). Clip and turn. Stuff fairly firmly. Close openings if necessary.

MATERIALS NEEDED:
Desired strings
Assorted trims
Stuffing

Figure 1

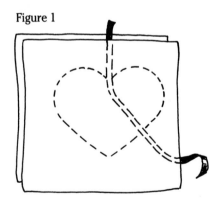

Figure 2

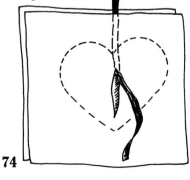

Embellishing the Hearts

The Cascading Hearts shown illustrate many ideas for embellishment. String bows (assorted and matching, single or double), appliquéd hearts (one, two, or three), and the Heart on a Twine Bow (see page 70) are the most frequently used. There are also buttons (singles and multiples), and one heart features a little contrasting ruffle.

Your own special likes will be easily incorporated. If you love doing embroidery, add it to the hearts. If you salvage lace trims and antique buttons, this is an ideal showcase. Potpourri advocates will enjoy aromatic Cascading Hearts.

Smaller Cascading Hearts can be made with four to eight hearts on shorter strings.

CASCADING MITTENS

This is a variation of Cascading Hearts.

Three sizes of mittens with heart, star, and kitten decorations can be combined to suit your fancy. For each mitten:

1. Sew the mitten front and back together, leaving open from the dot up on the side to the top.

2. Sew the facings together on one side.

3. With right sides together, stitch the facing to the mitten along the top edge only. When pressing, turn back a ¼-inch seam allowance on the facing.

4. On the facing side, stitch bias tape along the casing line. Turn back the edge of the bias tape, and stop the bias tape ⅝ inch from the seam on both sides.

5. With facing and seam on the outside, stitch as much as you can of the rest of the side seam. It will probably be easier to finish the last few stitches by hand. Press the seam allowances of the mitten under the facing, and close the facing by hand.

6. Insert ribbon for hanging. Run elastic through the casing. Lightly stuff the mitten below the elastic for a realistic look.

7. Add trims as desired. Heart and star trims (see page 80) are easy to fuse in place. Kittens will be more satisfactory if you appliqué faces in place. Stick folded ribbon ears under the top of the face before stitching down. Embroider the features.

RUFFLED SINGLE HEART

Using the full-size Americana Heart (page 140), add a 1¼-inch mock double ruffle and ribbon or fabric hanger for an individual hanging pillow. Cutting the heart from printed patchwork fabric is effective. (See the photo on page 66.)

MATERIALS NEEDED:
Same as for Cascading Hearts, plus ¼-inch elastic for wrists
Bias tape for wrists

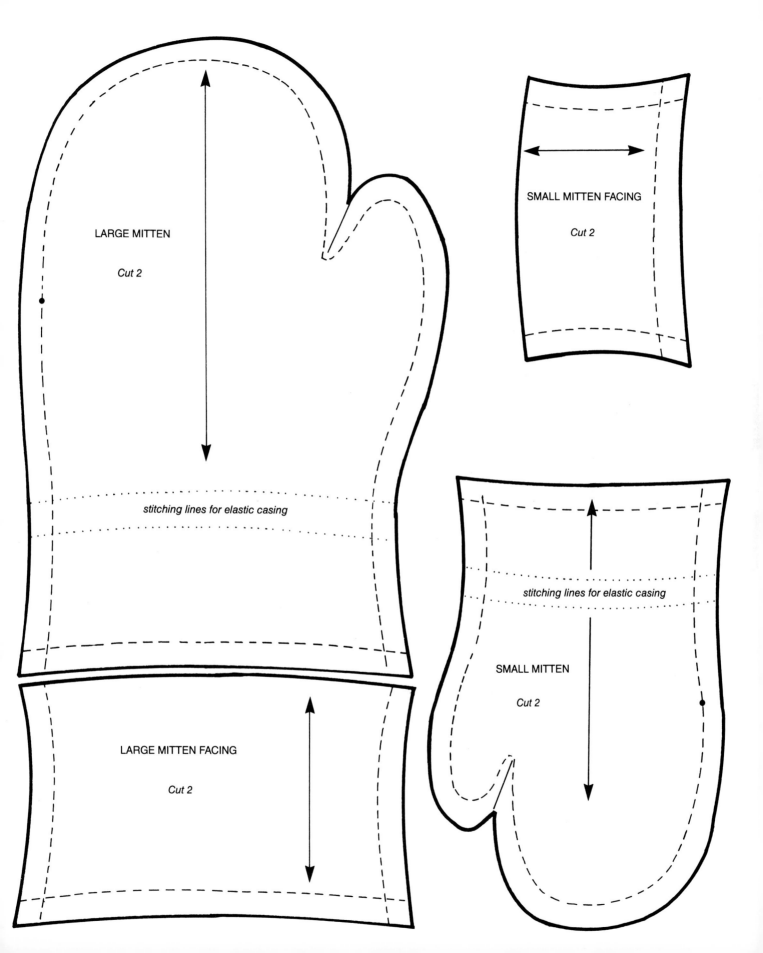

LARGE MITTEN

Cut 2

stitching lines for elastic casing

LARGE MITTEN FACING

Cut 2

SMALL MITTEN FACING

Cut 2

stitching lines for elastic casing

SMALL MITTEN

Cut 2

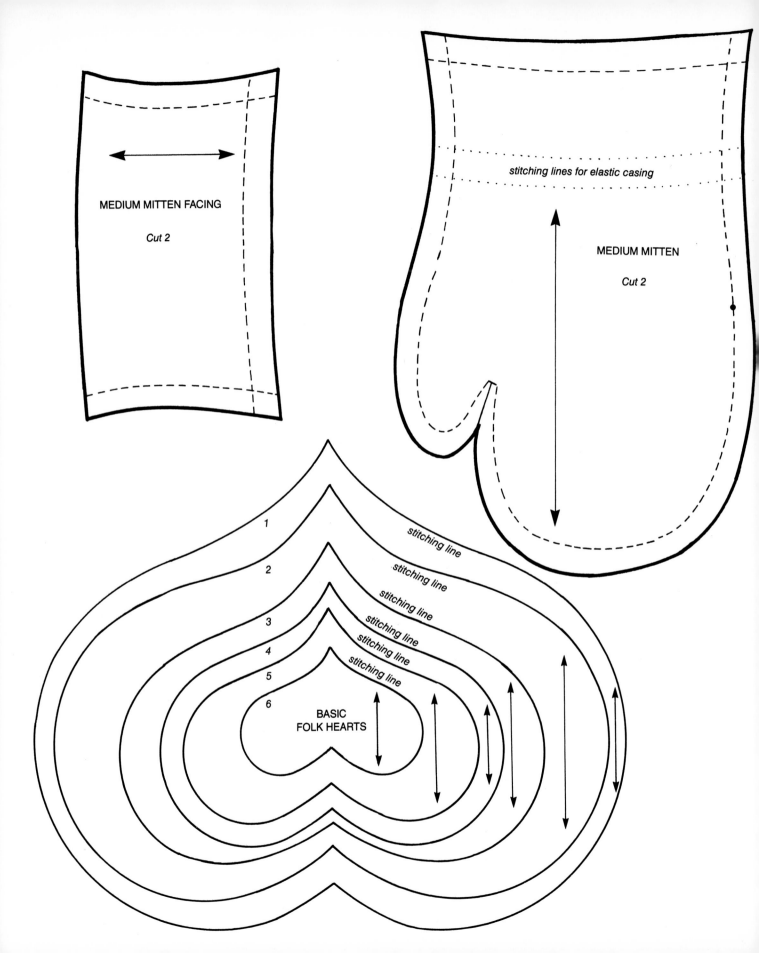

MEDIUM MITTEN FACING

Cut 2

stitching lines for elastic casing

MEDIUM MITTEN

Cut 2

1 *stitching line*

2 *stitching line*

3 *stitching line*

4 *stitching line*

5 *stitching line*

6 BASIC
FOLK HEARTS

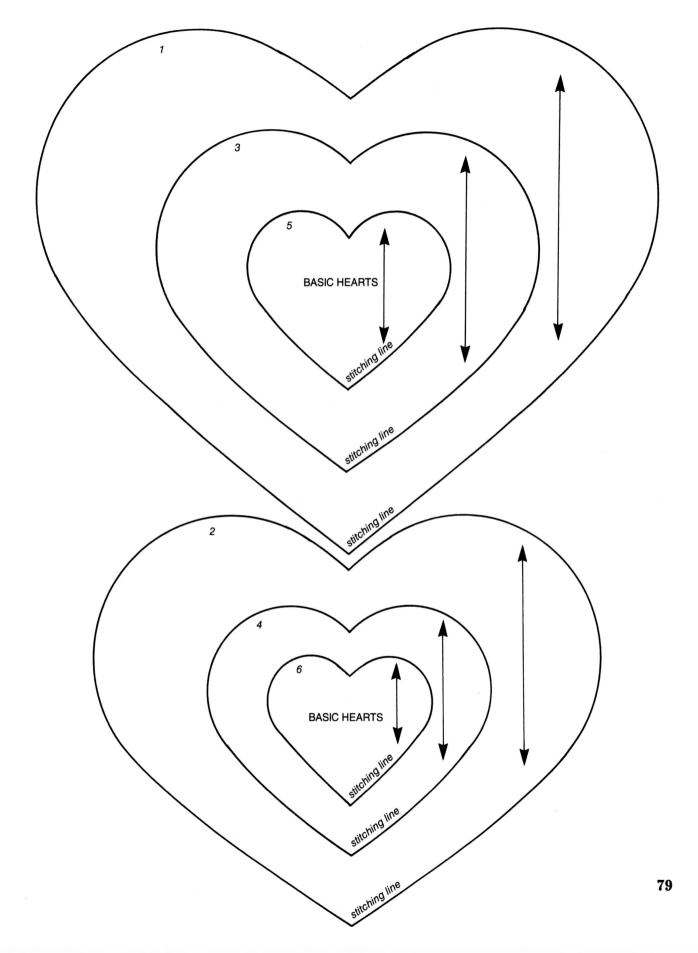

BASIC HEARTS

stitching line

stitching line

stitching line

BASIC HEARTS

stitching line

stitching line

stitching line

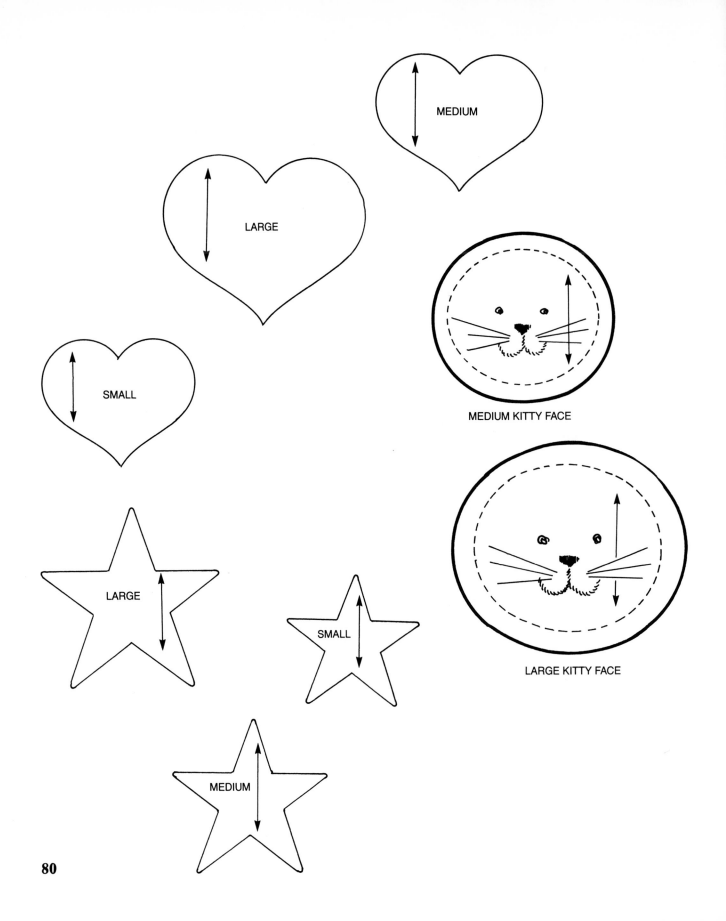

MEDIUM

LARGE

SMALL

MEDIUM KITTY FACE

LARGE

SMALL

LARGE KITTY FACE

MEDIUM

80

PRAIRIE DOLL IN A SWING

Making the Doll's Body

1. Fold the arms in half lengthwise. Stitch and turn to make a tube for each arm. (They are not stuffed.) Sew shoe pieces to the bottom of all leg pieces. Stitch right sides together, leaving open at the top. Stuff legs firmly.

2. Place one piece of the doll body right side up. Position the arms between the dots on either side of the upper torso. Put the other body piece right side down over the first. Stitch around the body and head, leaving open at the bottom.

3. Clip at the neck. Turn inside out and press. Attach the legs between the dots on the bottom of the body back. Press the seam allowance up around the bottom.

4. Stuff the body firmly. Stitch the front and back together across the bottom. Add lace if desired to simulate a petticoat.

5. Embroider the face. Cross-stitch the eyes. Use single stitch for the nose and outline stitch the mouth.

6. To make the hair, tear a strip of cotton 2 inches by 6 inches. Ravel the edges several threads deep. Tear across at ½-inch intervals. Ravel a scant ³⁄₁₆ inch on each side so that the remaining woven sections are also about ³⁄₁₆ inch wide. Tie single knots in the center of seven or eight little raveled strips. Position the knots across the seam line and secure in place with glue or thread.

Making the Doll's Clothes

1. Cut the sleeve/bodice piece. Cut the neck opening and turn back. Stitch by hand or machine to finish raw edges (see Figure 1). Narrow hem the sleeves.

2. Cut 6 inches of six-strand embroidery floss. Make gathering at the wrist by zigzag stitching over the embroidery floss. Position the floss ¼ inch from the hemmed edge, and start and stop stitching just a little more than ¼ inch from the ends. Do not gather until the dress is on the doll.

3. Hem the apron on three sides and center it on the skirt front. Gather the skirt sections to fit between the clipped notches on both sides of the sleeve/bodice. The dress is still flat and looks like Figure 2.

4. Fold right sides together. On both sides, stitch the underarm to the corner of the dress. Leave the needle in the fabric, lift the presser foot, and turn and stitch down the seam allowances on the skirt. Turn inside out and press.

5. Press the bottom of the skirt up ⅛ inch and hem.

6. Add ribbon apron straps and tie by hand. Allow approximately 2½ inches over each shoulder and the rest around the waist.

7. Put the dress on the doll. Gather the embroidery thread and tie in little bows at either wrist; trim away any excess length from the bows.

FINISHED SIZE:
doll approximately 6½ inches tall; with hanger and swing, 11 inches tall

NOTIONS NEEDED:
Embroidery floss for facial features
Embroidery floss for dress sleeves (looks like ribbon)
21 inches of ¼-inch wide ribbon for apron
¾ yard twine for swing
Balsa wood for swing seat
Hanger
Polyester loose fill
5 inches of ⅜-inch lace for petticoat (optional)

EXTRA TOOLS NEEDED:
Art knife for balsa wood
Brown broad felt-tip marking pen

Figure 1

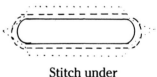

Stitch under

Figure 2

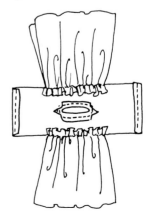

81

Making the Swing

1. Cut a balsa wood seat 1 inch by 4 inches. Cut swing holes with a craft knife or small drill. Thread 12 inches of twine through the swing holes. Knot on the same side of the board.

2. Tie the seat to the swing. Make sure the twine is equal in length on both sides. (A steam pressing can straighten twine that has been coiled.)

Assembly

1. Put the doll in the swing. Wrap her "hands" around the swing cords and stitch in place.

2. You may want to put dabs of glue on the tips of the doll's feet to hold them in place on the balsa wood seat.

Other Uses for Doll

The same doll can be fabricated as a black doll (see page 59). Another doll adorns the sewing basket on page 92. The size of the doll makes it perfect as a doll's doll. It sits nicely on a small chair or in a wreath. With a change of dress and hair, the Prairie Doll becomes a Native American Prairie Doll.

NATIVE AMERICAN PRAIRIE DOLL

The best fabric would really be a soft leather or suedelike material. You can substitute two pieces of broadcloth fused together. This gives a little more body and allows you to clip edges for a fringed effect without ravels, as if the material were leather.

1. Cut the bodice unit and make a slit at the neck. It is not necessary to turn under and stitch.

2. Topstitch the bodice onto the skirt section in a V shape, as in the pattern.

3. Fold the dress with right sides together. On both sides, stitch the underarm to the corner of the dress. Leave the needle in the fabric, lift the presser foot, and turn. Stitch skirt seams. Turn inside out. Press and the clip hem, bottom of the bodice, and sleeves to give a fringe effect.

4. Add optional bead trim on the dress bodice, embroider the face details, and braid perle cotton for the hair. The braid goes across the seam—it is not a full wig.

NOTIONS NEEDED:
Beads
Beading needle
Perle cotton or light yarn for hair
Feather

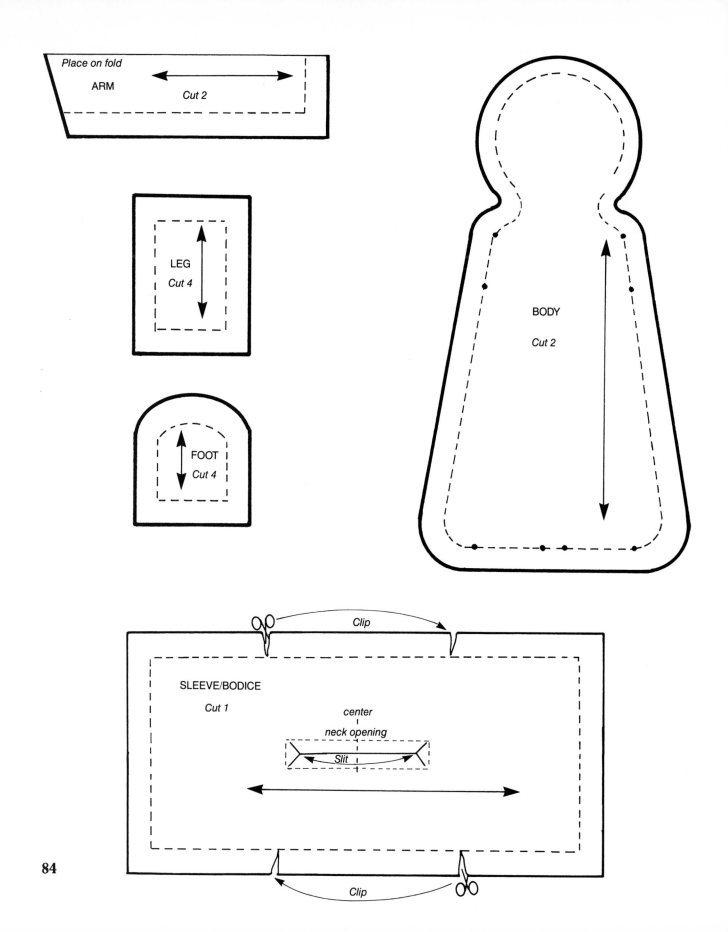

Place on fold

ARM

Cut 2

LEG
Cut 4

FOOT
Cut 4

BODY

Cut 2

Clip

SLEEVE/BODICE

Cut 1

center

neck opening

Slit

Clip

84

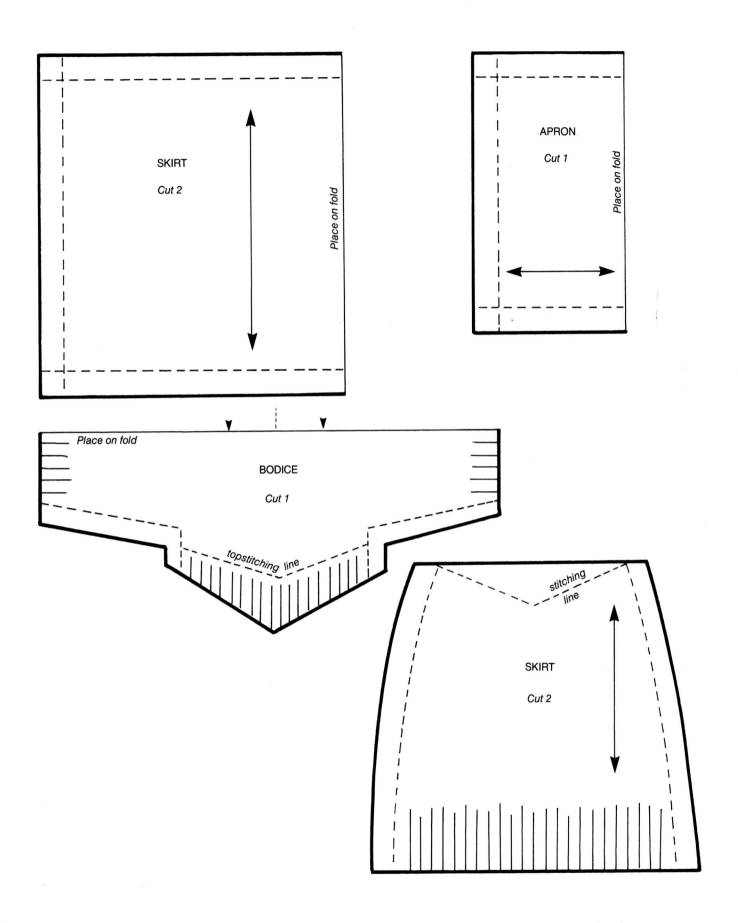

Sew a Treat for Yourself

PIONEER POCKETS

Pockets in dresses were not common in the turn-of-the-century prairie days. The items we call Pioneer Pockets were. Instead of wasting fabric to put pockets in every dress, one pocket could be worn with everything. It was really nothing more than a pocket on a waistband—today we call them pocketbooks or purses. Because they often held a lady's sewing supplies and because I am partial to sewers, I prefer to call them Pioneer Sewing Pockets. It was common for the pocket to be a little girl's first sewing project. As with many other everyday items, not many have survived to be handed down to our families and antiques shops.

While Pioneer Pockets are very functional, they can also be decorative. After seeing a real antique patchwork sewing pocket priced higher than many of the quilts in the same shop, I was inspired to take one very poorly made old quilt block I owned and turn it into a pocket to display with some of my collected antique sewing pieces.

MATERIALS NEEDED:
Pocket fabric
Batting and/or interfacing
Backing
Fleece (optional)
Fabric for binding

Cutting and Assembling the Pocket

1. Using the same pocket pattern piece, cut two of the front fabric. Cut one piece of fleece or two of lightweight interfacing for the front of the pocket. For the back, cut one of a heavy backing fabric like denim or two of regular-weight calico and one layer of interfacing. If you use the latter option, put the calico pieces wrong sides together and sandwich the interfacing between them, treating them from then on as one piece of fabric.

2. To make the slot pocket opening without cutting a slot, lay two fronts right sides together. Stitch on straight lines, take stitches in place at dots. (If using a lightweight interfacing, cut two layers and place one on each wrong side of the pocket front before stitching.) Separate layers by pulling each piece of fabric so the wrong sides touch and the right sides are exposed. Press carefully.

3. Topstitch around the opening. If using feather stitching or other decorative stitching on the binding, you may want to use it here also. If you are doing any optional decorating, complete it before the next step.

How much fabric? The only items listed with each project under Materials and Notions are notions and those fabrics that require more than ¼ yard to make as shown.

4. Stack pocket fronts and back together. Machine baste around the outer edge. Cut bias binding 1¼ inches wide. Fold in half and press some curve into the bias. Pin bias in place so that the raw edges of the bias match the raw edges of the pocket and it lies on the pocket front. Stitch in place. Roll the bias to the back so that the folded edge covers the machine stitching. Finish with a hidden stitch.

Back-to-Front Bias Option

Stitch bias tape to the back side of the pocket and press to the front. Instead of a hidden hem stitch, use embroidery thread and a feather stitch or buttonhole stitch to hold the bias in place.

Adding the Waistband

The simplest waistband is a 1½-inch-wide ribbon that is the length of your waist measurement plus 2½ inches. Overlap ends and use snaps or good old-fashioned pioneer Velcro. Sew an old button on top to disguise the Velcro, or if you love making buttonholes, make a regular narrow waistband and use a button and buttonhole to close.

Placement of Pocket on Waistband

Think about the relationship of the pocket to the closure. Most right-handed sewers want the pocket on the right side and the waistband closure at center back or the left side. You might prefer the closure right beside the pocket. Position the pocket on the waistband as desired.

LINED POCKET WITH ADDED HEART OPTION

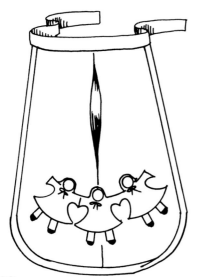

1. Make the pocket front as above.
2. Make line-and-turn heart (or hearts) to decorate the front. (The pattern for a single large heart is included here, or use the Basic Hearts or Basic Folk Hearts patterns in the preceding chapter.) Do as much quilting or decorative stitching as desired. When using multiple hearts, topstitch the smaller ones in place, leaving them open at the top for pockets.
3. Place back and front of the heart with right sides together. Stitch around the outside edge, leaving open at the top. Clip, trim and turn, and topstitch through all layers so that the raw seam allowances are enclosed.

> **MATERIALS NEEDED:**
> **Same as above except**
>   **eliminate binding fabric and**
>   **add heart**

OTHER POCKET VARIATIONS

As it happens, two other designs in this book would make nice Pioneer Pocket decorations. They are illustrated here, but shown in other forms later in the book. The Paper Dolls on page 148 could be appliquéd on the lower section, or use the pattern to cut a stencil and stencil a pocket front for everyone in your sewing circle. They get to embellish and finish them.

The Hearts and Roses Trapunto (see page 145) happens to fit the pocket perfectly. To be more decorative, make it in ecru like the pillow, or see the appliqué version of the same design in "Fun with Sweatshirts" (page 172).

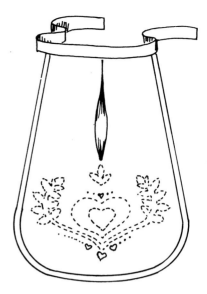

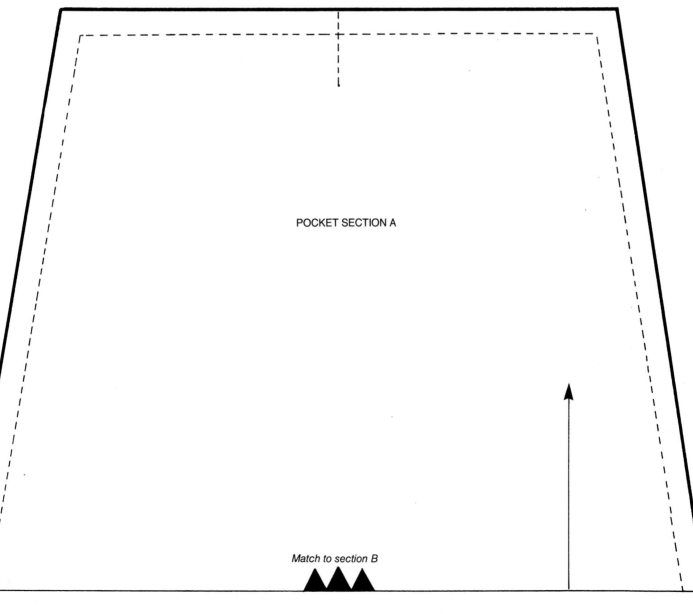

POCKET SECTION A

Match to section B

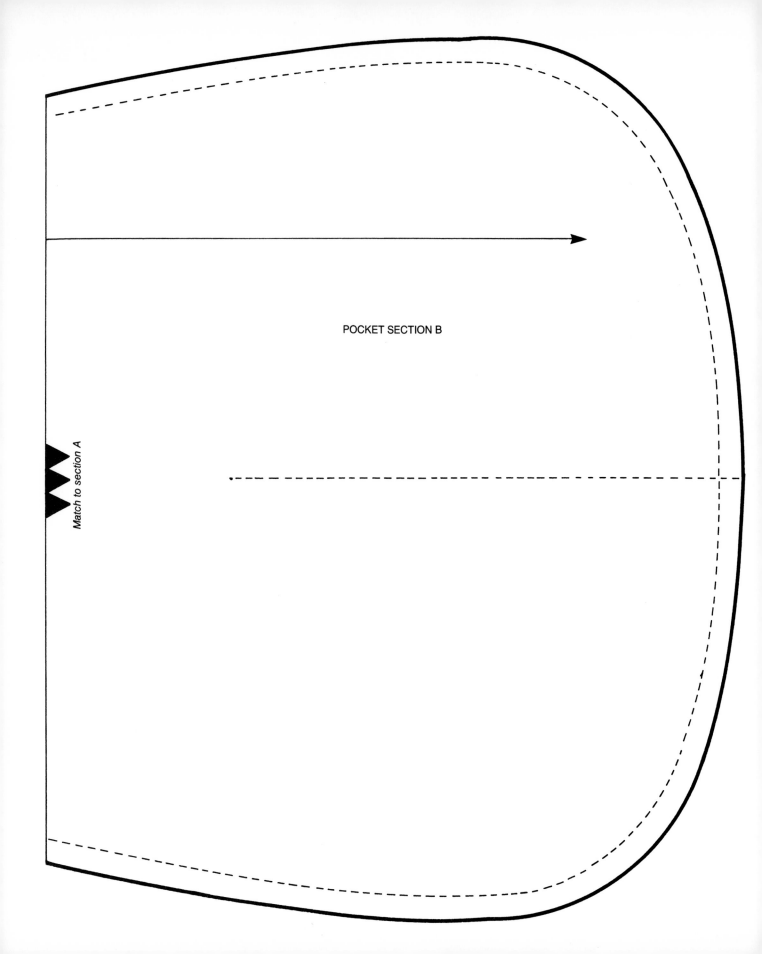

POCKET SECTION B

Match to section A

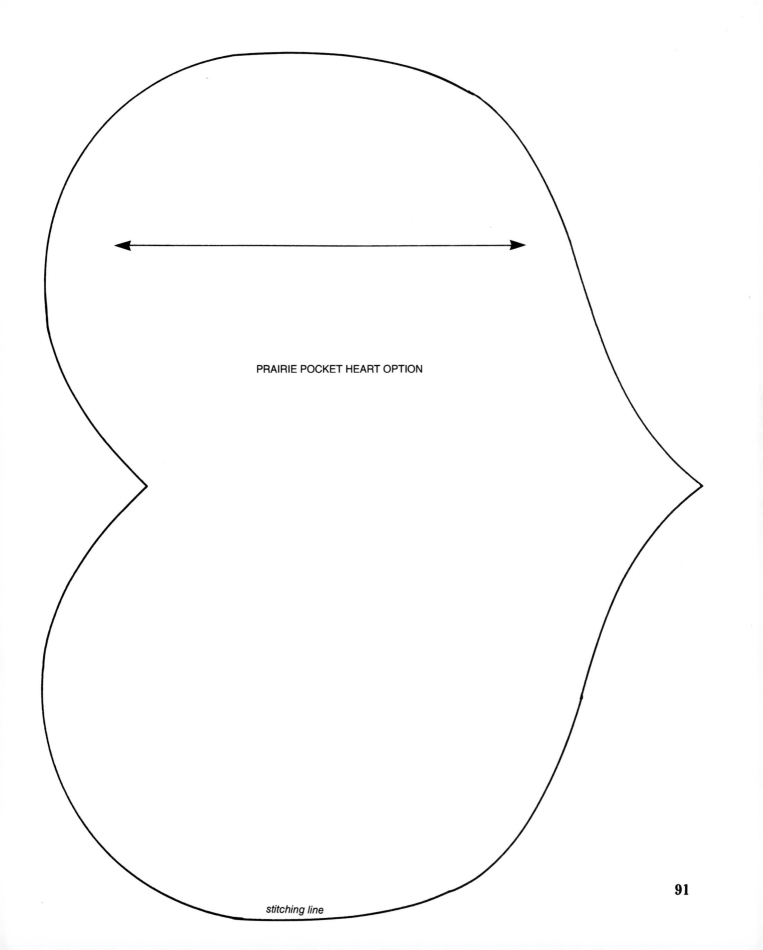

PRAIRIE POCKET HEART OPTION

stitching line

91

SEWING BASKETS

Sometimes pockets aren't big enough and sewing baskets are the best idea. Baskets are country, popular and plentiful. However, no two are exactly alike, so these instructions are therefore general rather than specific. When shopping, look for flat-bottomed, relatively straight-sided baskets or for those that lean outward slightly, but not with curved sides.

Measuring the Basket and Determining Fabric Needs

1. Measure around the basket at the top. The lining is gathered. The edge of the lining that stands above the top will look best if the lining is at least twice as long as this measurement. The sewing basket shown is 29 inches around the top.

2. Measure the height of the basket. Our sewing basket is 4 inches tall. After allowing ½ inch for gathering at the bottom, 1¼ inches for the ruffle above the basket, another 1¼ inches for the fabric to come back down to the basket top (self-facing), and 1 inch for gathering and finishing, the cut size of fabric needed is 8 inches high by 58 inches wide. Why not cut two pieces measuring 8 inches by 36 inches? That will allow for extra fullness.

If you want the ruffle facing to be a contrasting fabric, just substitute multiple pieces of fabric at this point. This is similar to the mock double ruffle concept shown on many of the pillows. Don't forget to allow for seams.

3. Because basket bottoms are often very irregular and the finish on this basket includes a padded covered bottom, the torn-paper pattern method is recommended. Put a piece of paper larger than the basket bottom into the bottom. Run your fingernail where the paper sides fold up, and carefully tear the paper on the resulting crease line. Put aside for the lining bottom pattern.

Making the Lining

1. Sew one pair of 8-inch ends of fabric together. Turn back and narrow-hem the other two ends. Leave the fabric flat for working. It's much easier to overlap hemmed ends than to gather a circle to fit a basket exactly.

2. Press under the ruffle facing and gathering allowance—in this case, 2¼ inches. Sew two rows of long machine gathering stitches at the bottom and at the point where the lining will touch the basket edge. Mark quarters of fabric. While the fabric is still flat is the time to consider topstitching trim in place.

3. Gather the bottom to approximately the bottom basket measurement—in our case 26½ inches around plus 2 inches for overlapping.

4. Gather the top to the basket top measurement plus 2 inches. Keep the last inch on both ends fairly flat. Keep the gathers even enough so that top and bottom quarters marks still line up.

5. Secure the top gathers and hide the stitching lines by topstitching ribbon band across the gathering on what will be the inside of the basket.

Adding Lining to Basket

1. Carefully glue the back of the gathered fabric to the inside of the basket at the top surface. When ends overlap, fold under the top and cover the raw edge. The bottom gathering will be folded and glued to the bottom of the basket, but it is best to do that after the top has dried.

2. Lift the ruffle and run glue around one-fourth of the basket. Pull the lining taut and hold in place. Continue until the bottom edge is secure. The raw gathered edge should be flat on the bottom of the basket, but will be covered.

3. Using your paper pattern, cut a cardboard or foam-core base and a layer of quilt batting. Lightly glue the batting to the cardboard, and then rough cut a larger piece of lining fabric (matching or contrasting) about 1 inch bigger all around. Wrap around to the back and glue in place.

4. Glue the bottom in place in the basket.

Making the Basket More Functional or Decorative

Adding pockets and elastic loops for thread makes the basket more functional. The little basket pictured on page 92 has elastic inside a fabric casing hot glued in place on the outside. To be more decorative it has a Prairie Doll watching over the contents. Just putting some stuffed bows on the handles would also be fun. I like decorated baskets because they become part of the decor and look at home by my favorite chair in the family room.

BIG PRAIRIE DOLL SEWING BASKETS

Still not big enough? What about this sewing basket affectionately called Benevolent Beatrice? The owner says, "Benevolent Beatrice belongs at every big sewing bee." It is her responsibility to ward off mistakes and oversee projects, something like a sewer's fairy godmother.

How to Have Your Own Benevolent Beatrice

1. Select a basket. We used one measuring 12 by 18 by 7½ inches. Make a pocket about 10 inches across and 6 inches deep, with a drawstring in the top. Add it to the lining while it is still flat.

2. Using the Betsy Ross pattern (see pages 103–107), make a half doll—we're talking the top half. When you get to the legs, just gather the bottom of the torso and close the doll.

3. Dress the doll in a dress from the same fabric as the basket lining. Instead of adding a gathered skirt to the bodice, add a strip of fabric 4½ inches wide and as long as the bodice is around. Gather this strip at the bottom of the torso also.

4. When the lining is put in the basket, make sure the pocket is positioned where Beatrice will be able to survey your projects comfortably. When the lining is completed, put the doll in the pocket and gather the drawstring around the bodice of the dress so that it looks as if the doll's skirt is lining your basket.

BUTTON JEWELRY

"Button, button, who's got the button?" was a game children played in simpler days. Now it is the cry of the sewer caught up in embellishing. Bite your tongue if you laughed about Grandma clipping buttons and now you are the lucky owner of the family button box. Almost every family has one. If yours doesn't, look for them at flea markets or garage sales. Once you start this, you'll love it and your need for buttons will jump dramatically.

Antique buttons are wonderful—antique pearl buttons are my favorite—but it's surprising what good results you can achieve with relatively inexpensive and readily available purchased buttons. When selecting, look for variety in texture, size, and shade. Plan on making several items or share with a friend to make the quantity purchased more acceptable. If you happen onto a button sale, don't be weak-hearted—stock up and think up projects!

Muslin fabric and pearl buttons are probably a favorite combination because they are so wearable with everything, but sometimes it's fun to make a piece you know can be worn with only one outfit but accents that perfectly. Think how effective a rust-colored checked heart with brown tone buttons will be with denim or turquoise or khaki.

Patterns are included for the heart, the small heart, the star, and a moon shape. Make all shapes using the stitch-and-line method. Turn through center back. Stuff lightly and whipstitch the center back shut.

Sewing Buttons in Place

The placement is most attractive to me when it is asymmetrical. It is nice with buttons on one side only—not completely encrusted. A few small buttons may spill out into the open area. Study the pieces pictured that you like most and then, thinking in terms of similar placement, start sewing. Generally, you will start with the largest button in the most heavily covered area and build out. It is a good idea to knot your thread after every button—just in case!

A faux sew method would be to take stitches in the button only with six-strand embroidery thread. Tie the thread at the back of the button. Then hot glue the buttons in place. This is about the only choice of procedure if you want a really thick, stacked-up, encrusted look.

Options

Other trims such as narrow lace sewn in the seam, French knots, and/or ribbon roses mixed in with the buttons could add very interesting looks. Flex your imagination!

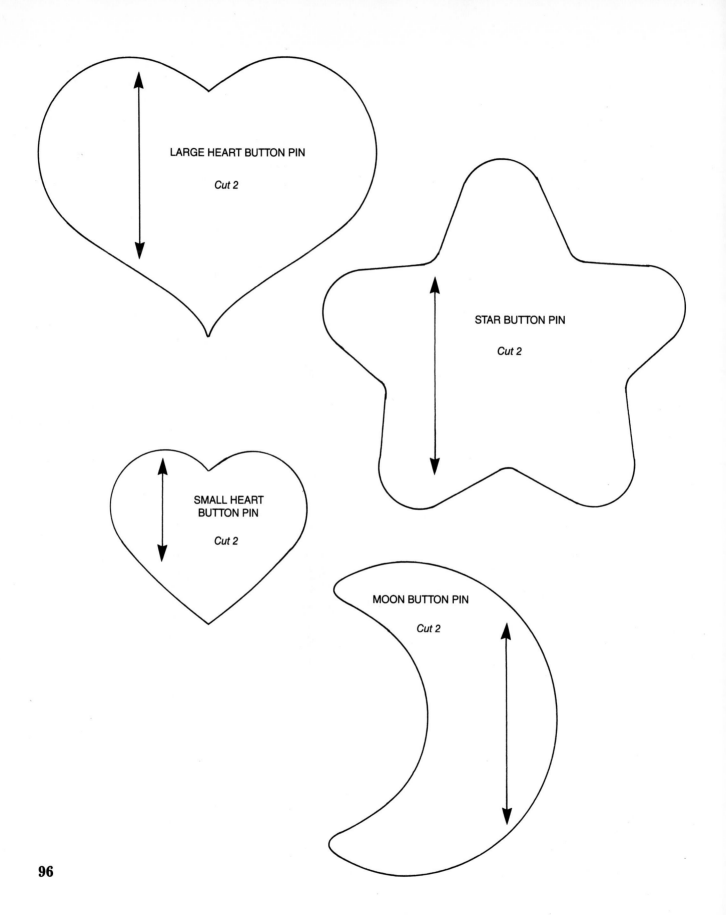

LARGE HEART BUTTON PIN

Cut 2

STAR BUTTON PIN

Cut 2

SMALL HEART
BUTTON PIN

Cut 2

MOON BUTTON PIN

Cut 2

96

The Americana Spirit

UNCLE SAM AND BETSY ROSS DOLLS

Uncle Sam and Betsy Ross have always been among my favorite American symbols. We love Betsy because of her alleged association with the flag, of course—plus we needleworkers relate to her as one of us. Researchers say Betsy's story is probably folklore. No one can validate that she really did show George Washington how to cleverly cut a five-pointed star and thus got the nod to make the first flag. The Betsy Ross story was first publicized shortly before the United States Centennial by a grandson of Betsy's, who said she made the flag in June 1776 for a secret group led by Washington.

Because historians have not found another explanation and the honor is not claimed by anyone else more likely, the Betsy Ross story lives, and I, for one, am glad.

While Uncle Sam is based on a real person, the Uncle Sam we've come to know and use to symbolize the United States government is mostly the creation of America's political cartoonists. Thomas Nast, generally credited with creating the modern political cartoon, drew his works during and after the Civil War for many prominent publications. It was his use of Uncle Sam to personify the United States government that cemented the relationship. His Uncle Sam's physique was definitely influenced by the lanky, bearded Abraham Lincoln. The stars and stripes clothes we associate with Uncle Sam were designed by Nast.

The Uncle Sam image we know best today, however, was created by James Montgomery Flagg. His World War I U.S. Army recruiting poster is perhaps the most famous poster in American history.

The man behind the image, by the way, was Sam Wilson, a popular New York meat packer who was called Uncle Sam by a host of friends and relatives. He contracted to supply provisions to United States troops during the War of 1812. He marked the casks of meat intended for the Army with the letters "U.S.," leading soldiers to joke that Uncle Sam had initialed their provisions and that they were thus "Uncle Sam's" soldiers.

Here we continue the common practice of paying tribute to folk heroes by making representational dolls.

How much fabric? The only items listed with each project under Materials and Notions are notions and those fabrics that require more than ¼ yard to make as shown.

Making the Doll Bodies

Before beginning, please review the **Line and turn** instructions in "Fabric Craft Basics." The body pattern pieces do *not* include seam allowances.

1. Mark seam lines and rough cut the doll's front torso. Select the face version you will use, put that pattern under the cloth and trace the features (see "Adding Facial Features," page 102).

2. Mark and cut out the combined back torso pieces. Sew them together down the center back seam. Press open at the top of the head. Sew the back and front together, matching drawn seam lines. Leave the bottom open. Trim away excess seam allowances, clip as needed, and turn right side out.

3. Start stuffing the head and shoulders. Pull off small walnut-size balls of filling. Pack a few at a time into the doll smoothly and evenly. Check the outer surface to be sure that you are not making a lumpy doll. Push the stuffing with your fingers, a dowel, or chopstick, but not with a sharp-pointed instrument or scissors or you risk poking through the fabric. The entire doll body should be stuffed very firmly. If you can push a hole into the stuffing with your finger, you need to add more stuffing. Take special care to make the neck rigid so the head won't wobble. Make the shoulders very firm, as the arms will be attached there.

For greater neck rigidity, you may consider adding a dowel in the dolls' necks (especially Uncle Sam's and especially if the dolls are strictly adult decoration dolls). The Uncle Sam shown has an 8-inch dowel carefully inserted during the stuffing process. It is in the middle of the stuffing from the waist to approximately the nose position of the head.

Making the Arms

1. Trace around the arm and hand pattern, and stitch matching pairs together on line except between dots at the shoulder. Clip and turn.

2. Transfer finger stitching lines to hands. One way of doing this is to lay the pattern on each arm and fold under most of the finger area, leaving the beginnings of the finger lines showing. From these points, you can lightly draw the finger stitching lines with a pencil or water-erasable pen. Do not forget to mark the appropriate thumb line.

3. To stuff the arm, fold or roll from the shoulder down to the wrist. Stuff the hand and finger area very lightly. Machine stitch the finger and thumb lines. The light stuffing will give them some definition. Unfold the arm an inch or two at a time, adding stuffing as you go. Stuff the arm firmly up to the very top, which should be stuffed lightly so it will fit over the shoulder.

APPROXIMATE FINISHED LENGTHS (WITHOUT HATS):
Sam 24 inches, Betsy 20 inches

MATERIALS NEEDED:
¾ yard body fabric
Stuffing
Heavy interfacing for shoe soles
Yarn for hair (see information with directions for hair)
Cardboard for yarn-winding templates
Notions for features on faces (see information with directions for faces)
Optional dowel for body support

4. Baste under ¼ inch at the top of each arm. Match arm seams to doll body seams and pin the arms on the doll. Sew the arm on with a blind stitch, adding more stuffing to the shoulder as needed.

Making the Hair

It is easiest to add the hair after the head and shoulders are complete, but before the legs are added. When selecting yarn for dolls, look for super high-bulk or brushed (mohair look) acrylic. It gives more body or fullness. The Uncle Sam doll shown has gray mohair, and Betsy has a high-bulk acrylic. The instructions here are for those yarns. If you use something else, it will probably be necessary to adjust. One skein of yarn makes a lot of hair. If you want to use leftover yarn, just cut and wrap the templates to see if you have enough.

Betsy's Hair
Making the basic wig:

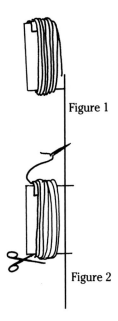

Figure 1

Figure 2

1. Cut a cardboard template 6 inches square. Cut a piece of body fabric 1 inch by 4½ inches and center it over one edge of the cardboard. Tape in place at each corner. Starting at one end of the fabric, wind the yarn smoothly and evenly—without pulling tightly—180 times around the template (Figure 1). Be sure the yarn covers the whole 4½-inch width evenly, not crisscrossing from one side to the other.

2. While the yarn is still on the cardboard, stitch it by hand to the fabric with small ¼-inch backstitches. This stitching will be the hair's exposed center part, so straight stitches are important. You can loosen one piece of tape, curve the board, and slide your hand up under the fabric to make stitching easier.

3. To remove the yarn, cut the yarn on the side opposite the fabric strip (Figure 2). Remove tape. Stitch under the raw ends of the fabric strip. Double-check—you may find it necessary to add some stitches so that each strand will be fastened to the fabric.

Adding the wig to the body:

1. Place the hair on the doll's head so the "part" is directly over the center back seam and extends onto the face ½ inch. Fasten the wig to the head by stitching down the length of the part into the doll's head. You may first want to tack the wig fabric strip to the head.

2. Smooth the strands over the head evenly, keeping the hair parted. Shape the front hair so it angles toward each temple, and pin it in place. Smooth the rest of the hair around the sides and back of the head and pin in position.

3. Loosely stay-stitch the hair in place about 2 inches on either side of the part. To do this, try to slide the needle *through* the strands of yarn for an inch, then take a stitch into the head, then through the strands, and so on, rather than stitching *over* the yarn.

4. Divide the hair on each side of the part into upper and lower sections, with the lower being somewhat thicker. Pin the upper sections out of the way (Figure 3). Divide the lower section into three equal parts on each side of the center part. Trim all this yarn to 4 inches in length. The hair is now going to be made into several small curls. Tie the lower end of each of the six curl sections with matching thread.

5. Starting at the back, on one side of the part, twist the section of hair into a spiral curl. Tuck the end under the upper part of the curl and sew in place, flat against the head. These back curls should cover the neck. Make the middle curls the same way, placing them low (Figure 4). The forward curls should be turned toward the face and placed below the temple area, both at the same height.

6. Let down the upper section of hair. If necessary, trim the hair so it ends 2 inches below the bottom of the lower curls.

7. Divide the upper section of hair the same way—three curls on each side of the part. Make the curls the same way. Place them overlapping the lower curls. Check each curl to be sure it is sewn securely in place. A few more stitches may be necessary.

Figure 3

Figure 4

Uncle Sam's Hair

Making the basic wig:

Use the same technique as for Betsy's wig, but with different template sizes, plus there is an additional hairpiece for the center back.

1. To make the center back hairpiece, make a template 3 inches by 4 inches. Cut a body fabric strip ½ inch by 2½ inches and center over the 3-inch side. Wind yarn around the template 34 times. Sew the yarn to the fabric strip while on the template. Cut the yarn apart on the side opposite the fabric strip. Turn in the raw ends of the fabric strip.

2. Keeping the hairpiece two layers thick, pin it to the center back of the head 3½ inches below the head seam (Figure 5). Sew the hairpiece in place securely. Then loosely sew the yarn to the head ½ inch below that stitching line.

3. To make the main wig, make a template 5 inches by 8½ inches. Cut body fabric strip 4¼ inches long and center over the 5-inch side. Wind yarn 80 times around template. Sew the resulting wig to the fabric strip and then to Uncle Sam's head in the same way as Betsy's. The back end of the fabric strip overlaps the hairpiece just slightly.

4. Smooth the yarn out from the part so that it doesn't crisscross over other strands. Pull the front 15 or 20 strands toward the temple area and tack in place behind the head seam line (Figure 6). Clip off the ends—they make too much bulk. Smooth the hair out from the part, over the temple and cut ends, and around to where it will overlap and blend in with the hairpiece. Look the head over carefully to make sure you don't have any unusually thick sections of hair.

5. Trim the ends evenly, but remember, Uncle Sam has shoulder-length hair!

Figure 5

Uncle Sam's Goatee

1. The goatee is made in the same way as the small hairpiece except for the number of times the yarn is wound around the 3-inch by

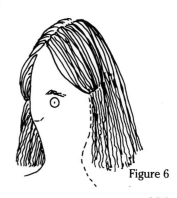

Figure 6

4-inch template. The goatee requires just 20 winds around the template, over a 1⅝-inch piece of body fabric centered over the 3-inch side of the template.

2. After sewing the yarn to the fabric strip, turn in the ends of the fabric and fasten. Keeping the goatee two layers thick, sew it very low on the face, about 5 inches from the seam line at the top of the head. Trim the goatee into a **V** shape, 2½ inches long at the sides and 4 inches long in the middle.

Adding Facial Features

There are three sets of features included for each doll. Pick the one most compatible with your skills and the desired look. Button or bead eyes and very simple embroidery stitches are the easiest. If there is any chance you will share these dolls with toddlers, do not use the removable features. Instead, select all embroidered features. If you happen to paint, you may prefer to paint features on the dolls.

A special tip on Sam's eyebrows: Try couching several short strands of the same yarn as used for the hair in position.

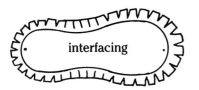

interfacing

Figure 1

Making the Legs

1. The dolls are designed with permanent shoes—you simply sew a different color fabric in the foot position to represent high-topped shoes. Sew a shoe section to the bottom of each leg piece.

2. Seam two leg pieces together, leaving open at both top and bottom. Push in fiberfill from both ends, but concentrate on making the lower leg very firm.

3. Cut fusible interfacing for the sole of the foot ¼-inch smaller than the pattern, and iron onto the sole fabric. Clip around sole to the edge of the interfacing (Figure 1). Match dot in center back of sole (at the heel) to the back leg seam and pin the sole to the foot, adding stuffing as needed to make it firm. Match the front seam and the other dot on the sole. Keep adding stuffing to make the foot firm. Blind stitch the sole in place (Figure 2). Do the second leg the same way.

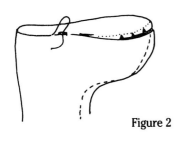

Figure 2

4. To make the knee joint, insert the needle through the knee at the dot from one side to the other (front to back) and pull thread tightly and knot. Pinch a small pleat on the side of the knee, stitch over four or five times, then knot the thread (Figure 3). Repeat on the other side of the knee, and then do the other leg. Measure to make sure the dots and subsequently the tucks—i.e., knees—are at the same height on either leg.

5. The knee and upper leg should be softer or looser. Match the front and back seams so they are both in the center of the leg, and baste the top shut with a good ¼-inch seam allowance. The area below the basting should be loosely stuffed or the doll won't sit well.

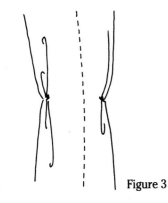

Figure 3

Attaching the Legs to the Body

1. Press ¼ inch under on the lower edge of the body. Push stuffing back into place, as it will have slipped down during the sewing of the hair. Add enough more stuffing to make a very firm body, down to within ½ inch of the bottom edge. Place the legs into the body opening, with the outside edges of each leg touching the body side seams. The legs will overlap about ¼ inch in the center. Check to be sure that the legs are the same length. Adjust up or down if necessary. Baste the legs to the back of the body to secure, then stitch in place. Add more stuffing. Stitch the body closed with a blind stitch (Figure 4).

2. Put the doll in a sitting position. It should be able to maintain an upright position. If not, you may need to remove some stuffing either at the top of each leg or at the bottom of the body. The knees should bend when the dolls are seated.

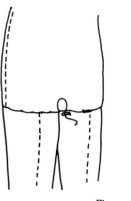

Figure 4

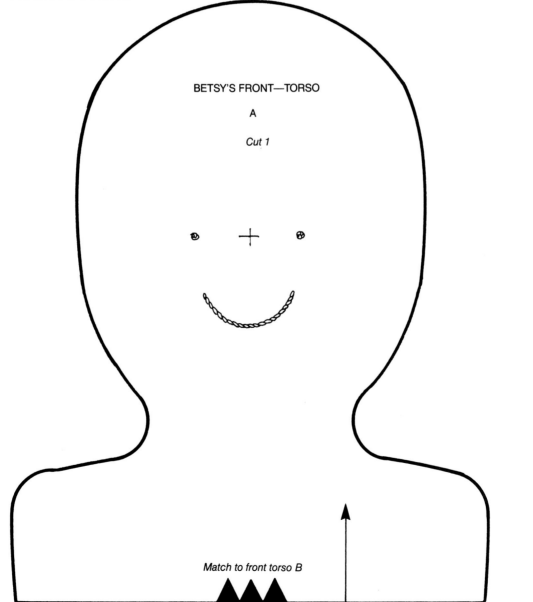

BETSY'S FRONT—TORSO

A

Cut 1

Match to front torso B

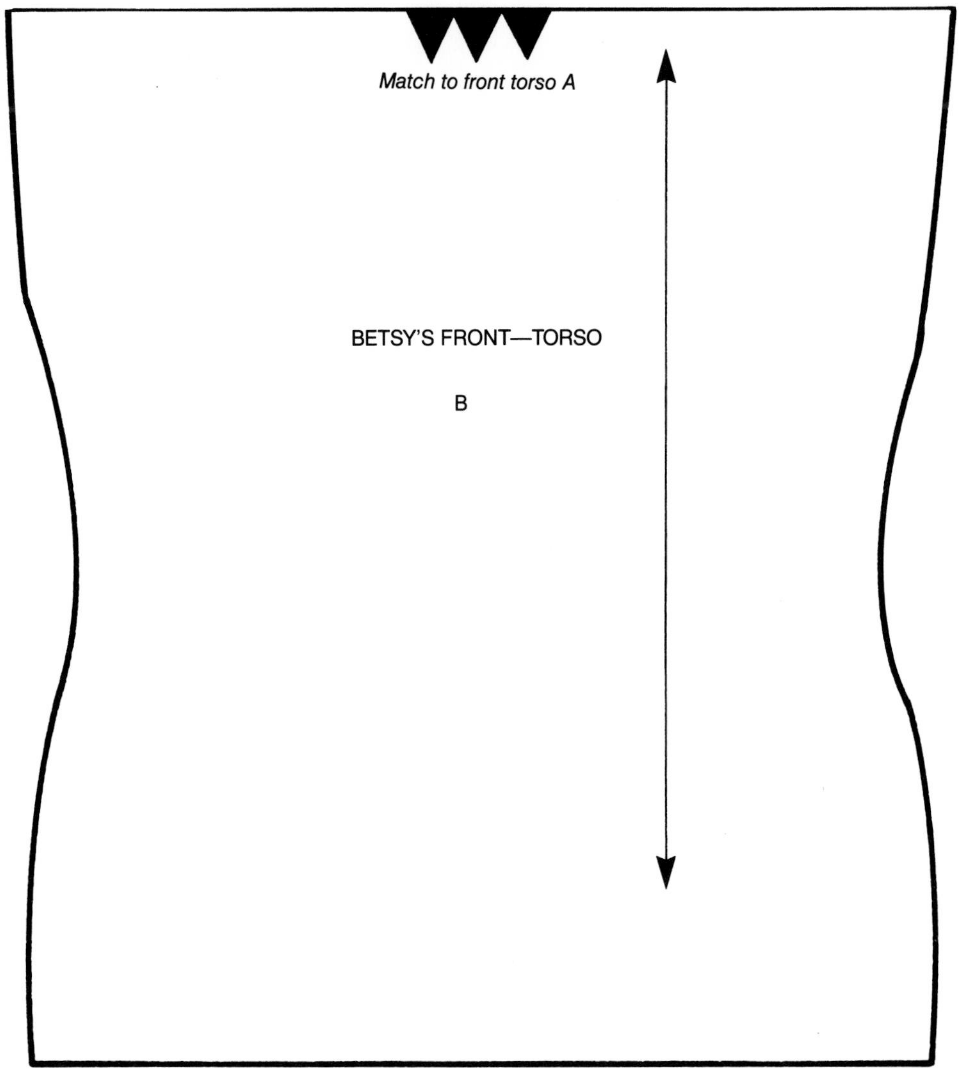

Match to front torso A

BETSY'S FRONT—TORSO

B

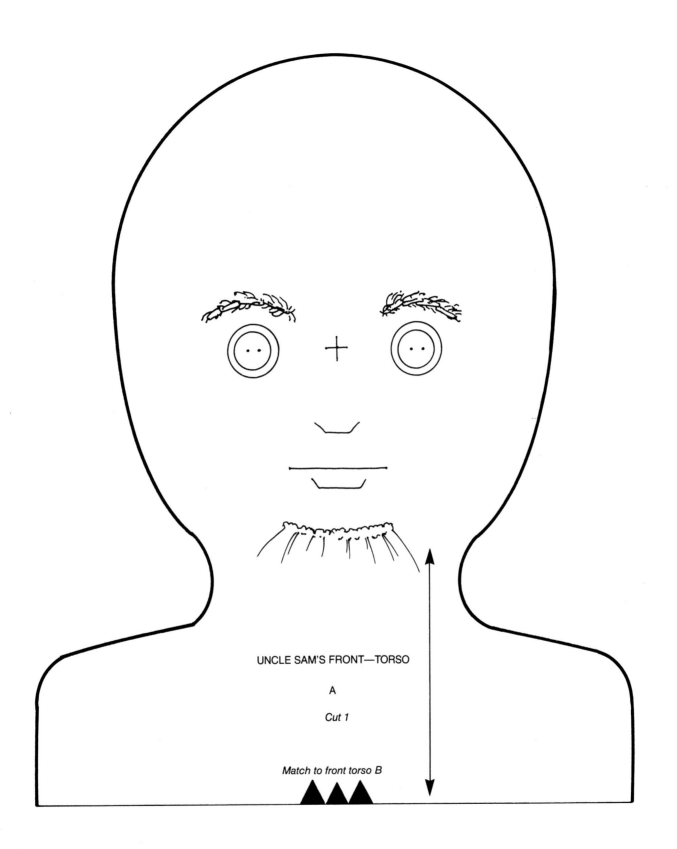

UNCLE SAM'S FRONT—TORSO

A

Cut 1

Match to front torso B

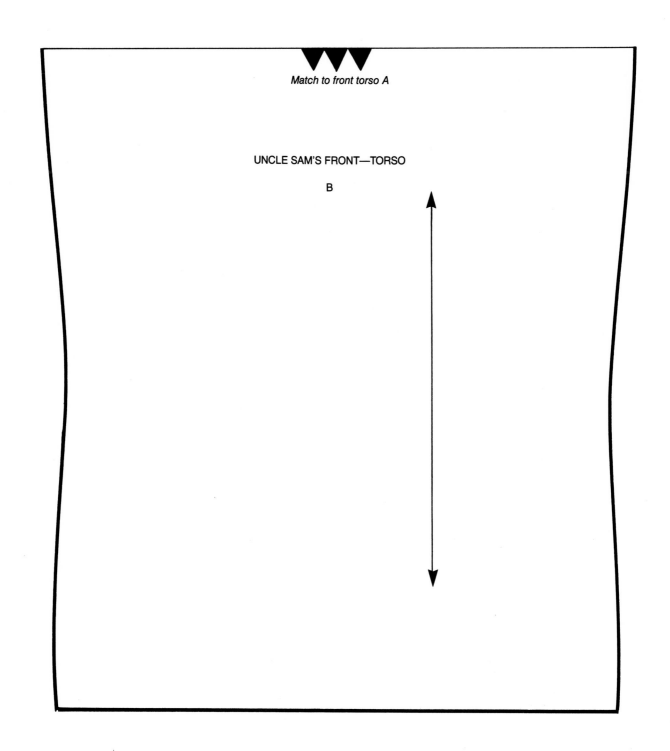

Match to front torso A

UNCLE SAM'S FRONT—TORSO

B

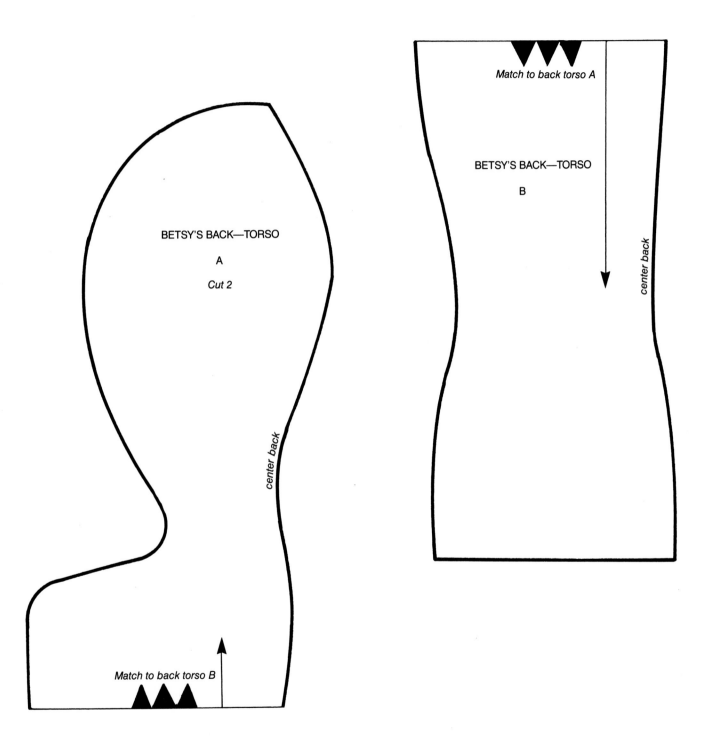

BETSY'S BACK—TORSO

A

Cut 2

center back

Match to back torso B

Match to back torso A

BETSY'S BACK—TORSO

B

center back

107

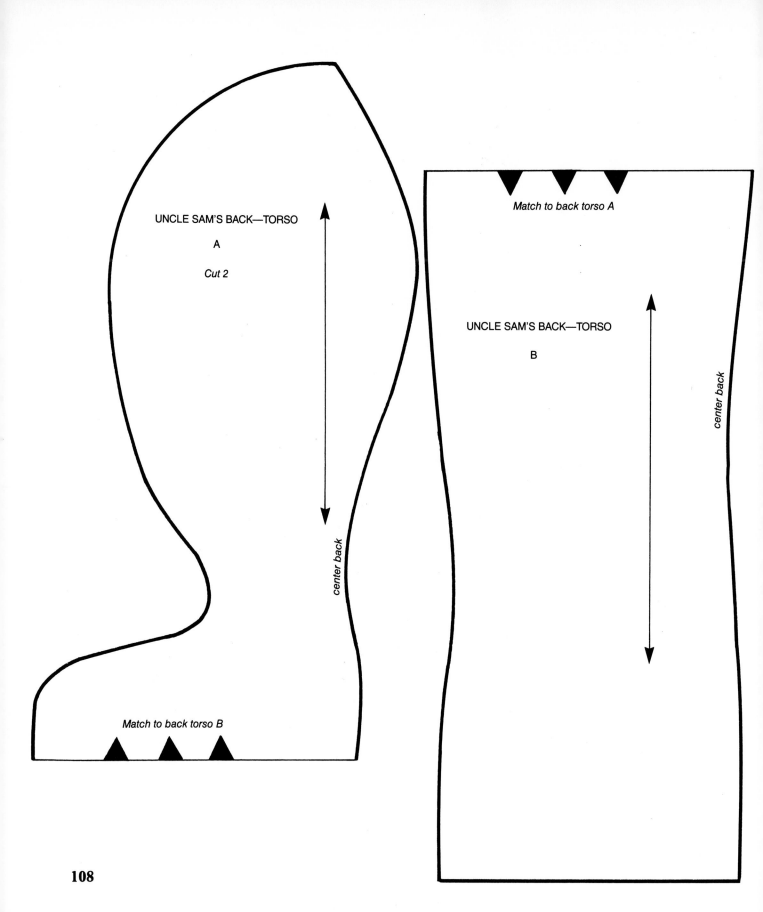

UNCLE SAM'S BACK—TORSO

A

Cut 2

center back

Match to back torso B

UNCLE SAM'S BACK—TORSO

B

Match to back torso A

center back

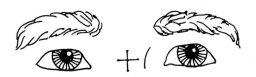
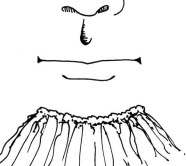

UNCLE SAM'S FACE—STENCILED AND STITCHED

UNCLE SAM'S FACE—PAINTED

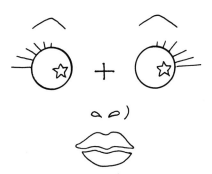

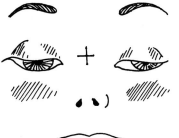

BETSY'S FACE—PAINTED

BETSY'S FACE—STENCILED AND STITCHED
Sew eyebrows, eyelashes, nose lines

109

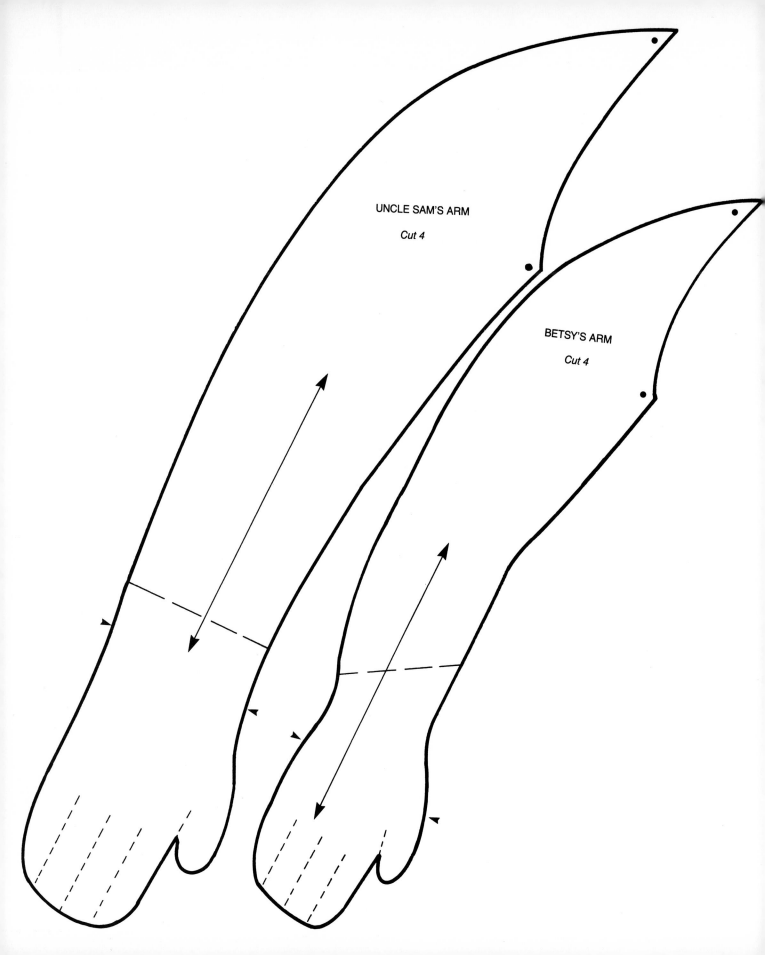

UNCLE SAM'S ARM

Cut 4

BETSY'S ARM

Cut 4

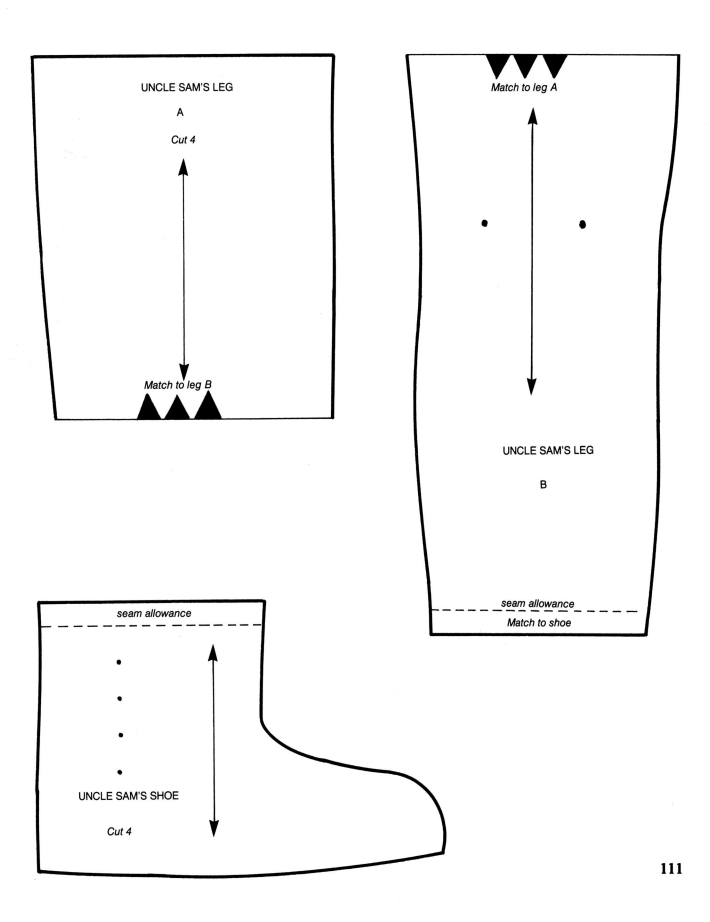

UNCLE SAM'S LEG

A

Cut 4

Match to leg B

Match to leg A

UNCLE SAM'S LEG

B

seam allowance

Match to shoe

seam allowance

UNCLE SAM'S SHOE

Cut 4

111

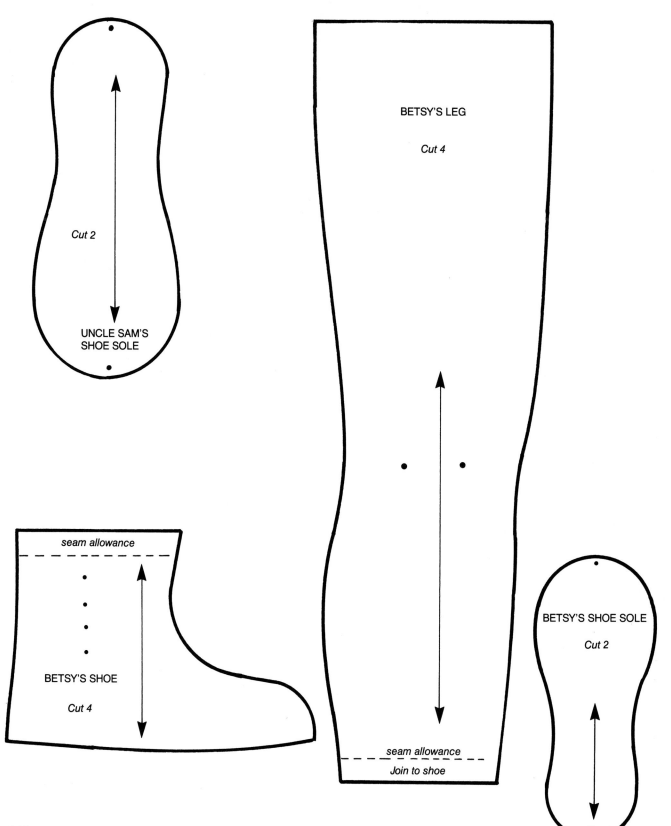

UNCLE SAM'S
SHOE SOLE

Cut 2

BETSY'S LEG

Cut 4

seam allowance

BETSY'S SHOE

Cut 4

seam allowance

Join to shoe

BETSY'S SHOE SOLE

Cut 2

BETSY'S CLOTHES

Betsy's clothes are made using several different fabrics. Each of the four fabrics shown has a piece that requires a 10½- to 11-inch length of fabric. If purchasing fabric, get ⅜ or ⅓ yard. The hat and petticoat could be cut from ⅜ yard of the same fabric.

ADDITIONAL MATERIALS:
1 yard round elastic for hat
6 inches of ⅛-inch elastic for sleeve
11 inches of ¼-inch elastic for petticoat waist
Two small snaps for dress
20 inches of preruffled 1-inch-wide edging for petticoat (optional)

Betsy's Cap

1. Cut two of the cap piece (one piece is lining). Stitch together ¼ inch from the edge, leaving a small opening in the seam for turning. Clip and turn. Press. Close the opening by hand.

2. Zigzag over round elastic about 1 inch from the finished edge. Pull up to fit Betsy's head after the hair is added. Secure ends and cut off the excess. Add ribbon and bows on top of the gathered area if desired.

Betsy's Petticoat

1. Cut an 11- by 20-inch piece for the petticoat. Seam the two 11-inch ends up the center back.

2. Press under ¼ inch and then ½ inch to make a waistline casing at the top.

3. Add a 1-inch ruffle at the bottom. (Make or purchase the ruffle.)

4. Run elastic through the waistline casing.

Betsy's Dress

1. Cut the bodice front and sew in the tucks. Cut two bodice backs. Sew the bodice front and backs together at the shoulders. Cut and sew facings together at the shoulder. Add facings to the neck edge of the bodice. Leave the center back edges extended.

2. Cut and turn up the sleeves, and sew in casing for elastic. Run 3 inches of elastic through each wrist and secure at each end. Gather the sleeve tops to fit the bodice armhole. Sew into the armhole.

3. Cut an 11- by 20-inch piece for the skirt. Seam the center back to 1½ inches from the top. Narrow-hem the skirt bottom. Gather the skirt at the top to approximately 12 inches.

4. To make the swag, trace both pieces of the swag pattern onto one piece of paper. Cut two. Make a narrow hem along each straight edge. Make six tucks as marked in the pattern on the curved edge (three on each side). Fold each tuck so the opening faces the center. Gather the curved edge evenly, except keep the tuck surfaces as flat as possible.

5. Pin hip swags and skirt together. Each hip swag goes from center front to center back. Pin in place on the bodice. Stitch the waist seam.

6. Turn back the center back seam allowances from the facings through the skirt and narrow-hem. Add snaps at top of the neck and waist. Add optional ribbon at the waist.

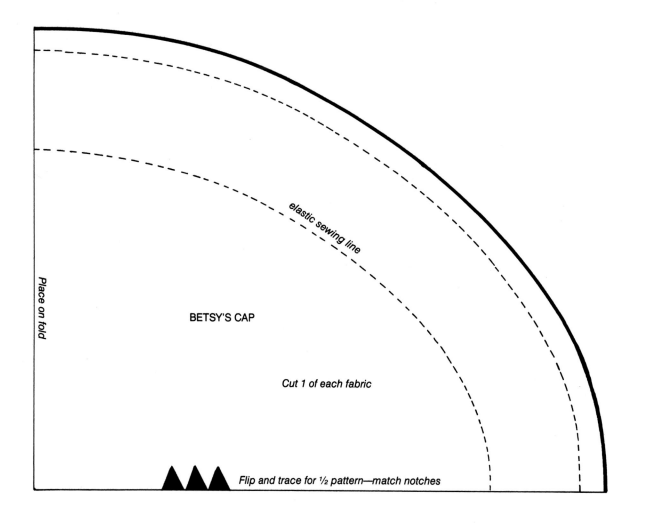

Place on fold

elastic sewing line

BETSY'S CAP

Cut 1 of each fabric

Flip and trace for ½ pattern—match notches

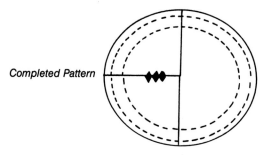

Completed Pattern

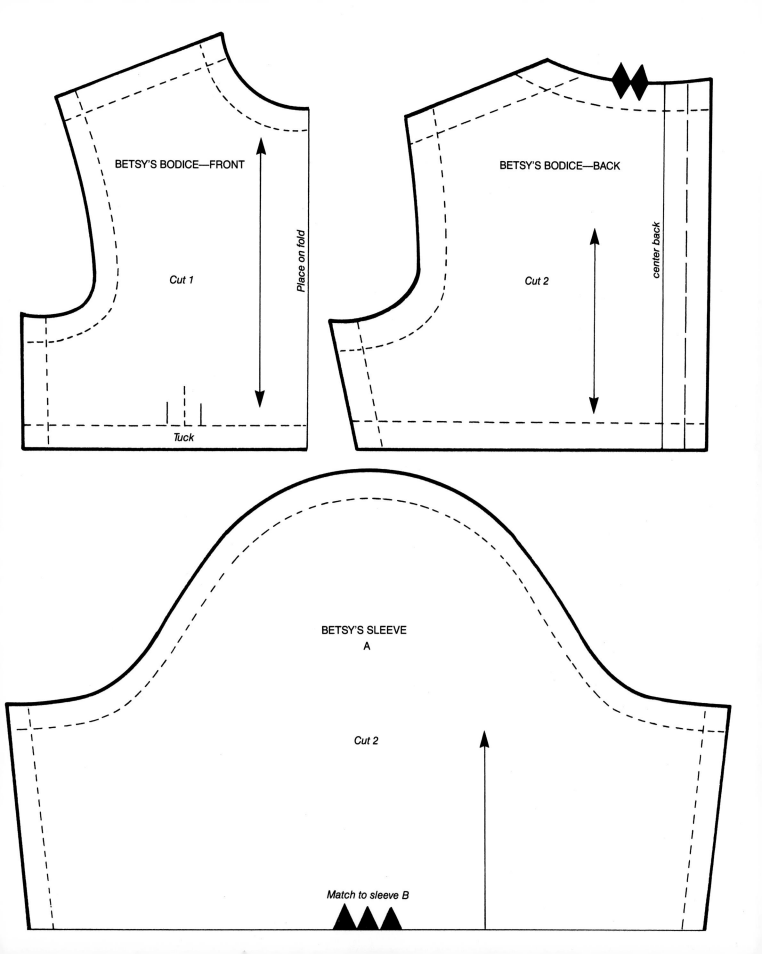

BETSY'S BODICE—FRONT

Cut 1

Place on fold

Tuck

BETSY'S BODICE—BACK

Cut 2

center back

BETSY'S SLEEVE
A

Cut 2

Match to sleeve B

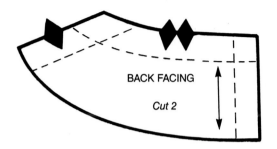

BACK FACING

Cut 2

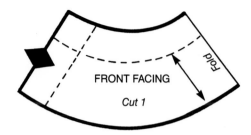

FRONT FACING

Cut 1

Fold

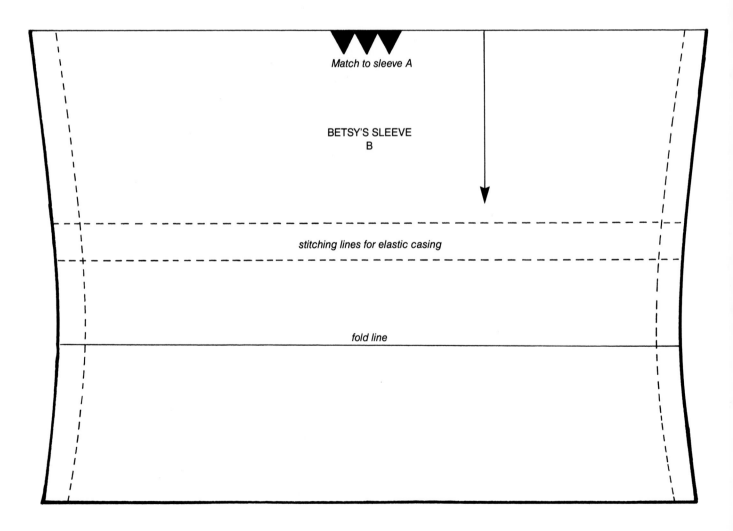

Match to sleeve A

BETSY'S SLEEVE
B

stitching lines for elastic casing

fold line

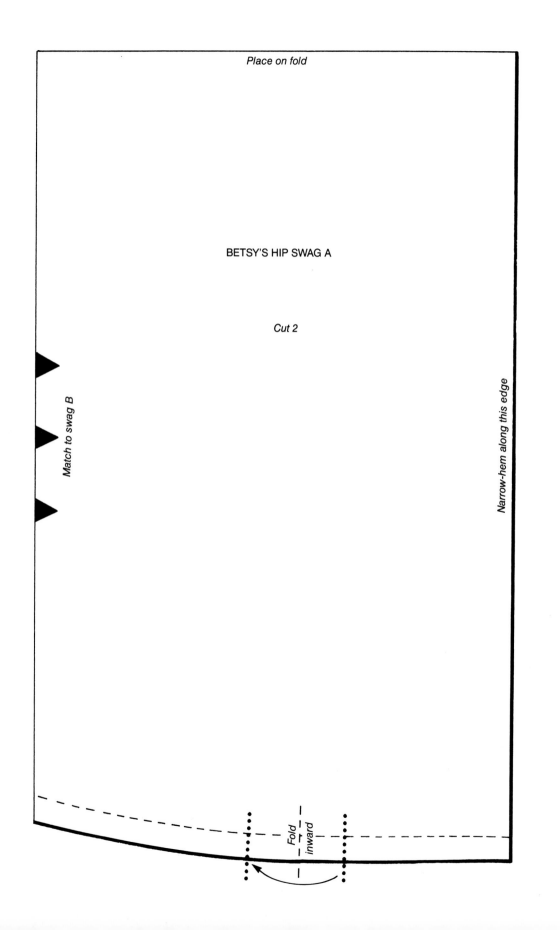

Place on fold

BETSY'S HIP SWAG A

Cut 2

Match to swag B

Narrow-hem along this edge

Fold inward

117

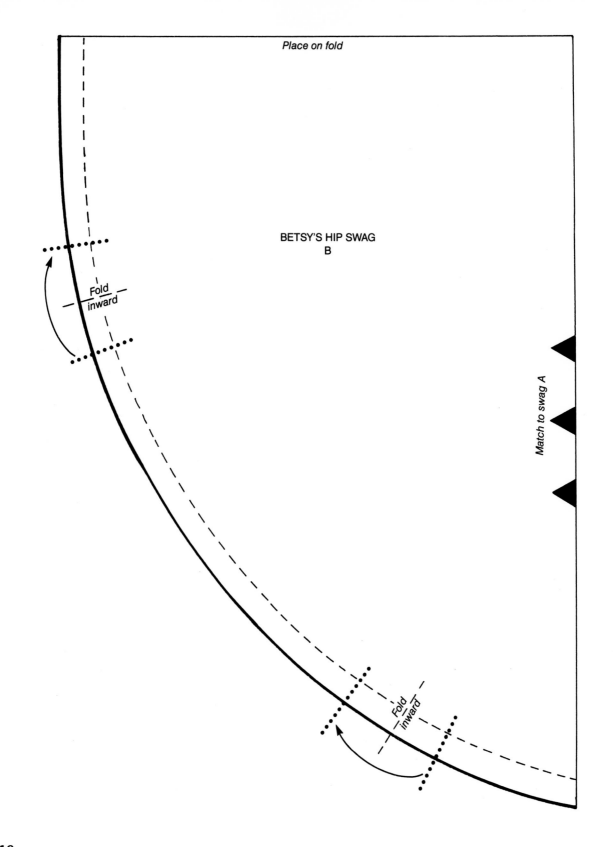

Place on fold

BETSY'S HIP SWAG
B

Fold
inward

Fold
inward

Match to swag A

UNCLE SAM'S CLOTHES

Both the jacket and the pants need ½ yard of fabric for the pieces to be cut on the preferred lengthwise grain. They will not use the full width.

Shirt and Tie Dickey

1. Cut four pieces of dickey. With the right sides together, line and turn two pairs, leaving open down the center front.

2. Join the two pieces at the center front. The raw seam won't show. Press the seam allowances open. The dickey only goes to the shoulder; it does not go around the neck.

3. Cut a 7½-inch piece of ribbon, turn under ⅜ inch on each end, and add a snap closure. Tack the center lower selvage of the ribbon to the center seam of the dickey—at the bottom of the collar. Use the rest of the ribbon to make a bow and tack it in place at the center front.

MATERIALS NEEDED:
½ yard of ½-inch ribbon for tie
Snap

Vest

1. Cut vest front and back pieces from both the lining and outside fabrics. Join the lining pieces at the shoulder seams. Join the outside fabric pieces at the shoulder seams.

2. With right sides of lining and vest together, stitch around all outside edges except the side seams (Figure 1). Clip and turn.

3. Join the underarm seams of the vest's outside fabric only. With right sides of the vest fabric touching, roll the garment to start stitching past the seam line into the lining as far as possible (Figure 2). You will be lucky to get three or four stitches. Stitch the vest section and then into the other side of the lining in the same way. Finish the rest of the lining seam by pressing the seam allowance back and stitching shut by hand.

4. Add decorative buttons to the right side of the vest. Close the center front with snaps.

MATERIALS NEEDED:
Four buttons or large beads
Four snaps

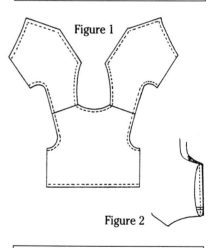

Figure 1

Figure 2

Pants

1. Match the two sections of pattern before cutting. Cut two pants legs, placed on the fold. Hem the bottom of each leg.

2. Stitch the inside seam allowance (up to the bend of the crotch) so that both legs are tubes. Now put one leg inside the other, with right sides together, and stitch the crotch seam. Clip the seams and turn right side out.

3. Narrow-hem the top, turn under at the fold line and stitch in place to make a casing. Run elastic through the waist and secure.

MATERIALS NEEDED:
Elastic

MATERIALS NEEDED:
Interfacing

Jacket

1. Match the two sections of the back pattern before cutting. Cut all pattern pieces from both lining and jacket fabric. Cut the front from interfacing as well.

2. Join the interfacing and front jacket piece together at the shoulder. Join front and back jacket pieces together at the shoulder seams. Repeat with front and back lining pieces. Stay-stitch the lining armholes and clip to the stitching line.

3. With right sides together, sew the lining to the coat at all seams except under the arms and armholes. (At this point, the jacket looks much like the vest in Figure 1 on page 119.)

4. Put gathering stitches into the top of the sleeve. Hem the bottom of each sleeve. Pin the sleeve into the coat armhole only. Stitch, but do not catch the lining.

5. Stitch the underarm seams of the sleeve and jacket, again leaving the lining loose. Close the lining underarm by hand to cover seam allowances and whipstitch the lining to the armhole seam allowances.

The collar rolls and makes a lapel in front. The jacket stays open in front to expose the vest. It can be worn so the collar of the dickey flares out over the lapel, or the dickey collar can be tucked neatly under the jacket. The jacket collar does not roll in back.

Uncle Sam's Hat

As you might expect, Uncle Sam's hat does not fall in the quick and easy category, but Uncle Sam wouldn't be Uncle Sam without the hat. It is so handsome and symbolic by itself that you might want to make it first and just use it as a shelf sitter until the doll is done.

If you are an expert glue user, there are several assembly steps where you may want to substitute gluing for tiny hand stitches.

MATERIALS NEEDED:
White florist wire
Paper-backed fusing agent
Stiff fusible interfacing
Felt
**Heavyweight nonwoven fabric
  or buckram**

1. Cut two brim shapes from white felt. Mark the dashed line on the felt. Shape wire to fit ⅛ to ¼ inch inside the outer edge of one brim. Tack into place every 1 to 2 inches. Overlap the ends of wire.

2. Cut paper-backed fusible in brim shape. Press onto the wired felt brim (over the wire) to hold it in place. Peel off the paper backing. Trim 1/16 inch off the outer edge of the stiff interfacing brim piece. Place this piece on the wired and fusible covered felt brim. Apply the second piece of paper-backed fusing agent to the other felt brim. Peel off the paper backing and fuse this brim to the first one, taking care to place the wire and stiff interfacing in the middle. Press all layers carefully and seal the edges closed.

3. Clip the brim on the inside to the dashed line every ½ to ¾ inch or so. Take this opportunity to fit the brim to your doll's head. Clip further if needed to fit properly. Press clipped edges so they stand up at right angles to the brim.

4. Cut two hat body pieces from felt and two pieces from heavy fusible nonwoven interfacing. Press together. Seam together along both curved edges. Press the seams open.

Steam makes felt flexible, which is usually one of its assets, but can be a detriment. When fusing and pressing, use an up-and-down movement with the iron, not a gliding motion. During the different steps, hold the hat carefully and do not bend if at all possible, so as to keep the stiff look intact.

5. Place the smaller end of the hat body over the clipped edges of the brim and pin in place. Sew by hand with tiny stitches as close to the brim as possible.

6. Cut the crown lining out of felt, stiff interfacing, and two layers of paper-backed fusing agent. Apply one piece of paper-backed fusing agent to the felt. Peel off the paper backing. Place the stiffener on the fused felt and press. Now apply the second piece of paper-backed fusing agent. Peel off the paper backing.

7. Cut the crown from felt. Clip to the fold line. Carefully center the crown lining within the clipped seam allowance, fusible side down and felt side up. Press the lining in place so that it adheres to the crown. Sew a basting thread through the clipped seam allowance and gather this edge up so the crown will fit into the top of the hat. Match the dots with the side seams.

8. Pin the crown in place along the upper edge of the hat body, catching the clipped edges inside the hat. Be sure the crown is flat and that the "clips" do not show. It is best to pin the crown in all the way around to be sure it fits evenly with no bunching up before you start to sew.

To hold the hat for sewing the crown in, place one hand inside the hat to hold the little clipped edges as you sew them. Using very small stitches, sew through the body into the crown without sewing over the edge where the body and crown meet.

Making the Hatband

1. Cut a 2¾- by 13½-inch band from blue fabric. Cut a ¾- by 13½-inch band of red fabric for trim. With right sides together, stitch these pieces together along one long edge. Press the seam allowance toward the blue. Fold and press the red fabric so that only ⅛ inch shows above the blue. Press back ¼ inch on the other long edge of the blue fabric.

2. Press paper-backed fusing web to your star fabric. Trace five stars on the paper side. Cut out and place one star in the center of the blue band, and space the other stars evenly 1 inch apart on either side of the center star. The stars have a direction—try to place all the stars with the arrow pointing up. Peel off the backing paper and press in place. It may be necessary to do double layers of star fabric to prevent the blue from showing through.

3. Fit the band around the hat just above the brim and pin in place. Turn under one end of the hatband and stitch by hand.

Optional Finishing Touches

1. To add a custom-made look to the hat, a felt binding may be sewn around the raw edges of the brim. Cut a 22-inch-long strip of ⅝-inch wide white felt. Fold the strip around the edge of the brim so that the top and bottom are equal. Whipstitch in place by hand. Stitch first the upper, then the lower side. If you are doing this, you will probably want to do it before the crown is added.

2. Since the brim is wired, you will be able to curve the sides upward with the traditional Uncle Sam flare.

Jumping Off with Sam and Betsy

Different fabric combinations can create different characters from the same patterns. A black suit and tie with a white shirt, dark hair, and straight stovepipe hat will make Sam into an Abe Lincoln figure. An all-white ensemble can be Mark Twain, while a gray suit can make him into Robert E. Lee. With the right materials, you could even make a skinny folk Santa.

Betsy can become any eighteenth-century lady, from Martha Washington to Marie Antoinette, with the right fabrics—and perhaps a change of hairdo. Add a shepherd's crook and she can be Little Bo-Peep, with all her sheep! Change the hip swag for a different apron and she could be transformed into Mrs. Santa.

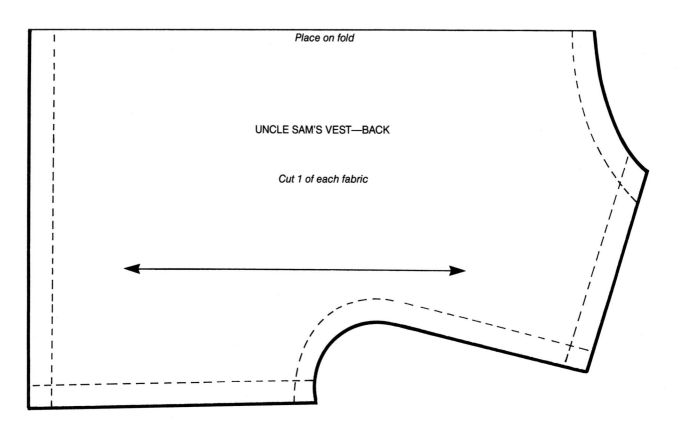

Place on fold

UNCLE SAM'S VEST—BACK

Cut 1 of each fabric

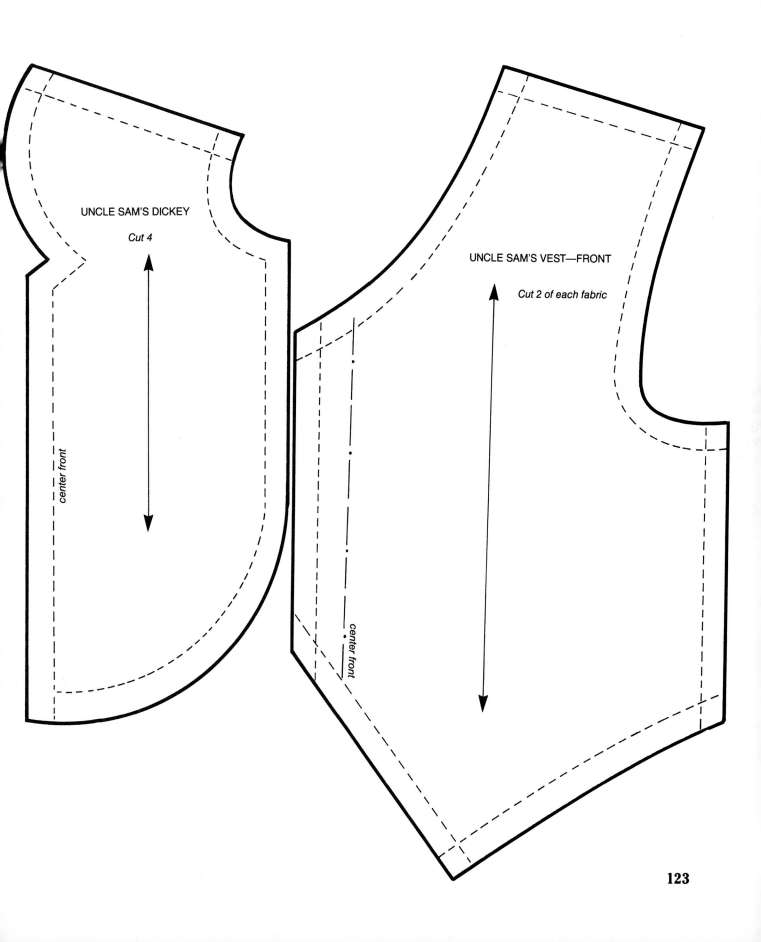

UNCLE SAM'S DICKEY

Cut 4

center front

UNCLE SAM'S VEST—FRONT

Cut 2 of each fabric

center front

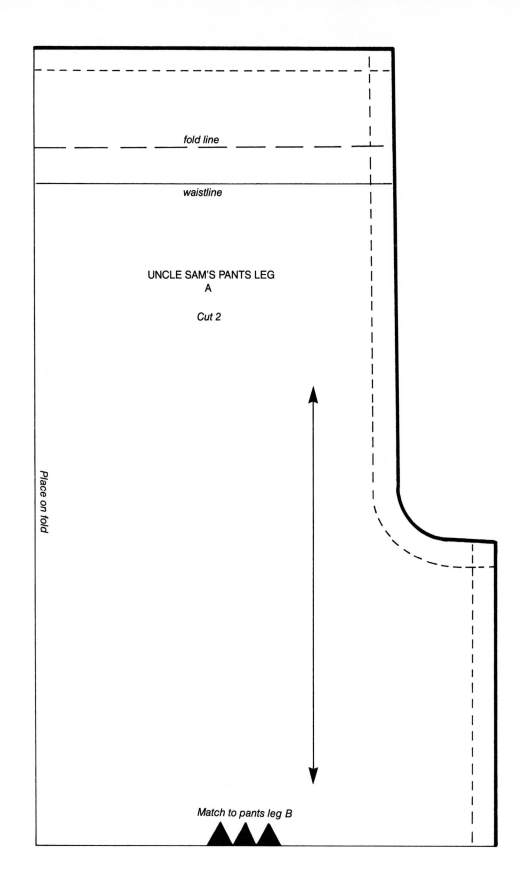

fold line

waistline

UNCLE SAM'S PANTS LEG
A

Cut 2

Place on fold

Match to pants leg B

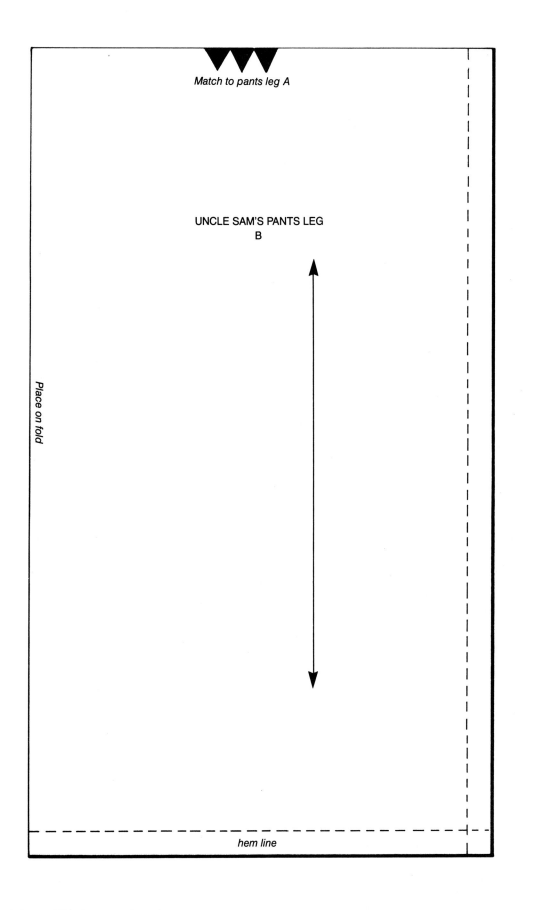

Match to pants leg A

UNCLE SAM'S PANTS LEG
B

Place on fold

hem line

125

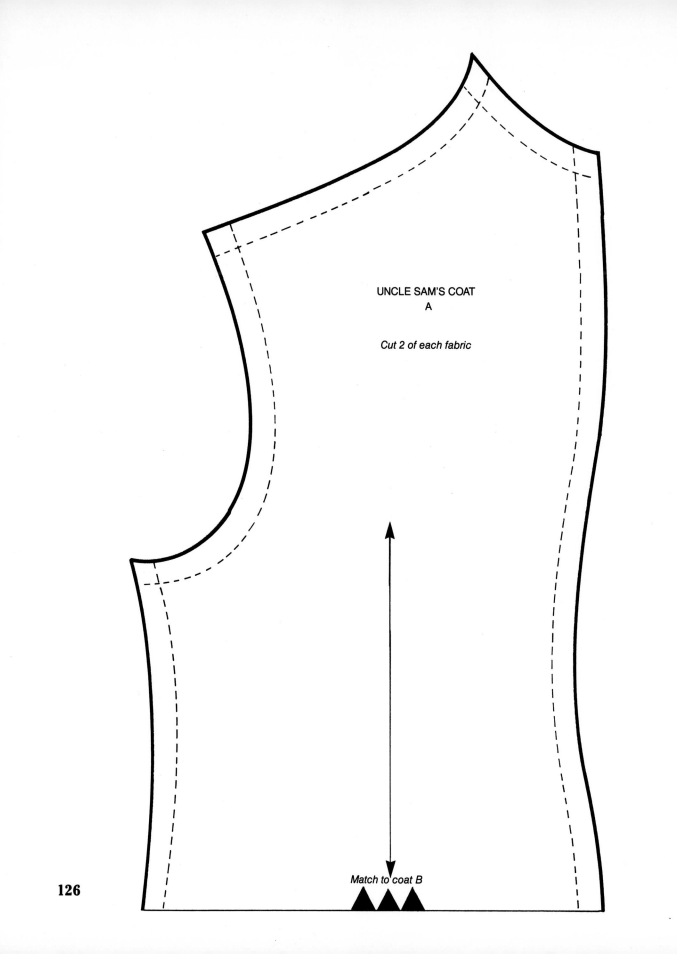

UNCLE SAM'S COAT
A

Cut 2 of each fabric

Match to coat B

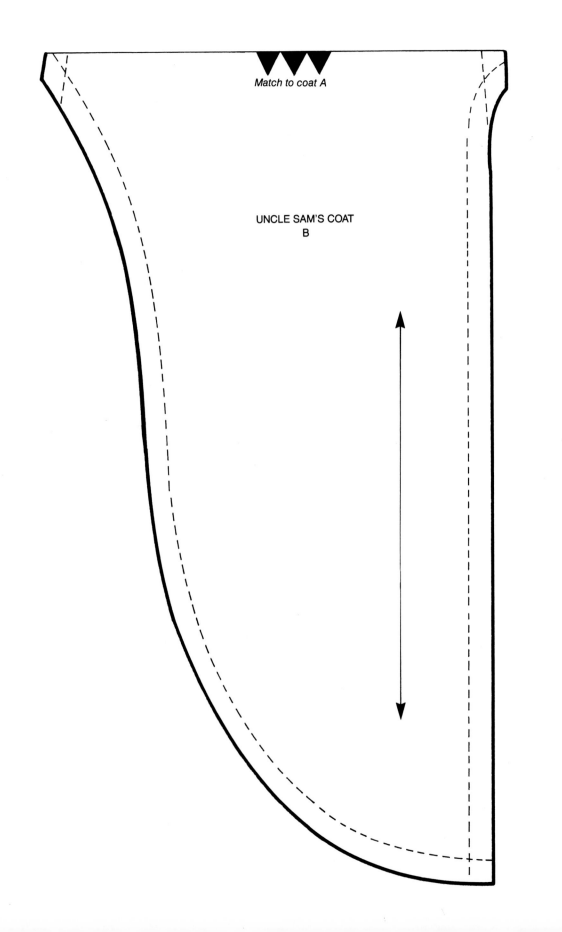

Match to coat A

UNCLE SAM'S COAT
B

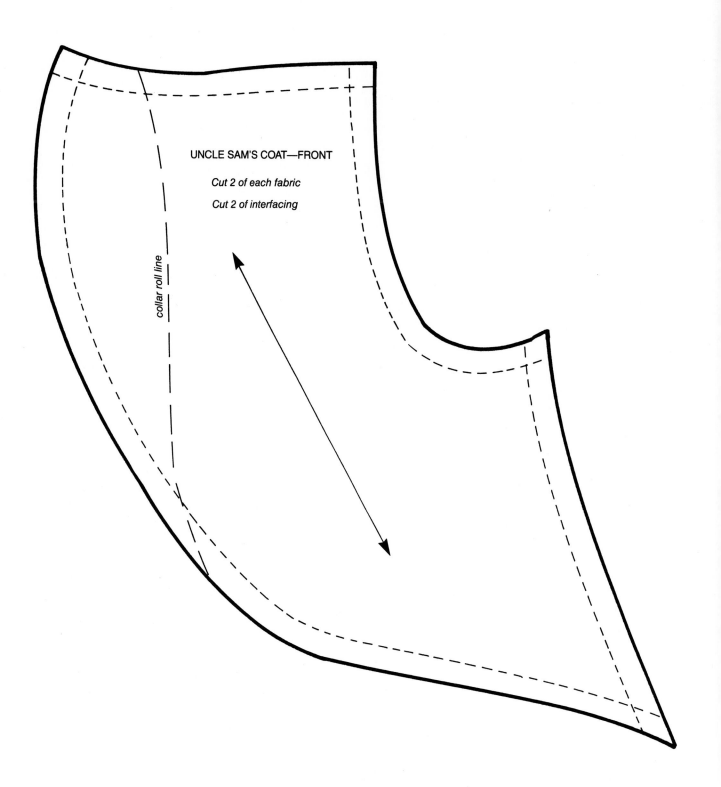

UNCLE SAM'S COAT—FRONT

Cut 2 of each fabric

Cut 2 of interfacing

collar roll line

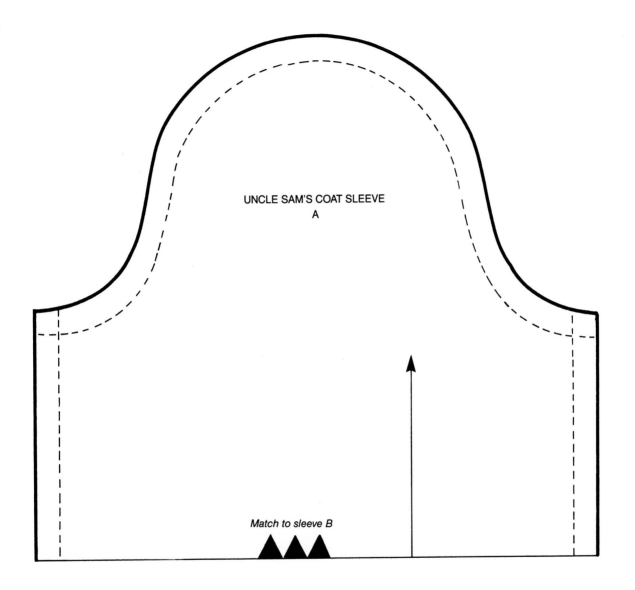

UNCLE SAM'S COAT SLEEVE
A

Match to sleeve B

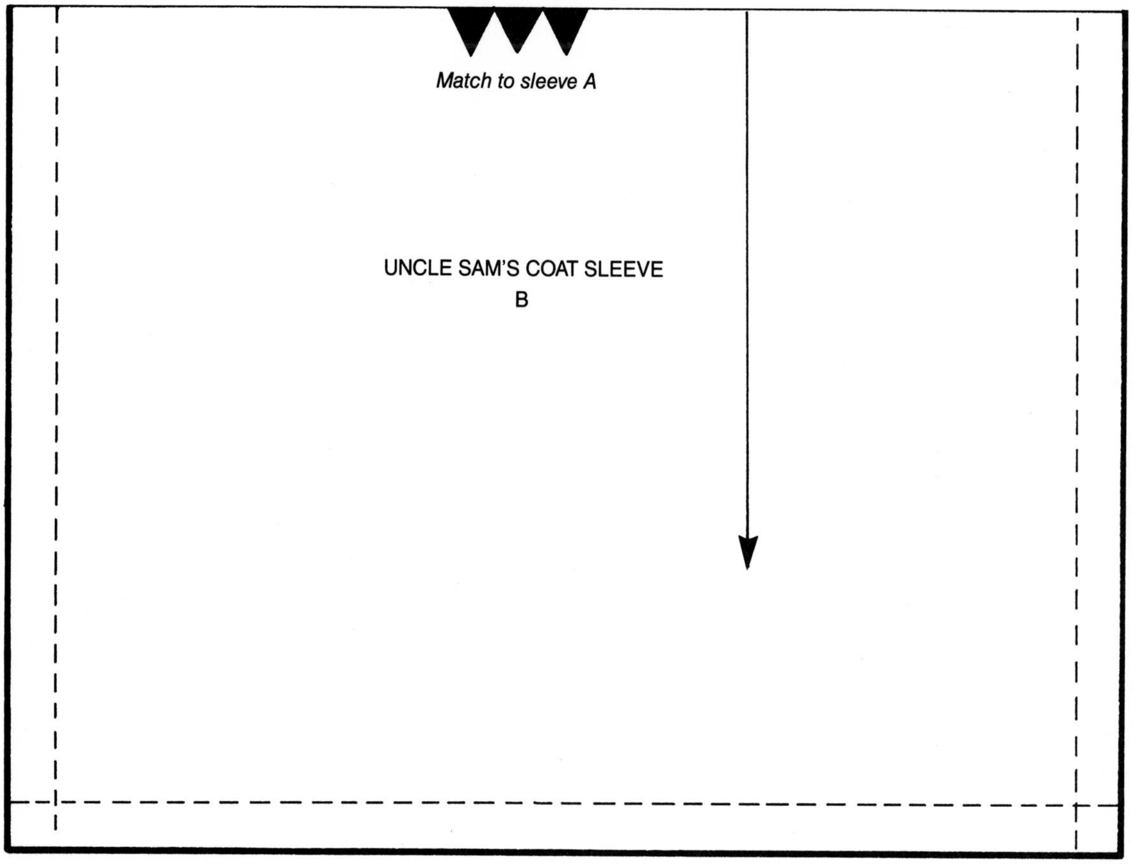

Match to sleeve A

UNCLE SAM'S COAT SLEEVE
B

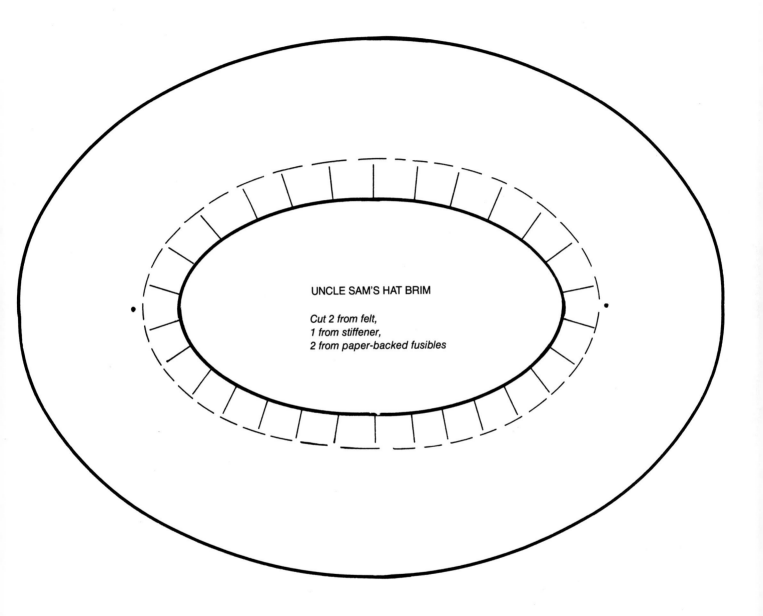

UNCLE SAM'S HAT BRIM

*Cut 2 from felt,
1 from stiffener,
2 from paper-backed fusibles*

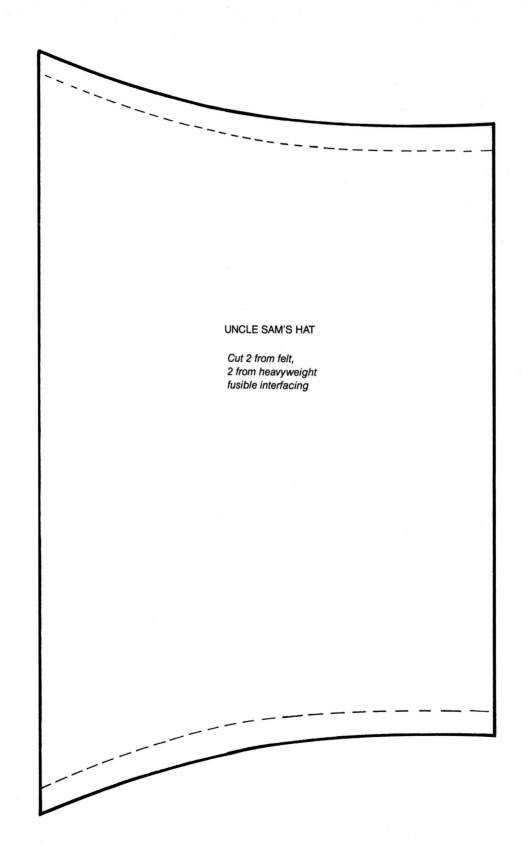

UNCLE SAM'S HAT

Cut 2 from felt,
2 from heavyweight
fusible interfacing

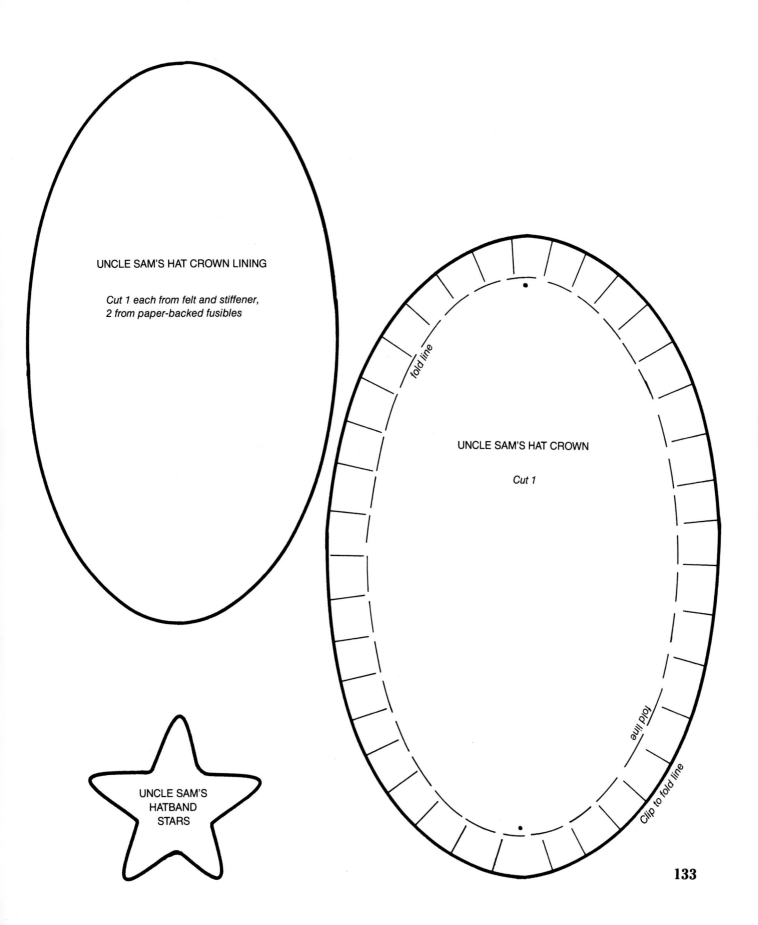

UNCLE SAM'S HAT CROWN LINING

Cut 1 each from felt and stiffener,
2 from paper-backed fusibles

UNCLE SAM'S HAT CROWN

Cut 1

fold line

fold line

Clip to fold line

UNCLE SAM'S
HATBAND
STARS

133

QUICKIE STARS AND STRIPES BANNER

The mini wall quilt pictured features one of the most available "helper" fabrics. Some people call printed fabrics that allow the sewer to get the desired effect yet eliminate some piecing "cheater" fabrics. I call them "helper" fabrics. Red and white stripes can almost always be found. The stripes in the fabric shown are ¼ inch. (Actually, the red is just under ¼ inch and the white is just over ¼ inch, but they look the same.) The idea works with any size stripe. The finished size will, of course, be different with different size stripes, and the patterns used here for the stars and hearts would need to be altered.

FINISHED SIZE:
14 by 17 ½ inches

MATERIALS:
Batting 15 by 18 inches
Backing 15 by 18 inches
Red and white striped fabric
(preferably ¼-inch stripes)

Making the Blocks

1. Each finished square should have thirteen stripes, starting and stopping with red. Cut ¼ inch on the outside of those red stripes. Measure how wide that is, then cut the strips that long to make a square. The striped square in the model was approximately 4 inches cut. While we know that the flag isn't square, the design doesn't work with rectangles.

2. The size for the blue field is determined by the width of seven stripes, starting and stopping with red, *plus* seam allowances on two adjacent sides only. The field in the model was 2 inches square and cut from fabric backed with paper-backed fusible web. The blue fields were fused in place in the upper left-hand corner of each striped square so that the square sat directly on the white stripe and the cut edges matched the cut edge of the larger square.

The hearts and stars are also cut from fabric made fusible, and fused in place, but it is easier to get proper placement for these after the squares are sewn together. Piece following the diagram. Fuse hearts and stars in place.

3. Cut batting and backing to allow for borders. Layer batting over backing, then center pieced squares on top. Quilt in the ditch between squares. Zigzag finish the fused edges of the fields, hearts, and stars.

4. Add borders using the quilt-as-you-sew method (see "Fabric Craft Basics").

½ inch finished red—cut 1 inch wide
½ inch finished white—cut 1 inch wide
1¼ inches finished blue—cut 1¾ inches
    wide
⅜ inch finished binding—cut 2 inches
    for French fold

This would be a perfect project to tea dye in its entirety to obtain a wonderful antique color. It's psychologically hard to do after the quilt is made. It is easier to tint the fabric first and work with stained fabric.

NOTE: Betsy's little flag pillow/pincushion is just one more square made like the squares for the little quilt. It was tea dyed, backed, and stuffed.

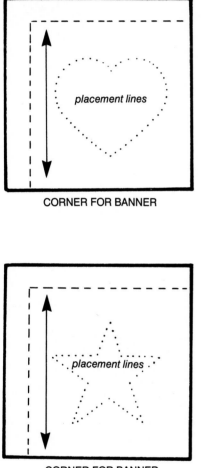

CORNER FOR BANNER

HEART

STAR

CORNER FOR BANNER

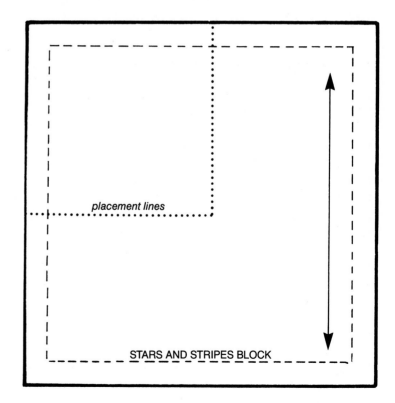

placement lines

STARS AND STRIPES BLOCK

AMERICANA PIECED HEARTS

The method for making the Americana Pieced Heart (for either the square pillow or the hanging heart) incorporates an easy sew-before-you-cut process.

1. Cut two red and two white strips 1¼ inches wide and 18 inches long. (Models photographed were made with muted colors.) Starting with a red strip, sew them together alternating red and white strips. Press seams toward red strips. If you are working with smaller scraps, sets four strips wide and 5½ inches and 9½ inches long will also work.

2. Using the pattern for the heart lobe, cut one piece from the pieced fabric. Make sure that a white strip is at the bottom and the pattern is flipped so that the curve at the top is correct for the upper right-hand corner of the pillow. Do not cut any of the bottom white strip, just line the edge of the pattern with the edge of the fabric.

3. Using the same pattern piece, but this time as shown, cut one piece of blue field material. Seam the two pieces at the center.

4. The bottom of the heart is also cut from the pieced strips. It needs a red strip at both the top and bottom. Sew a short scrap of a red strip (2½ to 3 inches long) in the center of the outside white strip of your pieced fabric. Then position the bottom heart pattern with its top edge aligned with the edge of the top red strip. Mark and cut the bottom heart and sew to the top half of the heart.

5. Appliqué the contrasting heart on the blue field. When positioning the heart, fold under the outside seam allowance to make sure the heart is properly positioned. Stuff lightly as you finish appliquéing.

THE AMERICANA HANGING HEART

1. Make one Americana heart front as above. Use the completed heart front as a pattern to cut the back. Clip at the dots and press under the seam allowance between the dots on both heart front and back where streamers will hang.

2. Make assorted strips for streamers. The heart shown has fourteen strips assorted in size and fabrics. They are mostly ⅝ inch to ¾ inch wide and 12 inches to 16 inches long. They will be trimmed after the heart is completed. In addition, there are seven pieces of assorted ribbons in the streamers.

3. Arrange streamers as desired, right side up on a piece of tear-away background stabilizer (ask for it where you buy interfacing). When satisfied, machine baste the streamers in place on the stabilizer, roughly following the curve of the heart. Put the finished heart front on top of the streamers and topstitch the edge that is folded under onto the strips. This is where the tear-away comes in—simply tear away the stabilizer.

4. With right sides together, stitch front to back between the dots in the other direction. Turn and stuff.

5. Finish the bottom by hand. Add ribbon or fabric hanging strips at the top of the heart.

FINISHED SIZE:
heart 8 inches wide by 6 inches high plus streamers

MATERIALS NEEDED:
Stuffing
Assorted ribbons (optional)
Background stabilizer (preferably tear-away)

137

FINISHED SIZE:
12 inches square plus 1⅝-inch ruffle

MATERIALS NEEDED:
12½-inch square of background fabric, batting, and backing

AMERICANA PILLOW

1. Make the heart following the instructions above.

2. Cut four strips of contrast fabric and corner pieces. With right sides of fabric together, match notches and piece strips and corners (Figure 1).

3. Mark the center of each side of the background square. Position a pieced corner right side down from the center of one side to the center of the adjoining side (Figure 2). Stitch the corner in place using the stitch-and-flip technique (see "Fabric Craft Basics"). Proceed around the pillow, finishing each corner the same way. Trim the corners to make the pillow 12½ inches square. Trim away excess background square fabric under the corner pieces, if desired.

4. Position the pieced Americana heart in the opening and appliqué in place.

5. Add the ruffle and finish as desired. The pillow shown has a mock double ruffle, with cut widths of 1¾ inches and 2⅛ inches and lengths at least twice the circumference of the pillow. (See **Ruffles** and **Pillow finishing** in "Fabric Craft Basics.")

Figure 1

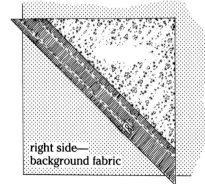

Figure 2

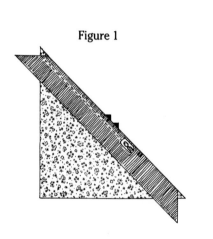

right side—
background fabric

I PLEDGE ALLEGIANCE PIN

This fun pin is made using the hand of Betsy Ross (see Betsy's arm pattern on page 110 and cut using the optional line at the wrist) and appropriate ribbon and button scraps. Any red, white, and blue ribbon(s) will work. Individual streamers of each color, a tiny fabric flag, or even an embroidered appliqué might be usable. A heart button could substitute for the star, etc. If you want a larger pin, use Uncle Sam's hand.

Making the Pin

1. Make the hand as for the doll, except leave open at the wrist edge. When stuffed lightly and the fingers are stitched in, close the wrist with hand stitching.

2. Attach ribbon trims at the back. Add button.

3. Sew a safety pin to the back or use the sewable pin backs available in most notions sections.

Other Hand-Held Accessories

If you have a hand collection, as I do, one hand pin may not be enough. See illustrations for other pin ideas and for a belt. Use Uncle Sam's hand pattern (also marked with a straight cutting line at the wrist) for the belt. Insert ribbon, belting, or even braided cording at the wrist before closing. Put Velcro on the hands to close.

139

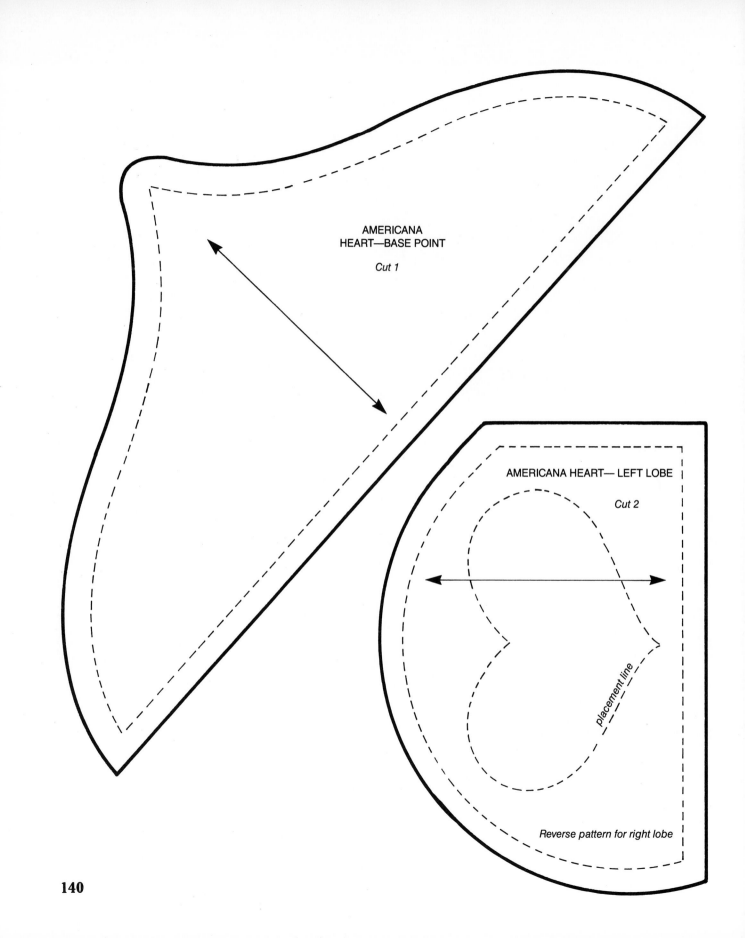

AMERICANA
HEART—BASE POINT

Cut 1

AMERICANA HEART— LEFT LOBE

Cut 2

placement line

Reverse pattern for right lobe

140

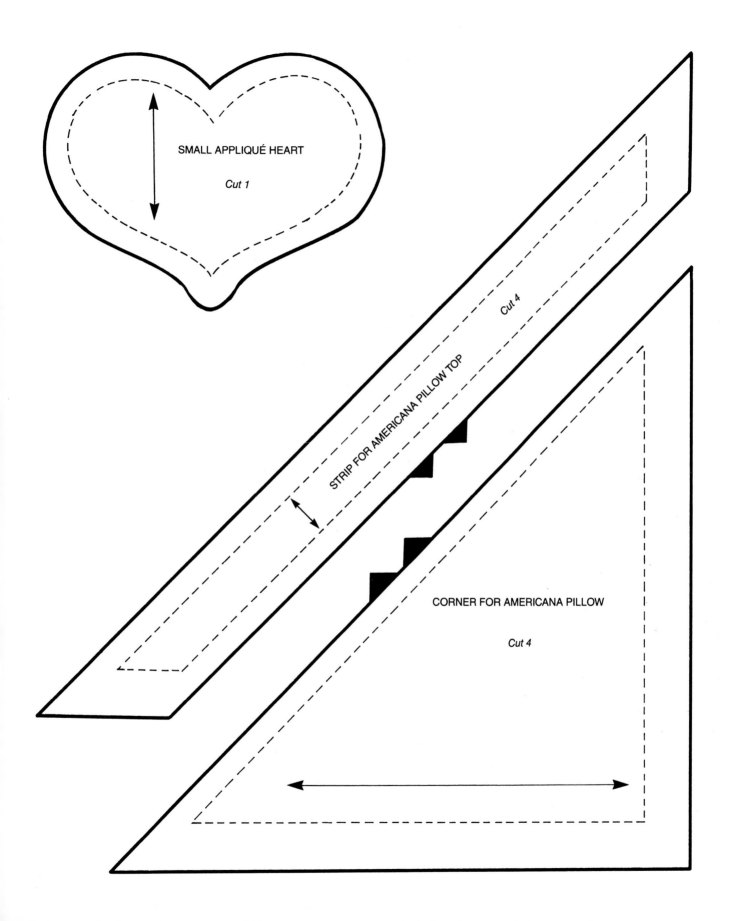

SMALL APPLIQUÉ HEART

Cut 1

STRIP FOR AMERICANA PILLOW TOP

Cut 4

CORNER FOR AMERICANA PILLOW

Cut 4

Bears and Other Fun Things

HEARTS AND ROSES TRAPUNTO PILLOW

Making the Trapunto Design

The decorative form of quilting used here is called trapunto. It is accomplished by stitching two layers of fabric together and then filling the stitched area with batting or cording to cause the dimensional surface design. It is further embellished with embroidery, buttons, and ribbons.

Marking the Design Area

1. From the pillow fabric, cut at least 10 inches across the width of the fabric. Set this aside for ruffles. From the remainder, cut two pieces 11 inches by 15 inches. Set one aside for the back.

2. Fold the pillow top fabric in half, then in half again, making light creases to mark the centers. Unfold the fabric and lay it over the full heart placement guide, making sure center folds align and all edges are straight. With a water-erasable pen (or some other nonpermanent marker), trace all placement lines.

3. Use the outside edge of the heart to align tracing with the corner placement guide. Again, center folds should align. Mark quilting and cording lines for lower right corner. (The outside, square-cornered lines indicate the seam line and the outside cutting line of the pillow.) Flip the pattern to trace the lower left corner. Reposition the pattern as necessary to trace placement lines for the top half, omitting curled quilting lines.

Stitching the Design

Nearly all the stitching holding the two layers of fabric together and making the channels is done by machine. Only the scrolls at the bottom and the three petals at the top center were hand quilted on the pillow shown.

FINISHED SIZE:
14 by 10 inches plus 2-inch-wide ruffles

ADDITIONAL MATERIALS AND NOTIONS:
⅝ yard main fabric
45 inches lace trim, ⅜ inch wide
Contrasting embroidery floss
Purchased ribbon roses
Six small buttons (sizes may vary)
Stuffing
78 inches lightweight yarn or cording and tapestry needle
10 inches each, two colors ⅛-inch satin ribbon
11- by 15-inch quilt backing fabric

How much fabric? The only items listed with each project under Materials and Notions are notions and those fabrics that require more than ¼ yard to make as shown.

1. Position the marked pillow top over the quilt backing fabric, marked side showing. Baste the two pieces together along center folds and diagonally from corner to corner.

2. Using a small machine stitch along each marked line (except for the bottom scrolls and the three center petals at the top), sew through both fabrics.

3. Hand quilt the two bottom scrolls and the petals at the top, making stitches as small and uniform as you can.

Filling the Design Areas

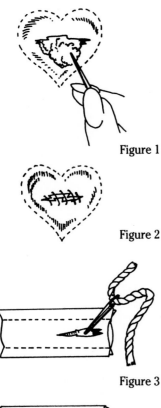

Figure 1

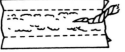

Figure 2

1. The shading on the heart placement guide indicates areas to be stuffed. Make a little slit in the backing at the center of each area, being very careful not to cut through the top fabric. Pull apart tiny wisps of stuffing and push them into the empty space (Figure 1). You might use the blunt end of the tapestry needle to push stuffing into the points.

2. When the area seems nicely padded, close the opening with a loose whipstitch (Figure 2).

3. Cord the stitched channels using the tapestry needle and yarn. Make tiny slits in the backing fabric, as before. Insert your needle between the layers and draw the yarn through the channel (Figure 3). Leave a short tail outside the backing (Figure 4). Close the slits with a whipstitch.

4. Finish the pillow top with buttons, French knots, and Lazy Daisy embroidery as shown on the placement guide. Sew lace trim in place. Add ribbon roses at top corners and at the center, tacked over ribbon streamers and bow.

Figure 3

Figure 4

Ruffles

The ruffle here is a mock double ruffle with a flap insert at the seam (see "Fabric Craft Basics," **Ruffles** and **Flapping**.)

1. Cut two strips across the width of the fabric 2 inches wide and two strips 4 inches wide. Seam each pair end to end to make two strips at least 84 inches long. (A third strip will make a fuller ruffle if you have enough fabric.)

2. Make a strip for the flapping that is the same length and 1 inch wide. Press the strip in half lengthwise, right sides out.

3. Match the raw edges of all three strips, with the flapping strip in the middle. The right sides of the ruffle strip should be facing. Stitch a ¼-inch seam. Turn to the right side and press the joined ruffle in half lengthwise.

4. Run two rows of gathering along the bottom of the ruffle strip. Gather the strip to approximately 50 inches long.

5. Add the ruffle and pillow back. Stuff and close the pillow.

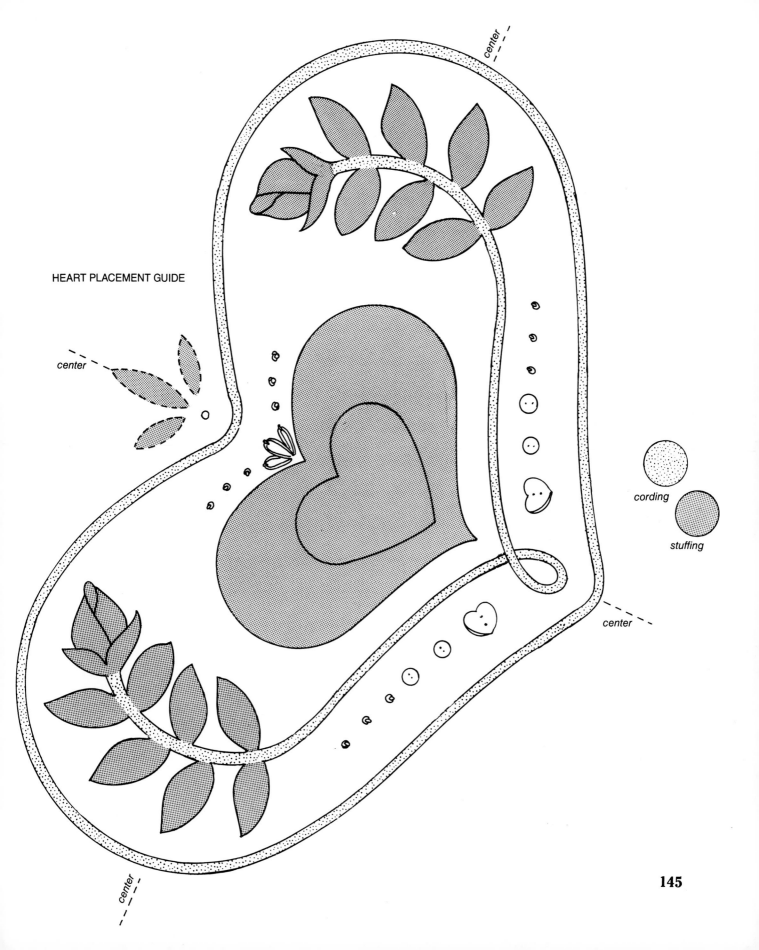

HEART PLACEMENT GUIDE

center

center

center

center

cording

stuffing

145

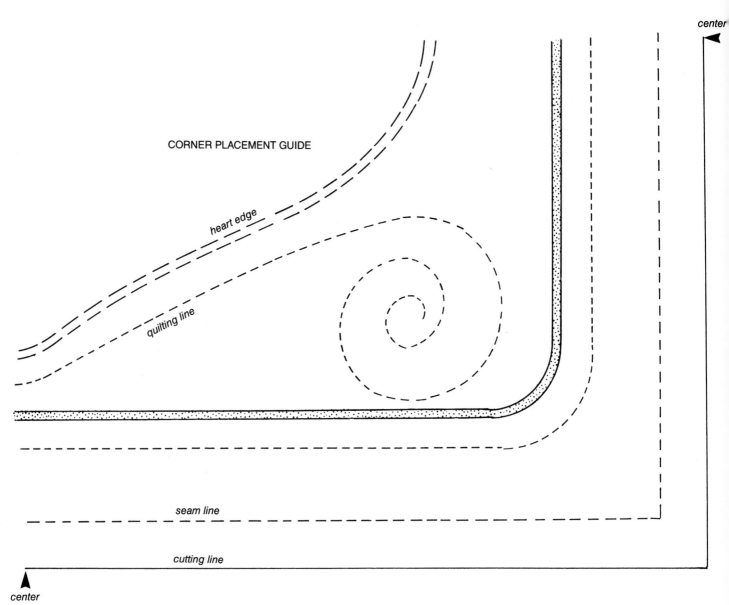

CORNER PLACEMENT GUIDE

center

center

heart edge

quilting line

seam line

cutting line

146

PAPER DOLL CHAIN

Paper doll chains have always fascinated me. This group was designed originally to represent the friendship and unity quilters share worldwide.

1. Apply fusing agent to the back of the selected fabric(s). Trace the design on the backing paper and cut carefully.

2. Fuse in place on an 11- by 15-inch background. Embellish as desired. Legs, faces, and dress trims are all optional.

3. Using a purchased shaped frame enhanced the design in the photograph, but if you can't find one, don't let that stop you. The Paper Doll Chain will fit into the same heart as the Hearts and Roses Trapunto pillow, and these little girls would make a sweet pillow, too.

4. An easy way to hold fabric in a frame is to cut a foam core scrap the same size as the frame interior. Put batting behind the picture and quilt if desired. Position the finished item on foam core and push into the frame opening. It should stay with no further work.

5. If you would like to make the optional mock double ruffle, do not trim away excess background fabric, but mark around the edge of the frame and use that as the stitching line.

MATERIALS NEEDED:
Paper-backed fusing agent
Ribbons
Buttons
Purchased frame
Scrap of foam core (optional)
Quilt batting
Small sharp scissors

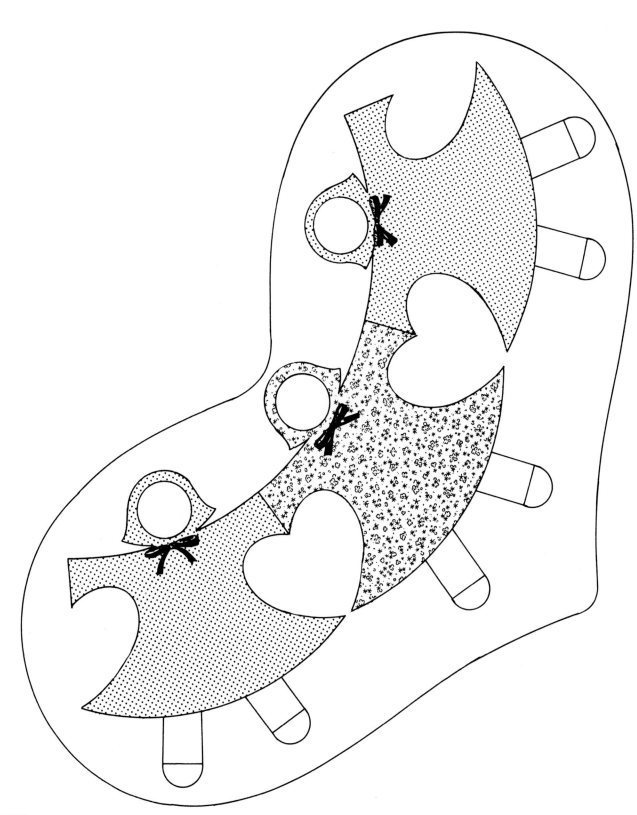

THE THREE BEARS—A FAMILY SAGA

Just like the most famous bear family in literature, our bear family has three sizes. Their finished sizes are approximately 5½ inches, 6¼ inches, and 7 inches tall. If you like the idea of making a "family members" garland or Christmas decorations and you want to establish a greater variety of sizes, add ⅛ inch all around the pattern pieces and proceed. You can also do ⅛ inch smaller. In reality, it is the clothing and accessories you choose that really tell the story of the family member, and worrying about that many different sizes may not be worth the effort.

Instructions for Teddy Bear Bodies

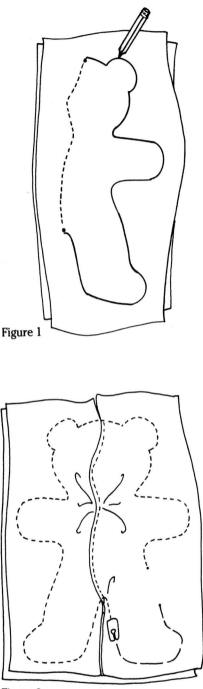

Figure 1

In case you are looking for bear back pattern pieces, don't. Because of the sewing technique we use, there is only one pattern piece for each size bear. After the front is completed, it becomes the pattern for the back.

1. Trace the selected size of bear front. This is the seam line. Draw around the pattern on the wrong side of one piece of *rough cut* fabric. Put a second piece of fabric under the drawn bear outline, right sides together, and stitch from A to B. This is the center front seam and the seam that gives dimension to the bear's front. Turn the sewn front pieces over and line the pattern center front with the sewn seam and trace the rest of the bear's body on this side of the fabric (Figure 1). Trim and *clip* the sewn seam only so that you can spread the bear front nearly flat on a third piece of fabric, right sides together. The nose and tummy areas should not be touching the bear's back.

2. Sew around the bear on the drawn seam line, leaving it open between notches (Figure 2). Now trim the excess away, but leave a ¼-inch seam allowance along the side opening for finishing. Clip the curves and angles and turn the bear right side out. You may want to press the bear if it is badly wrinkled. Stuff with fiberfill. Fold in the raw edges along the side and stitch.

3. To define the ears, take two or three small stitches at the base of each ear from the front into the stuffing, but not through to the back. Make French knots for the eyes where indicated on the pattern. Add mouth, nose, and heart embroidery. The positioning shown may be used on all three bears or slightly reduced for baby and slightly enlarged for papa.

WARNING: The bears invite adornment. Keep in mind your own needs for childproofing these little critters. We don't want to create a hazard of accidental swallowing—as with buttons that might be pulled loose.

Figure 2

BEAR FACE

150

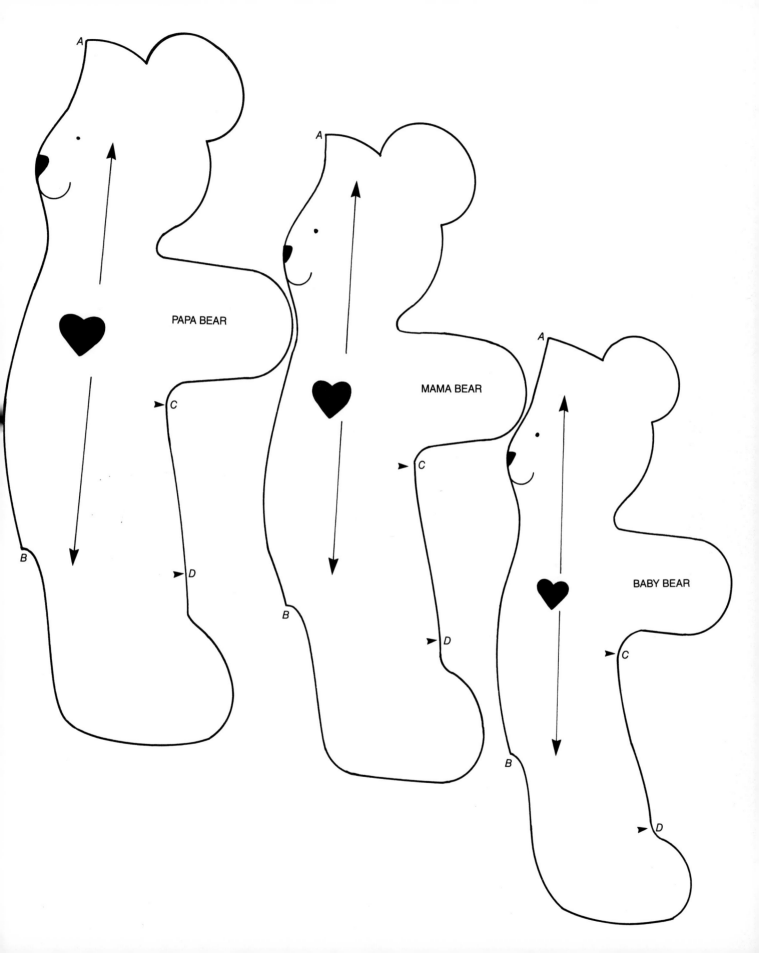

PAPA BEAR

MAMA BEAR

BABY BEAR

Introducing Flex-Fit

There may be a considerable difference in the actual finished size of the teddy bears. A slight discrepancy in the seam allowance and differences in the amount of stuffing used will make the size of the bears and their parts vary considerably. There's not much information available on altering patterns for small bears. Therefore, our bear garments, while all designed for a particular size bear—and that size is identified with each garment—are designed with a relaxed fit. Several of the garments may fit different size bears just by changing snap locations, hem lengths, etc. The dress that is loose and long on the middle bear will be short and tight the next size up. If you find it desirable to make a garment for a bear of a different size, you will probably need to make small adjustments. Taking a tuck in the back of the baby's bonnet, trimming a little off the shoulder line of the sailor collar, or changing the length of a dress may be all that is necessary.

What About the Seam Allowances?

Watch your pattern pieces carefully, as some garment patterns are given with seam allowances while others are not. The reason is that there are three different methods for constructing the bears' clothes. The two used most frequently require marking the sewing line, not the cutting line. The third method starts with a pattern piece that incorporates the seam allowance. The pattern pieces reflect the recommended construction method. Keep in mind that if you are changing fabrics, you may want to change construction techniques also.

The methods are:

● **Felt.** When constructing the garments with felt, the edges are often, but not always, whipstitched together by hand; no seam allowances are allowed or needed. In some of the felt garments shown, we have made regular seams. The patterns reflect exactly how the garments were made.

● **Faux felt.** Many people really like felt, others don't. One of my best friends has always been so negative about felt that I've developed a woven fabrics substitute for felt. It simply involves completely lining each garment piece before whipstitching the pieces together as if they were felt.

Start with a finished size (no printed seam allowance) pattern piece. Trace it onto the wrong side of a firmly woven fabric, allowing at least ¼ inch all around. Place the fabric over a second piece of fabric the same size, with right sides together. *Rough cut* both pieces. Cut a small slash in the center of the second piece. Using a smaller machine stitch (10 to 12 stitches per inch), stitch completely around the shape on the seam line. *Clip* the seams as necessary and turn through the cut slit. Carefully push at the seam line from inside so the finished shape follows the pattern line. Press. Whipstitch the slit shut or secure with a piece of paper-backed fusing agent. You now have a completely lined piece of fabric with finished edges that can be whipstitched together just like felt.

● **Regular sewing.** Some things, like the little play apron, are just as easy to make by simply folding under and stitching the raw edges.

PRESSING TIP: Pressing these little creations can be difficult. A rolled-up magazine, tied with string (rubber bands may melt) and covered with a washcloth or kitchen towel, will fit into places ironing boards won't.

PAPA'S CLOTHES

The items that follow are designed to fit the largest bear.

Vest (faux felt method)

Because this vest is designed with a lap front closing, the front pieces are not symmetrical. Men's clothes lap left over right. Following the directions for faux felt, make one each of the back, left front, and right front vest pieces. (When cutting the left front, place the pattern *printed side up* on the wrong side of the fabric, then follow faux felt directions. When cutting the right front, place the pattern *printed side down* on the wrong side of the fabric, then follow faux felt directions.) Whipstitch together at the shoulders and underarms. Add two small snaps for closure.

Necktie and Collar (regular sewing)

The collar is made of two pieces cut on the bias. The easiest way to make this is to sew before you cut.

1. Fold a 6- by 10-inch piece of fabric in half crosswise. Place the pattern on it diagonally and trace around the edge. Stitch on the traced line, but leave open on the straight edge between dots (Figure 1).

2. Use the pattern to cut a piece of iron-on interfacing from the fold line to the nonstraight edge of the collar and apply to one collar piece only (Figure 2). Clip and turn. For crisp points, poke corners carefully but diligently.

3. Turn the open edges under and close with a hand stitch. Press flat and then press on the fold line. Taking advantage of the bias, form a slight curve to the collar. Sew a snap on both ends of the neck band.

MATERIALS NEEDED:
Because our teddy bears are small (4 inches to 5½ inches), most of their bodies and clothes can be made with small scraps. Pieces of fabric 11 by 18 inches or larger would be listed, but otherwise our materials listing only includes notions.

NOTIONS:
Two snaps

NOTIONS:
4½-inch piece of ⅜-inch grosgrain ribbon

Figure 1

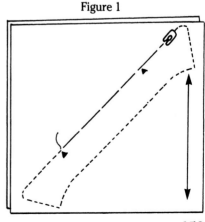

Figure 2

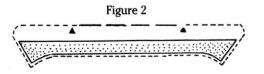

Figure 3

NOTIONS:
One snap

4. Make a tie by folding the 4½-inch piece of ⅜-inch grosgrain ribbon in half lengthwise. Make the "knot" by taking a small stitch in the ribbon about ¼ inch from the fold and wrapping the thread around the ribbon, tightening as you wrap (Figure 3). Trim both ends to a point. Sew the tie to the neck band so the collar points slightly cover the knot on both sides when closed.

Nightshirt (regular sewing)

1. To make the nightshirt, sew both front pieces together at the center below dot A. Sew under the seam allowance above the dot. Fold left side over right at the dot, making a ⅛-inch pleat, and sew across. Sew front to back at the shoulders. Press the seam open.

2. Hem the sleeves. Sew the side seams to dot B. Clip at the underarms. Sew the hem. Sew under ⅛ inch at the neckline. Sew on snap at the center front.

Nightcap (regular sewing)

The nightcap fits jauntily over one ear.

1. Turn up a ⅛-inch hem on the bottom, curved edge. With right sides together, sew the straight edges together. Turn right side out.

2. Put the cap over one bear ear and fold down the top part of the cap to fit the bear snugly. Tack the fold in place. If desired, make a little tassel using fine yarn or embroidery floss, and sew it to the point of the cap.

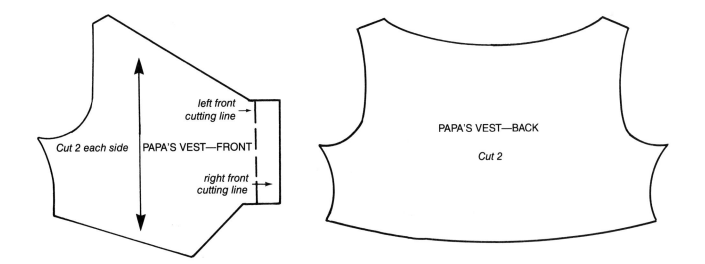

Cut 2 each side PAPA'S VEST—FRONT

left front cutting line

right front cutting line

PAPA'S VEST—BACK

Cut 2

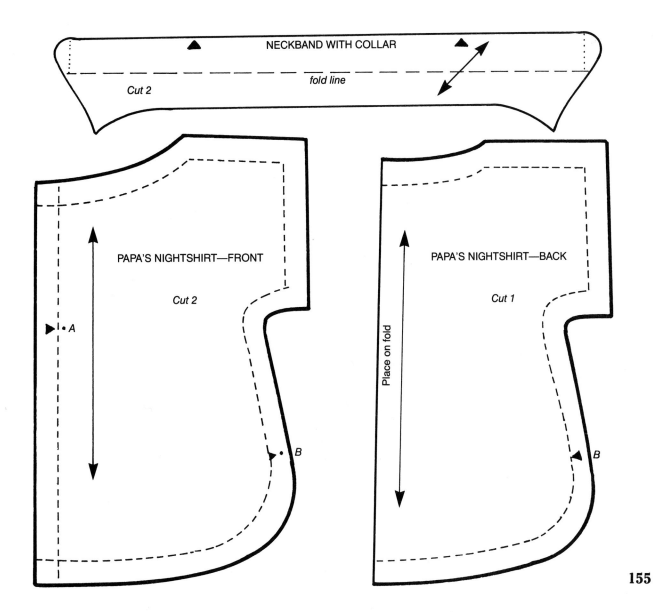

NECKBAND WITH COLLAR

Cut 2 fold line

PAPA'S NIGHTSHIRT—FRONT

Cut 2

• A

• B

PAPA'S NIGHTSHIRT—BACK

Cut 1

Place on fold

B

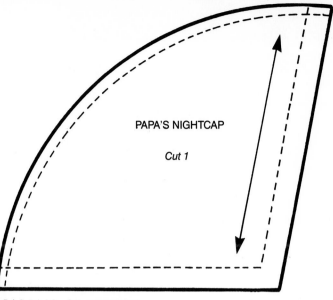

PAPA'S NIGHTCAP

Cut 1

MAMA'S CLOTHES

The items that follow are all designed to fit the middle bear.

Heart Apron (regular and faux felt techniques)

1. Use the pattern to cut the skirt. Turn under ¼ inch and hem one long and two short sides. Gather along the other edge until the skirt measures 3½ inches long, working ⅛ inch from the edge. Center ⅜-inch ribbon over gathers on the right side of the skirt. Sew one edge of ribbon to the skirt. Turn in the ribbon ends. Fold ribbon over the raw edge of gathers and sew down by hand.

2. Make the heart using the faux felt method. Center on the skirt, position according to the line on the heart pattern, and stitch in place. Sew one end of each 5-inch ribbon to the side of the hearts as in the diagram here. Cross ribbons in back behind the bear and sew to opposite ends of the waistband, adjusting the length as necessary to fit the bear.

Mother's Nightgown (regular sewing)

1. To make the nightgown, join front pieces to back at the shoulders from the sleeve edge to dot A. Gather the neckline from dot B on one front, around the neckline to dot B on the other front. Press open. Hem the sleeves. Sew underarm seams. Clip curves. Hem the lower edge of the gown.

2. Turn under the center front and neckline edges. Stitch, attaching lace at the same time on the right front and neckline. The lace need not extend down the left front edge, as that will be covered by the right front.

3. Put the gown on the bear. Using double thread, make small running stitches and gather each cuff up to fit. Gather the neckline from the dot on one front to the dot on the other. Sew snaps at the neckline and waist.

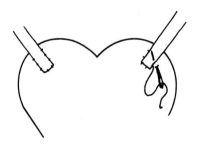

NOTIONS:
5 inches of ⅜-inch ribbon for waistband
Two 5-inch pieces of ⅛-inch ribbon for shoulder straps

NOTIONS:
Two snaps
28 inches of straight lace ¼ inch wide

Mother's Nightcap (regular sewing)

1. The nightcap is two fully lined pieces. Press both pieces on the fold line and mark ear openings (Figure 1). Open each piece and place right sides together with fold lines matching. The outer edges will not match—while the pieces match at the fold line, the back section is an oval and the front a circle (Figure 2). Sew along the fold line, leaving the two ear spaces open. Backstitch at the beginning and end of each section. Fold front section halves together; fold back section halves together (Figure 3), with all fabric right side out. Try the cap on the bear to be sure the ear holes fit. Remove and press flat.

2. Pin the raw edges together. Stitch layers together very close to the edge or zigzag. Topstitch lace trim over the stitching.

3. Sew one row of gathering thread around the cap ½ inch from the outer edge. Sew another row just inside the first (Figure 4).

4. Put the cap on the bear and gently pull the gathering threads up so the cap fits snugly. Make secure knots. Starting at the center front, attach ribbon over stitches with fabric glue or small stitches. Make a dainty bow and sew it on at the center front over the ends of the ribbon band.

NOTIONS:
14 inches of lace ¼-inch wide
12 inches of ⅛-inch satin
    ribbon

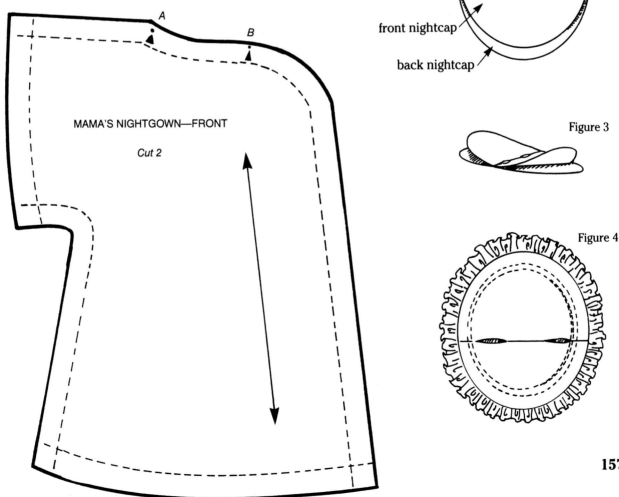

Figure 1

Figure 2

front nightcap

back nightcap

Figure 3

Figure 4

A

B

MAMA'S NIGHTGOWN—FRONT

Cut 2

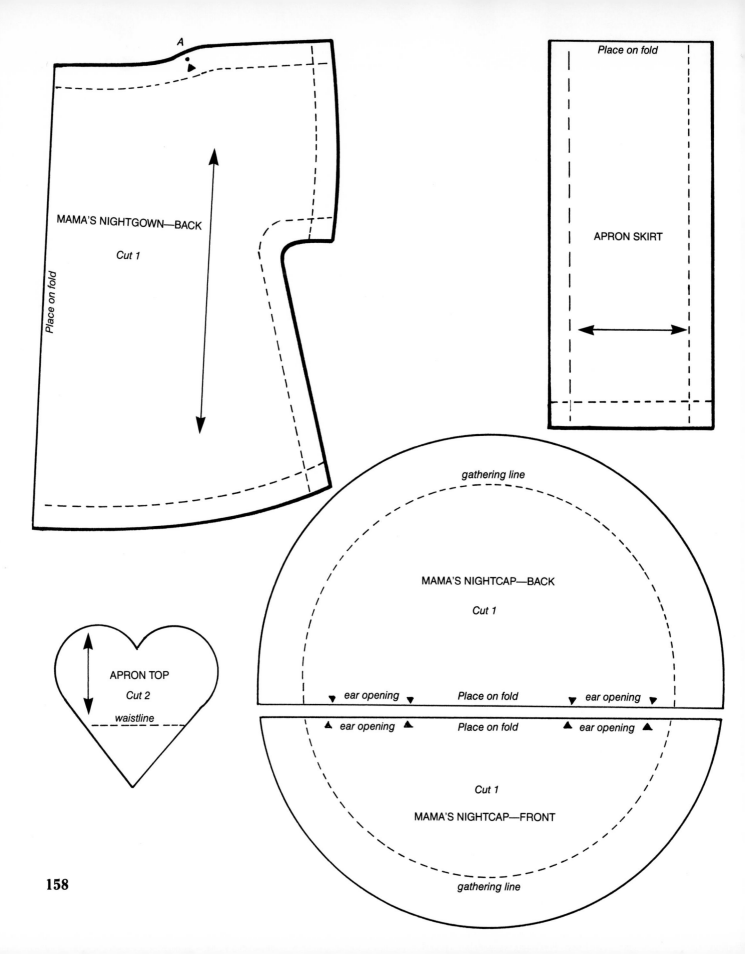

A

MAMA'S NIGHTGOWN—BACK

Cut 1

Place on fold

Place on fold

APRON SKIRT

gathering line

MAMA'S NIGHTCAP—BACK

Cut 1

ear opening   Place on fold   ear opening

ear opening   Place on fold   ear opening

Cut 1

MAMA'S NIGHTCAP—FRONT

gathering line

APRON TOP

Cut 2

waistline

CHILDREN'S CLOTHES—MEDIUM

The overalls, play apron, ballerina outfit, and ballet slippers were designed to fit the medium bear.

Overalls (regular sewing)

1. Sew the center front seam from top to dot. Press the seam open. Turn under the side and upper edge seam allowances, and topstitch a hem, clipping at the underarm curve as needed.

2. Sew under the seam allowance at the top edge of the back. Sew front to back on each side, matching upper and lower edges. Press open. Sew under seam allowances on lower edges. Pin the front and back cuff edges together. Stitch the inseam, clipping at the point if needed. Turn right side out.

3. Put the overalls on your bear. Attach the two straps (4 inches each) in the same way as with Mama's Heart Apron.

Toy or Play Apron (regular sewing)

1. Cut one apron piece. Turn under ¼ inch at the bottom and stitch the hem. Then fold to the back along the first fold line and press. Next fold to the front side on the second fold line to make a pocket flap. Stitch the pocket flap along the second fold line and press. This makes the pockets. Stitch along the outer edges to hold the pocket layer in place. Hem all remaining edges by turning under ¼ inch and topstitching in place. Clip at curves as necessary. Stitch the pocket layer on the vertical lines to make dividers. (See diagram.)

2. To make the straps, cut two 4½-inch-long pieces of ⅛-inch or ³⁄₁₆-inch ribbon. Sew a ribbon to each upper corner of the finished apron angled out over the shoulder. Put the apron on the bear. With the center pocket seam lined up with the center seam of the bear, pin the apron in proper position. Cross the ties in the back and adjust to the correct size. Pin each ribbon end to the opposite lower armhole corner and stitch in place.

NOTE: To make the toy apron fit the baby bear, just trim ⅛ inch from the top and armhole edges of the pattern, and shorten the apron straps accordingly.

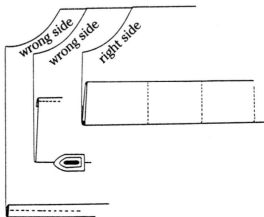

159

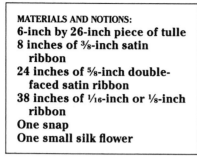

Ballerina (regular sewing)

1. To make the tutu, fold the 6-inch by 26-inch piece of tulle (a little finer than nylon net) in half lengthwise, twice. It will be approximately 1½ inches by 26 inches. Sew one row of long gathering stitches ¼ inch from the last folded edge (Figure 1). Gather to fit the bear's waist. (Measure your own teddy's waist, but the approximate measurement is 6 inches). For the waistband, cut ⅜-inch satin ribbon 1 inch longer than the waist measurement. To secure the tulle inconspicuously to the ribbon, hand stitch it in the woven edge, leaving ½ inch of ribbon free at each end (Figure 2). Turn the ribbon ends under and sew a snap at the center back.

Carefully cut the tulle skirt open along the bottom fold. If any of the gathered edge shows above the waistband, trim it away carefully.

2. To make straps, use double-faced satin ribbon ⅝ inch wide and 11 inches long. Fold into a **V** shape in the middle of the ribbon (Figure 3). Stitch the bottom of the fold to the bottom of the ribbon waistband at center front. Secure the straps at the top of the waistband. With the tutu on the bear, fit the straps to the correct length and secure to the waistband in the back. At the waist, add a tiny flower and bow with long streamers, using approximately 6 inches of 1/16-inch ribbon (Figure 4).

Figure 1

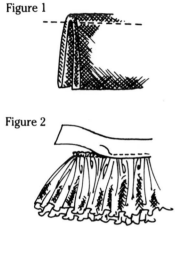

Figure 2

Figure 3

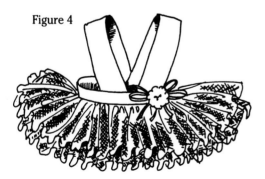

Figure 4

Ballet Slippers

1. For each slipper, fold 4 inches of ⅝-inch ribbon in half crosswise and whipstitch along one long side and up the cut ends to make the shoe shape. To fit the shoe to your bear, put it on right side out and mark individual contours—the satin will retain a pin or fingernail mark long enough to turn inside out and stitch by machine. Turn right side out, check fit.

2. Find the center of a 15-inch piece of ⅛-inch or 1/16-inch ribbon; sew that point to the back of the shoe at the top of the seam. Put the shoe on and wrap the ribbon around the leg one and a half times and tie in a bow.

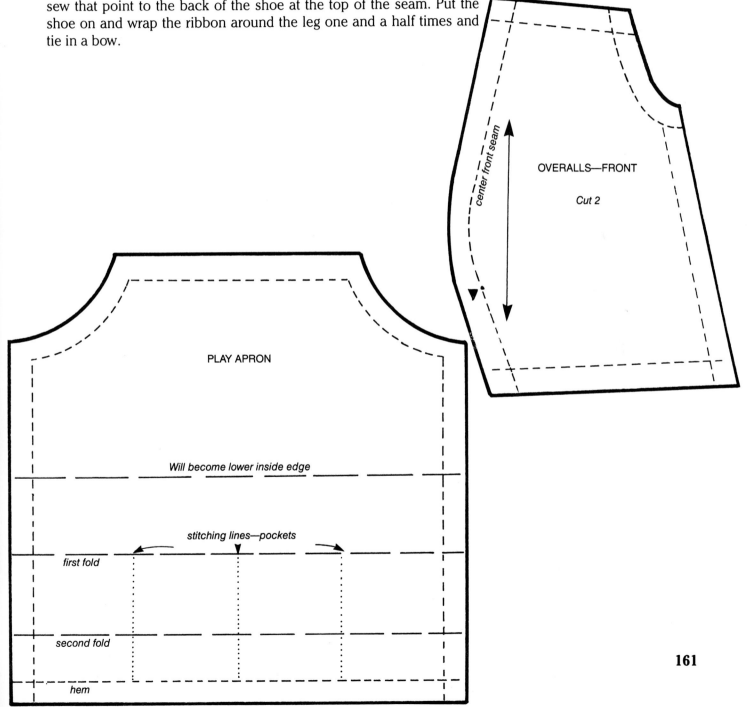

center front seam

OVERALLS—FRONT

Cut 2

PLAY APRON

Will become lower inside edge

stitching lines—pockets

first fold

second fold

hem

NOTIONS:
Two 4-inch pieces of ⅝-inch satin ribbon
Two 15-inch pieces of either ⅛-inch or 1/16-inch satin ribbon

161

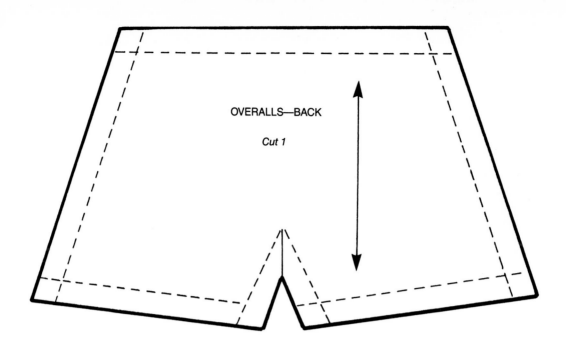

OVERALLS—BACK

Cut 1

CHILDREN'S CLOTHES—SMALL

These clothing items are designed to fit the small bear.

NOTIONS:
One snap

Figure 1

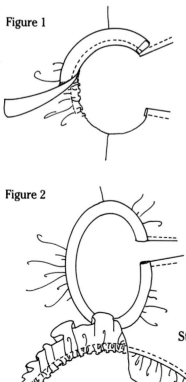

Figure 2

Stitch in place, then turn under and topstitch

Little Girl's Dress (regular sewing)

1. Cut two backs, two sleeves, and one front. On the front, sew the gathering stitches between dots A. Seam the center back from dot B to the hem. Press the seam open and the seam allowances down. Topstitch along both sides of the back neck opening. Sew the front and back together at the shoulders. Press the seam open.

2. Pull the front neckline gathers up to measure 1 inch wide. Sew a ¾-inch by 7-inch bias strip to the neckline, with right sides together, edges matching, and ends turned in (Figure 1). Turn the raw edge under ¼ inch and hand stitch to the inside of the neckline.

3. Keep each sleeve piece folded as cut, right side out. Gather sleeve ruffles along the curved edge until they fit the armholes. Sew in place, matching right sides and raw edges. Pull the ruffle away from the dress and topstitch seam allowances in place under the dress (Figure 2).

Stitch the underarm seams.

4. Turn up a ¼-inch hem in the skirt and stitch. Sew a snap to the neckline at center back.

Little Boy's Sailor Collar (faux felt)

1. Trace one collar. Most collar fabrics will be transparent enough to lay on the pattern and trace. This gives a nice line for beading a row of *fabric glue* or positioning ¹⁄₁₆-inch ribbon for stitching. Make sure the ribbon extends at least ¼ inch beyond the traced edge of the collar so it will be caught in the seam.

2. Put the ribbon-trimmed collar face-down on the second piece of collar fabric and proceed with the faux felt construction. Sew a snap at center front—the collar tips will overlap.

Make a tie with the ⅜-inch ribbon and sew on over the snap.

Baby Layette (faux felt)

Kimono

Make the entire kimono piece using the faux felt method. Whipstitch the side seam together. Sew a 5-inch piece of ⅜-inch gathered lace at the neck. Attach one 5-inch length of ¹⁄₁₆-inch ribbon to each side of the neck at center front.

Bonnet

1. Make the bonnet body using the faux felt method. Pin to the back of the head so the center front extends ¼ inch beyond the bear's head seam and the side edges are just barely in front of the head seam (Figure 1).

2. To make the brim, use single-fold bias tape 5 inches long with the ends folded inside ¼ inch and a 4½-inch piece of ⅜-inch gathered lace sewn in between the two long edges (Figure 2). You can use purchased tape, or make your own. With the bonnet still pinned to the bear, place one end of the brim even with the lower edge of the side of the bonnet, keeping the lace edge toward the face. Whipstitch the bonnet and brim together up one side. Then place the brim in front of the ear and sew the brim to the center section of the bonnet. Again place the brim in front of the ear, and continue sewing the brim to the bonnet from the ear to the lower edge of the bonnet.

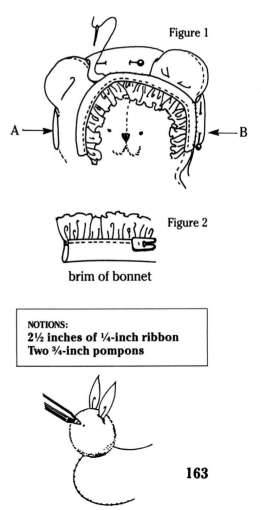

Figure 1

Figure 2

brim of bonnet

Bunny Slippers (felt method)

Cut four pieces of felt. For each slipper, whipstitch together two pieces from A to B around the bottom. Using fabric glue, fasten the pompons at point A.

To make the ears, cut ¼-inch-wide ribbon into four pieces ⅝ inch long. Trim one end of each piece to a point and glue two near the back of the pompon. Use a black felt fine-line marker to make the eyes and nose.

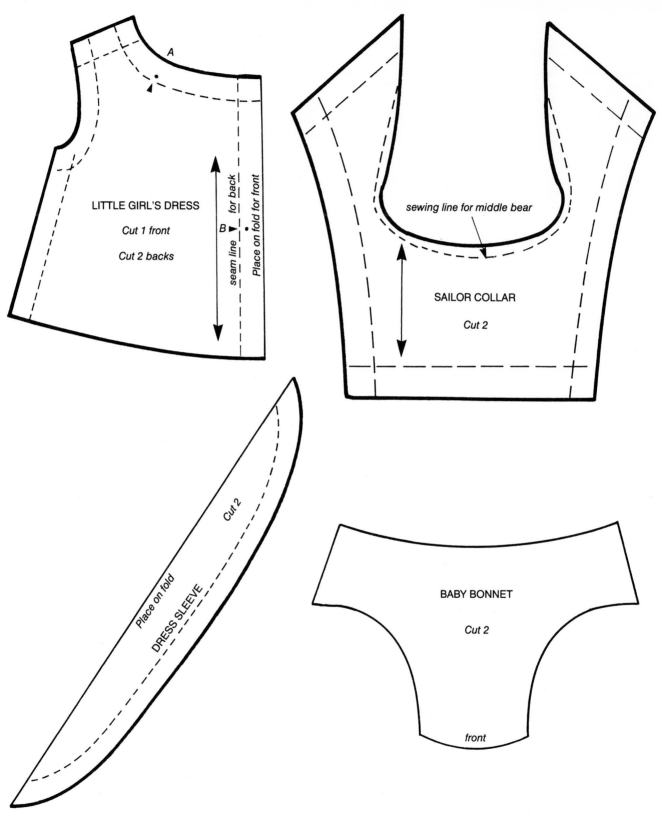

LITTLE GIRL'S DRESS

Cut 1 front

Cut 2 backs

A

seam line

for back

B

Place on fold for front

SAILOR COLLAR

Cut 2

sewing line for middle bear

Place on fold

DRESS SLEEVE

Cut 2

BABY BONNET

Cut 2

front

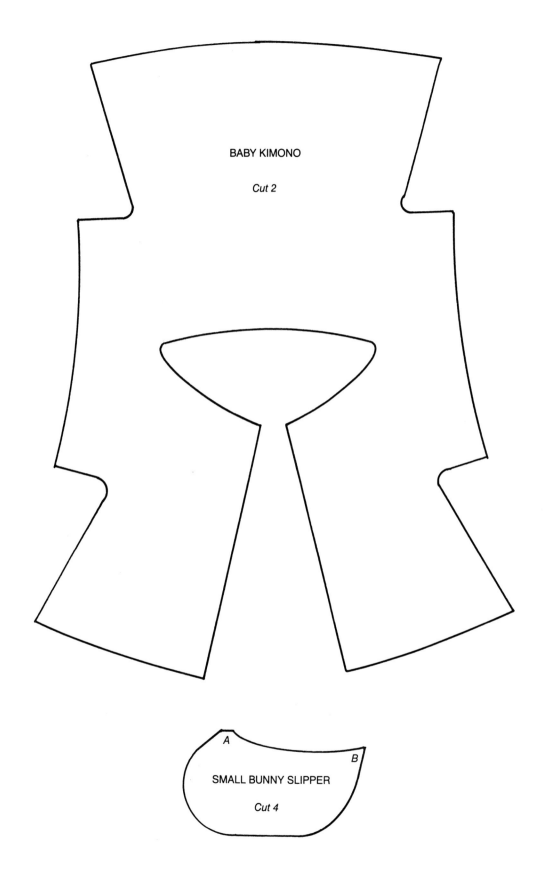

BABY KIMONO

Cut 2

A
B

SMALL BUNNY SLIPPER

Cut 4

165

Where Shall I Put the Bears?

Each little bear is darling alone. It makes a sweet pocket toy or adds to any collection of bears.

Groups of bears tell an even better story than individual bears. Bear Family Garlands are among my favorite ways to group the bears. Develop bears to represent the members of your family. They can all be made from the same fabric and outfitted, or sometimes the fabric that makes the bear's body is enough to tell the story. Gray Glen Plaid wool, worn-out denim, hot pink satin, calico, velveteen, and other fabrics all evoke different family member personality traits.

When the bears are assembled, either whipstitch their paws together or make a stitch in each hand with a long piece of six-strand embroidery floss. Put hearts and ribbons at each end for hanging. Or dress the bears in outfits that represent family members and they make very personal Christmas ornaments.

For additional variety to the clothes given here, you can make all sorts of things that don't really require patterns—a fringed woolen neck scarf, a big ribbon hair bow behind one ear, leg warmers, baby blankets, etc.

Holidays and special occasions call for bear outfits, too. For Christmas clothes, see the next chapter.

MASKED BEAR

For trick or treat, this mask and cape outfit could be made into many costumes for your Halloween teddy. In black it is just sinister; made in red and complemented with a pipe cleaner fork, it is devilish; use blue satin and a yellow S, and it's Superman!

Putting the Cape Together

1. Sew both front pieces to back at the sides, leaving open between the dots. Press the seams open. Repeat with the lining pieces. Place the cape and lining right sides together, matching seam lines and armholes. Pin in place.

2. Stitch all around the outer edge, leaving 2 inches open at the hem edge in the center back. Trim the seam allowances and clip where necessary. Turn right side out. Press edges flat.

3. Slip-stitch lining to the cape at the armholes and the 2-inch opening in the hem.

4. Machine stitch a gathering line around the neckline where marked. With the cape on the bear, pull the gathers up so the front pieces barely meet. Pin the ribbon on top of the gathers so that the ends extend 5 to 6 inches for tying. Topstitch ribbon in place over the gathers.

Felt Mask

Cut the mask out of felt. Cut out eyeholes. Fit the mask on the bear, pinning it in back. Stitch the ends together and trim any excess. Press the seam open.

NOTIONS:
17 inches of ¼-inch ribbon for cape

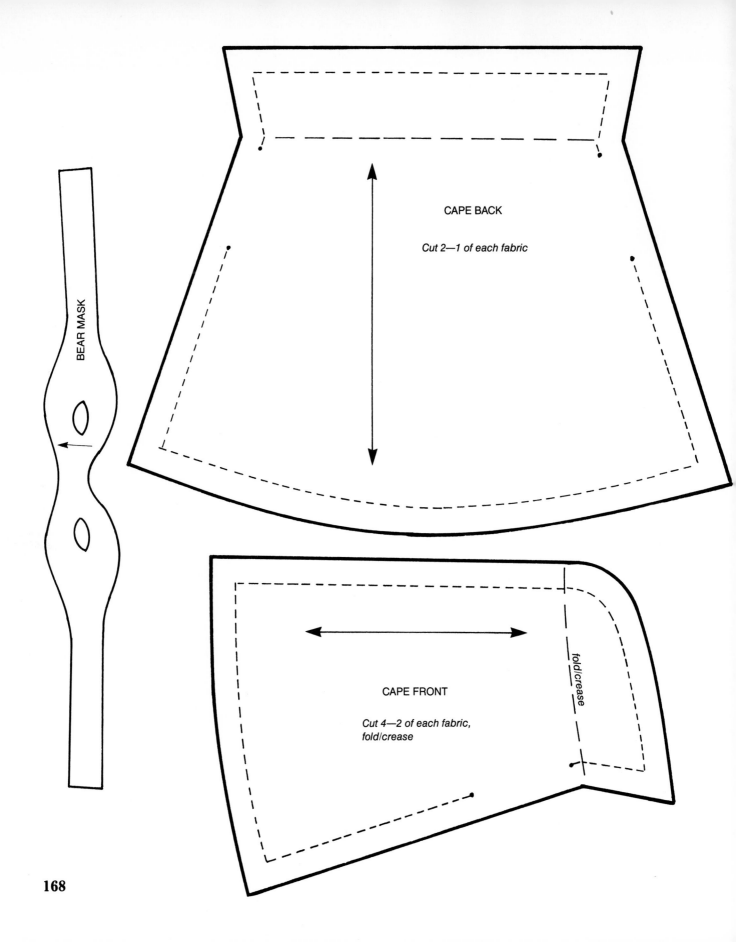

BEAR MASK

CAPE BACK

Cut 2—1 of each fabric

CAPE FRONT

*Cut 4—2 of each fabric,
fold/crease*

fold/crease

168

EASTER RABBITS

While an Easter basket could certainly hold bears, it seems they *must* hold rabbits, hence our rabbit versions. There are two sizes of rabbits. Make the rabbit body using the same technique used for the bear. The tail for the baby rabbit is made with the fringelike ball on Santa's cap (see page 211). Make the larger rabbit's tail the same way, except your starting strip should be 1 inch by 5 inches.

CARROT FOR BUNNY GARLAND

What's a rabbit without a carrot? Whether you're making a garland or a single bunny, a cute carrot accessory is always appropriate.

1. Trace the carrot pattern onto paper-backed fusible. Fuse it in place on the carrot fabric. Cut out carrots and fuse to any scrap backing fabric. Trim away any excess backing.

2. Sew straight edges together. Trim the seam allowance down to ⅛ inch and turn the carrot right side out.

3. By hand, run tiny gathering stitches around the top edge. Push a little stuffing into the tip, then insert pipe cleaner. Stuff the rest of the carrot around the pipe cleaner, stopping just short of the top. Pull gathers tight around the bottom of the pipe cleaner and secure.

4. Glue the pompon to the top of the pipe cleaner.

> **ADDITIONAL MATERIALS:**
> **1¼ inches of green pipe cleaner**
> **¾-inch green pompon**

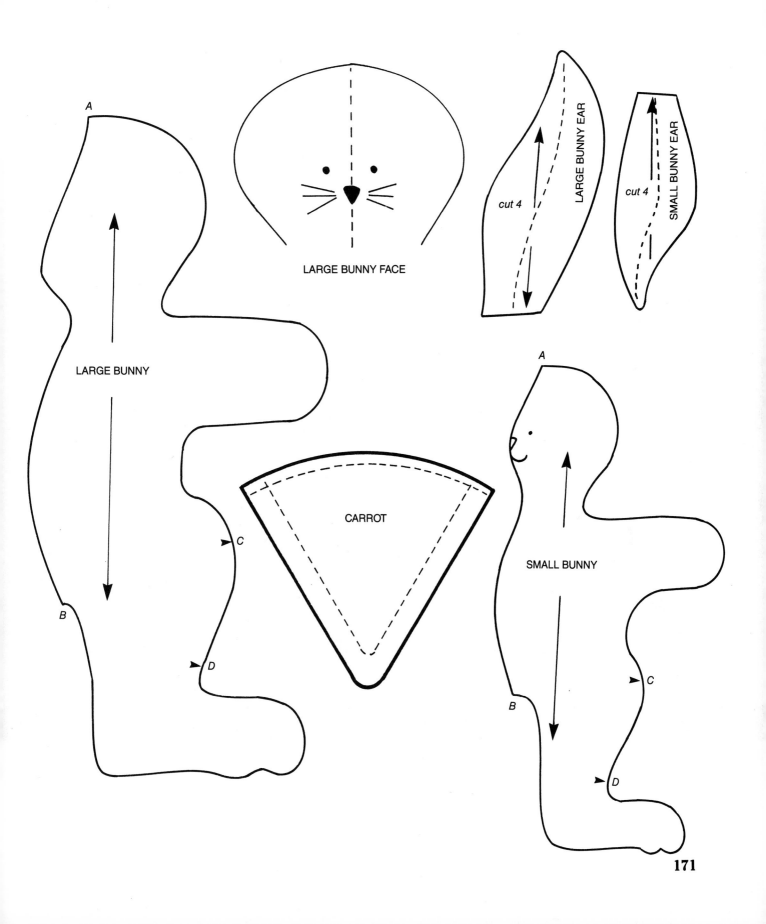

A

LARGE BUNNY

B

C

D

LARGE BUNNY FACE

LARGE BUNNY EAR

cut 4

SMALL BUNNY EAR

cut 4

CARROT

A

SMALL BUNNY

B

C

D

171

FUN WITH SWEATSHIRTS

Here are some ways to use the patterns and designs throughout the book as a bonus for ideas for decorating sweatshirts.

PAPER DOLL CHAIN APPLIQUÉ

The paper doll chain from earlier in this chapter can be fused in a single set of three on the front of a sweatshirt. Add twine or ribbon at each end and garnish with little stuffed bows at the end (Figure 1).

Want the dolls to go all the way around the shoulders? Ten will make a nice circle. (It may be necessary to adjust slightly.)

HEARTS, HEARTS, AND MORE HEARTS

Using any of the hearts from the basic heart designs in "Things That Look Great on Hooks and Pegs," make a bottom border and sleeve chevrons for a sweatshirt (Figure 2). Hearts shown are from the Folk Heart group in two sizes. They could be fused, lined and turned, and then appliquéd, or a combination where you leave some of the lined hearts open at the top to make pockets.

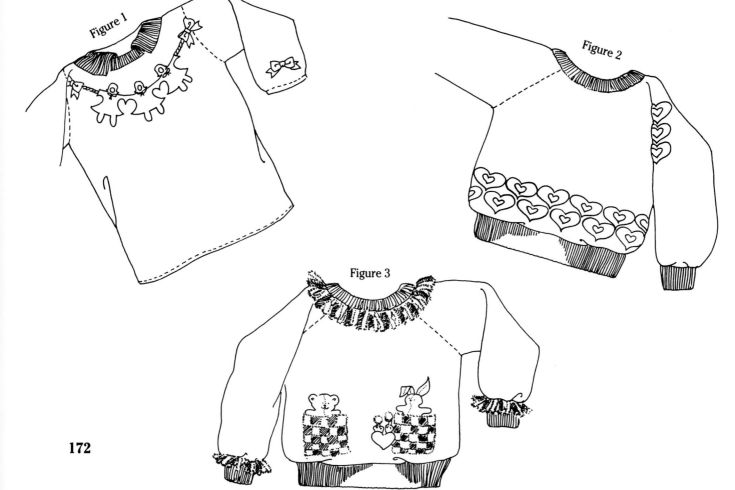

Figure 1

Figure 2

Figure 3

TEDDY BEARS AND/OR RABBITS IN POCKETS

To make the frayed fabric strip pockets, weave strips upside down and fuse a pocket-size backing on the weaving. Leave slightly extended ends of the strips. Topstitch pockets in place and then fray the extended ends. Make them the right size to hold one of the bears or rabbits (Figure 3).

To make the neck and sleeve decorations, make frayed strips twice as long as the resulting fringe. Center the open strips on the desired stitching line. Stretch the sweatshirt while stitching the fringe in place to the amount the fringe strips will need to stretch in putting on and taking off.

THE HEARTS AND ROSES TRAPUNTO

The trapunto design can be interpreted in fusible appliqué, but it is really worth the effort for traditional hand appliqué with ribbon pieces folded under the leaves for roses. Add extra lace around the seams and neck. Consider cutting off the waistband ribbing and hemming the sweatshirt bottom. Then add an elastic casing at the waist (Figure 4).

BUTTONED-DOWN SWEATSHIRT

Remember the soft jewelry in the "Sew a Treat for Yourself" chapter? Using the same pattern shapes—mix or match—appliqué or stencil shapes for button backgrounds randomly or in a definite pattern. Stitch ribbons from the neck to the shape. Add buttons in the same way as described for a separate stuffed piece (Figure 5).

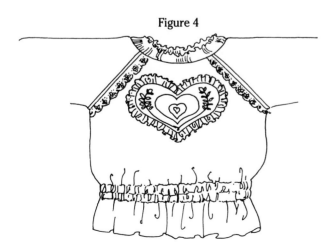

Figure 4

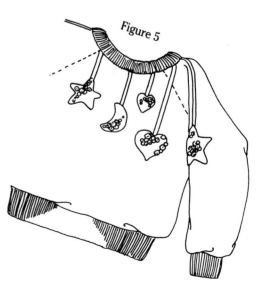

Figure 5

A Special Scrap Quilt

1890s NINE PATCH CRIB QUILT

This up-to-date remake was inspired by a delightful turn-of-the century American patchwork quilt (shown on rack in picture). When this project began, my goal was not to make an exact replica, but to create an "antique-looking" quilt using modern quilting techniques.

To capture the old-fashioned quality in the new version, it was important to study the original. Look carefully for clues. What colors were used? How were print fabrics used together? How many squares make up the quilt? How are the squares laid out?

It is easy to see that the antique quilt was constructed using Nine Patch squares and alternate plain or empty blocks. They are placed in a "diagonal set." This means that instead of laying out the squares so they are flat on one side, they are set on their points. Each Nine Patch patchwork square consists of nine smaller squares—five dark and four light squares sewn together in a checkerboard pattern. Each of the matching alternate blocks is a square as big as the completed patchwork block.

When the original quilt was made, each square of the Nine Patch was cut out and sewn separately, by hand. Instead of that laborious method, our instructions use a technique called "strip piecing." This involves cutting strips of fabric as wide as the desired square (finished size plus two ¼-inch seam allowances) and sewing them together in rows. By cutting across the sewn strips the same width as the original strips into final square size, the result is prepieced squares. The benefits of using this strip method are that you will save time, be more accurate, and the process is easier.

(Just in case having free time is not your problem and you would prefer to make this quilt piece by piece, the actual patterns for cutting pieces instead of using the strip techniques are included. When you get to the borders, please use the measurements included in the border instructions, as the pieces are too big to reproduce realistically in this book.)

In the antique quilt, there were eighty Nine Patch squares set

How much fabric? The only items listed with each project under Materials and Notions are notions and those fabrics that require more than ¼ yard to make as shown.

diagonally. Each of the little Nine Patch squares was ⅞ inch. By making each of them only ⅛ inch bigger and by adding a 1-inch border, the same size interior section can be made using only sixty-three Nine Patch squares. Instead of eight rows with ten squares each, you will be working with seven rows of nine squares, a considerable time-saver. No matter how fast your techniques, the best way to save time is to do less work without sacrificing quality of design.

In finishing, a wider final border was added, and the new quilt is several inches larger in both directions than the old one.

While analyzing the original quilt, I discovered that it was not uncommon for the same Nine Patch square to be used three or more times. By making at least three patchwork squares using the same fabric combinations, the time-saving strip techniques can be advantageously incorporated. Careful placement of the finished squares prevents the repetition from being obvious.

Selecting Scrap Fabrics

Select at least forty-two fabrics—that is, twenty-one contrasting pair combinations of fabrics. (You will use each pair combination three times to make a total of sixty-three patchwork blocks.) They may have one dark fabric and one light, a medium and a light fabric, or a dark and a medium. The same fabric may be the darker material in one unit and the lighter in another. However, following the guide of the antique quilt, the darker fabric always occupies the outside corners and the center block of the Nine Patch. The strip-piecing technique will save so much time that you may wish to complete more combinations. Then you can select your favorites for this quilt and set aside the others for a different project.

If you were making a reproduction quilt, each of the fabrics would need to match the original as closely as possible, which would entail a long, exhausting fabric search. By creating a quilt that just looks antique, you don't make such a time commitment. You will want to select fabrics in the general color families and styles and omit prominent colors that are not in the original quilt.

Making the Nine Patch Units

1. For each fabric pair, cut two 1½-inch by 9-inch strips and one 1½-inch by 5-inch strip of the darker fabric. Cut one strip measuring 1½ inches by 9 inches and two 1½-inch by 5-inch strips of the lighter fabric. (I prefer the length of the strips to be on the lengthwise grain of the fabric.) Because 9 inches is the exact measurement needed for the longest strip, ¼-yard pieces of fabric will work, unless they are skimpy. If you have enough fabric, cut 9½-inch-long strips—that allows you to straighten every edge. Don't forget, the rotary cutter method is a great help (see "Fabric Craft Basics").

FINISHED SIZE:
47 by 56 inches

ADDITIONAL MATERIALS:
1⅜ yards background fabric
¾ yard border and binding fabric
Batting, 48 by 58 inches
2¾ yards backing fabric (includes sufficient fabric to cut borders and binding—if purchasing fabric)
Invisible nylon thread for machine quilting

2. Using a ¼-inch seam allowance, sew each set of alternating light and dark strips together so that the dark strips are on the outside of the long set and the light strips are on the outside of the short set (Figure 1). Press all seam allowances toward the dark fabrics, not open as in dressmaking. This is very important.

3. With right sides together and one end matching, place one short strip set on top of one long strip set (Figure 2). Now carefully align the seams. The seam allowance will be pressed in opposite directions, serving as "automatic pins," and all because you pressed the seam allowances toward the dark fabric in the previous step.

Cut three 1½-inch strips across the stacked sets and three more from the remaining section of the long strip. The rotary cutter is again the ideal tool because it cuts through the fabric while that is perfectly flat, leaving little room for distortion.

4. Next, the pairs that were cut facing each other are ready to be seamed on the long edge, using a ¼-inch seam allowance (Figure 3). Press toward the dark corners. Do all three pairs consecutively.

5. Sew one of the additional rows to the opposite side of each unit to make the checkerboard, and press the seam allowances toward the dark corners to complete the Nine Patch square (Figure 4).

6. Repeat Steps 1 through 5, using different fabric combinations until you have created sixty-three Nine Patch units.

Joining the Nine Patch Units to the Alternate Blocks

When you have sixty-three Nine Patch units, you are ready to join them to the alternate fabric blocks. It may seem as if the step of making the blocks was omitted, but a contemporary piecing technique known as "chain piecing" will be used here. This method greatly streamlines the process of joining the patchwork blocks to the alternate blocks. Instead of cutting the alternate blocks first and then sewing them to the patches, you will sew the patches to a long strip of the background fabric and then cut the blocks. What you gain from this approach is perfectly sized squares, because you use the Nine Patch as the cutting line for the alternate fabric block. Check the size of your blocks. They should be 3½ inches. If so, that's great—proceed. If the blocks are slightly larger or smaller but consistent, the quilt will finish larger or smaller, but you will need to make only minor adjustments as you proceed. If your squares are a different size, use that measurement instead of 3½ inches in the next step.

1. To begin the chain piecing process, cut four strips of fabric that measure 3½ inches in width and 43½ inches long or a total of 175 inches in length (see cutting diagram). Place a Nine Patch square right sides together with the background fabric strip and stitch, using the ¼-inch seam allowance, along the length of the background fabric strip.

2. Place a second Nine Patch unit on the fabric directly against

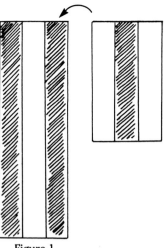

Figure 1

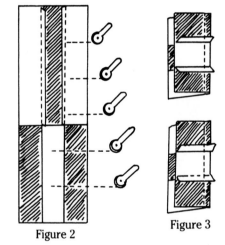

Figure 2

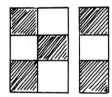

Figure 3

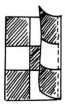

Figure 4

the bottom edge of the first Nine Patch and stitch in the same fashion. Continue placing the Nine Patch squares on the long strips of fabric and stitch them one after another. You will only sew forty-eight of the Nine Patches this way. The remaining Nine Patch squares will be used to complete the diagonal rows. When you have finished piecing, take the sewn pieces to the ironing board and press the seams toward the nonpieced square (Figure 5).

3. Now, using a rotary cutter, ruler, and protective mat, you will cut through the solid fabric strip. First take the opportunity to "square up" your patches. Put a horizontal ruler line on the seam line, center the Nine Patch, and trim one side, if necessary. Repeat on the next side and with each block. You should now have forty-eight patch/block combinations. The Nine Patches and the background squares are already joined and their edges should be even. There is much greater accuracy in this method than if you were to cut the alternate blocks separately and then stitch them to the Nine Patch units.

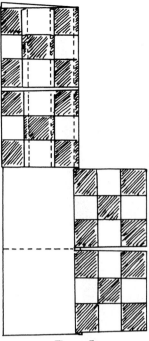

Figure 5

Cutting Layout A—For Background, Corner Triangles (C), Setting Triangles (S)

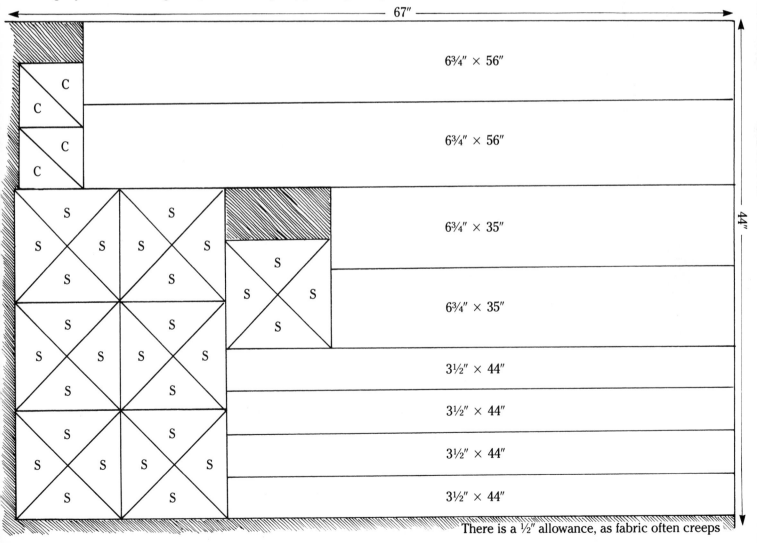

6¾" × 56"

6¾" × 56"

6¾" × 35"

6¾" × 35"

3½" × 44"

3½" × 44"

3½" × 44"

3½" × 44"

67"

44"

There is a ½" allowance, as fabric often creeps

The Diagonal Set Layout

After joining the Nine Patches with the strips of alternate block fabric, and cutting, you can begin laying out the diagonal rows that will make up the quilt. Arrange the forty-eight pairs and the fifteen leftover Nine Patches as diagrammed. I use the floor, as it allows me to stand back and study the arrangement. Much of the antique quilt's charm is due to the random fashion in which the blocks were laid out. To achieve that authentic look, do not overplan the placement of your patches in terms of color or pattern.

Diagonal Set Layout

Making the Setting Triangles

A quilt that is set on the diagonal is almost always more interesting when it's complete. During the layout process, however, surprise triangular spaces are formed on the outside edges. In order to complete the quilt, these spaces need to be filled. Probably your first inclination in making the setting triangles is to take a block the size of the Nine Patch and cut it in half diagonally. This would give you a triangle that would almost fit the space, but the outside (longest) edge of the new triangle would be on the bias. You do not want the outside edge of the quilt top to be on the bias if at all possible. Because of the stretchiness of the bias edge, distortion is more likely to occur.

To eliminate the bias edge, take a larger square measuring at least 9 inches and cut it in half diagonally, then cut the new pieces diagonally again (Figure 6). You will need twenty-eight triangles to complete the rows, so you need to make seven 9-inch squares. The triangles you have just created will fit into the empty spaces of the layout, with outside edges on the straight grain. Do not worry that the triangles seem bigger than necessary, they are "floating" triangles; they will be finished to the correct size later.

Piecing the Diagonal Rows

1. The easiest and least confusing way to join the diagonal rows is to start by joining the patch/block combinations within each row, right sides together.

2. The next step is to sew the setting triangles in the appropriate spaces. Each diagonal row will begin and end with one of the twenty-eight setting triangles. (The four triangles that make up the four corners of the quilt will not be added until the border has been attached—refer to step 7.) Line up the right angle of the setting triangle with a corner of the patchwork block so that the hypotenuse (longest edge) will become the outside edge of the quilt. The tips of the triangles will extend beyond the patchwork in both directions (Figure 7). Stitch and press toward the triangles.

3. When the pieces within each diagonal row have been sewn together, the completed rows can be stitched one to another following your layout pattern. Begin in the upper left corner with the single Nine Patch in row 1 and, with right sides of fabric together, sew it to row 2 (Figure 8). Row 3 is then joined to row 2, and so on until all the diagonal rows have been sewn together (Figure 9).

NOTE: When joining the rows, the extending tips of the triangles will need to be sewn one over the other, thus creating the effect of floating triangles. Press all seam allowances back. Trim off the stitched triangle tips and excess seam allowances before placing the quilt top over the batting and backing fabrics.

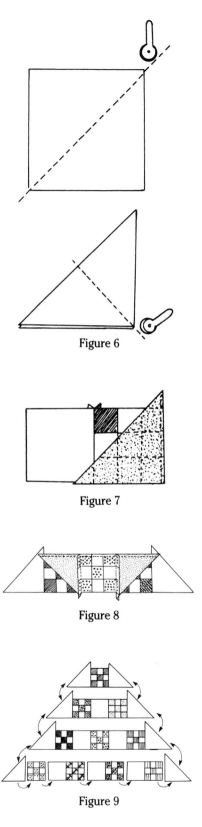

Figure 6

Figure 7

Figure 8

Figure 9

Hand Quilting or Machine Quilting?

If you are going to hand quilt, you will want to complete the borders before quilting. The quilt shown was quilted entirely by machine. If you want to follow that procedure, you are now ready to place the quilt top onto the batting and backing fabrics. The borders are added with the "quilt-as-you-sew" method. The machine quilting is done in the ditch. In other words, you will machine stitch over the existing seams between the squares.

Some people go "No, no!" at the idea of machine quilting. A few years ago, I might not have accepted machine quilting as true quilting, either. It is, of course. Now I am more realistic, especially in budgeting my time. It is more important for me to complete a project than to wait until I have time to hand quilt. In the case of a baby quilt, it is much more practical and really more substantially prepares the quilt for washing. The real proof is in looking at the quilt. If you would be delighted to hear someone say, "It's yours!", you should try machine quilting. It is not really easier, but it is much faster.

I am also doing many quilts where I combine hand and machine quilting. Generally, I quilt in the ditch by machine and save my hand quilting for the background squares where I can be more creative. Most people don't even notice the machine quilting.

Preparing the Backing Fabric for Quilting

Cut two pieces 29 inches by 48 inches (see cutting layout B). Seam them together to make one piece 48 inches by 57½ inches. Press the seam open.

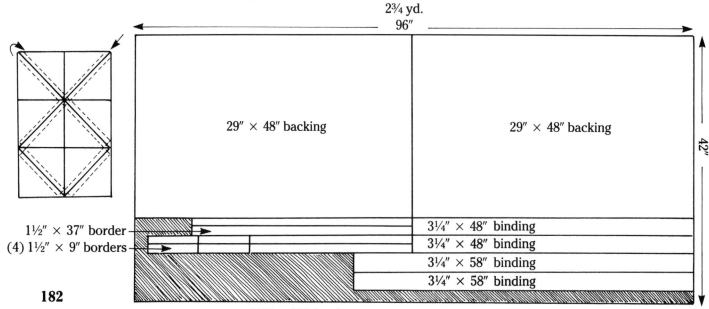

2¾ yd.
96"

29" × 48" backing   29" × 48" backing

42"

1½" × 37" border
(4) 1½" × 9" borders

3¼" × 48" binding
3¼" × 48" binding
3¼" × 58" binding
3¼" × 58" binding

182

1½" × 28" border

Cutting Layout B—For Backing, Border, and Binding

Selecting and Preparing the Batting for Quilting

If you will be doing machine quilting, select a medium-weight bonded polyester quilt batt that retains a medium loft. This is also the batting I generally use for hand quilting and the one I recommend for beginners. It holds its loft and does not demand as much hand quilting to look puffy. It is easy to quilt an average 8 to 10 stitches per inch on this kind of batting. Some hand quilters who are seeking a smaller stitch prefer a thinner batting, but I think thin batts require much more quilting to look good.

1. Lay the backing fabric face-down on a large flat surface, with the center seam crosswise. Place the batting on the backing fabric. Center the quilt top over the two layers. At this point, the batting and backing will extend approximately 6½ to 7 inches beyond the quilt top on all sides.

2. Pin or baste in place. I recommend using rustproof safety pins to secure the quilt top to the batting and backing. (Hint: Don't do this on good furniture. An old beat-up table is perfect for the job.) It is very important to keep the fabrics taut while pinning to avoid lumps and bumps between the layers. Begin by pinning near the center of the quilt top. Pin outward in one direction toward an edge. Return to the center and continue pinning in another direction. Check regularly to ensure that the fabric remains taut.

3. When you have completed pinning in all directions, you will machine quilt across the quilt top and around the edges, following the existing seam lines before adding the borders.

To handle the quilt more easily, roll it up to handle the bulk, unrolling it as you go to expose only the part that is being quilted. With this quilt, you will actually roll diagonally, in order to follow the existing seam lines (Figure 10). In addition to quilting in the ditch between blocks, this quilt was machine quilted in straight lines that were developed by continuing the lines of the Nine Patch seams.

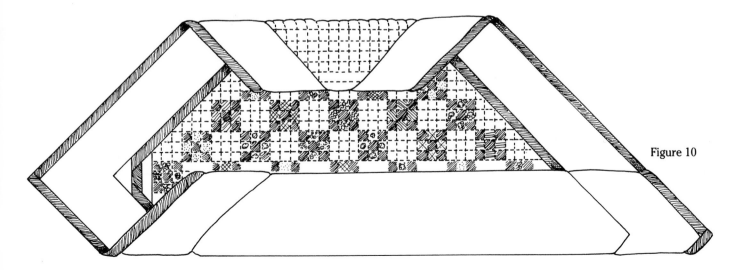

Figure 10

It is advantageous to machine quilt around the edge of the quilt before adding borders so that your edge seams can be hidden under the border fabric. Use invisible thread for the quilt top and thread that matches your backing fabric in the bobbin. Machine quilt in the ditch of the seams. Trim away all threads. I like to trim them as I go so that they don't get sewn into other rows. It is easy to do while checking the back for puckers or other irregularities.

Adding the Borders and Corner Triangles (Quilt-as-You-Sew)

The larger setting triangles have developed a space in the quilt that looks like a narrow border that matches the alternating blocks. That visual border is complete everywhere but at the four corners.

Figure 11

1. To make the matching corner border strips, cut four strips measuring 1½ inches wide by 9 inches long from the background fabric. Cut four strips the same width and 7 inches long for the corner contrasting border pieces. These corner strips give the border its octagonal shape.

2. When sewing the strips to the quilt top, place right sides together. Use a straight line in the quilt pattern to position the edge of the border. This should give you a straighter seam. When stitching, you will be sewing through four layers: quilt border, quilt top, quilt batting, and quilt backing. (See **Stitch-and-flip technique** in the "Fabric Craft Basics" chapter.) After joining the border pieces, press the seam back very lightly and trim any excess fabric at the ends.

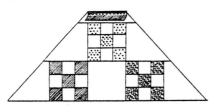

Figure 12

Add the matching border corner strips first (Figure 11). Repeat for the contrasting border corners (Figure 12). Make sure these pieces cover the edges of the border strips already joined to the quilt top.

3. After the short corner strips are complete, add the contrasting borders (Figure 13). Press each seam lightly and trim away any excess fabric.

4. An unusual touch for a quilt top is the corner triangle design. These triangles are cut from the same fabric as the background squares. You will need two 5⅛-inch squares of fabric. Cut each square in half diagonally to form the four corner triangles. In this case, you *want* the longer edge of the triangle to be on the bias. It will be inside and the other two sides (those on the lengthwise and crosswise grain) will be on the outside edge.

Figure 13

With right sides together, sew the corner triangles to the quilt top and inner border (Figure 14), sewing through all layers. Trim away any excess. This should square off the quilt top.

5. The outside borders are cut from the same fabric as the background squares. (See cutting layout B.) The cut width of these border strips should not exceed 6¾ inches. (This will finish to be 6¼ inches, some of which will be covered by the binding.) The short border pieces are attached first in the same "quilt-as-you-sew" manner as the

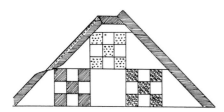

Figure 14

narrow contrasting border pieces. First add the top and bottom, then the remaining two sides. The end result is that the long edge pieces overlap the other two border pieces for a blunt corner finish.

Marking the Border for Quilting

The border quilting design is ideal for continuous quilting, either by hand or machine. The easiest way to mark the borders is to line up the X pattern along every other Nine Patch (see the layout diagram on page 182) and then connect the legs with straight lines. For the corners, just extend the straight lines until they meet.

For machine quilting, keep the quilt rolled, exposing only one border at a time. Be sure to check your bobbin thread before beginning—you don't want to have to stop and rewind your bobbin in the middle of this.

Binding the Edges

See "Fabric Craft Basics" for instructions on binding the edges.

This quilt turned out a slightly awkward width—47 inches—which means you either have to piece a backing or buy 60-inch-wide goods for the backing. This backing was, in fact, made larger and this quilt was actually finished by bringing the backing fabric around and binding the edge, even though if you read the "Fabric Craft Basics" chapter, you know that binding from the back is not my favorite way to finish a quilt.

Whether you are adding a separate binding or bringing it around from the back, the quilt would not look right if the binding did not match the small border. If you don't have enough fabric to make the back and the little border, or if you just prefer to do it this way, you can cut a separate French fold binding. The width would be 4¾ inches.

As described in the "Fabric Craft Basics" chapter, the binding is finished by hand. If you want to finish by machine, add binding to the back, then bring it forward and topstitch by machine. A machine hemming stitch with the invisible thread on the top is an option you might want to try. As machines vary on how they make the hemming stitch, another decorative stitch might work best for you.

It's Not Done Until It's Signed

Let's assume that your quilt will be a treasured antique a hundred years from now. We should give our descendants and their quilt historians a boost by always signing and dating our quilts. Most often, this is done on the back, in a corner if you prefer. You can be elaborate and sew on a cross-stitched or embroidered signature, but the simplest method is to sign your name and date using an indelible marking pen or laundry marker on a scrap of prewashed muslin. Add any personal information or inscription that you like. Then hand stitch the muslin to the back of the quilt.

SMALL NINE PATCH PATTERN PIECE

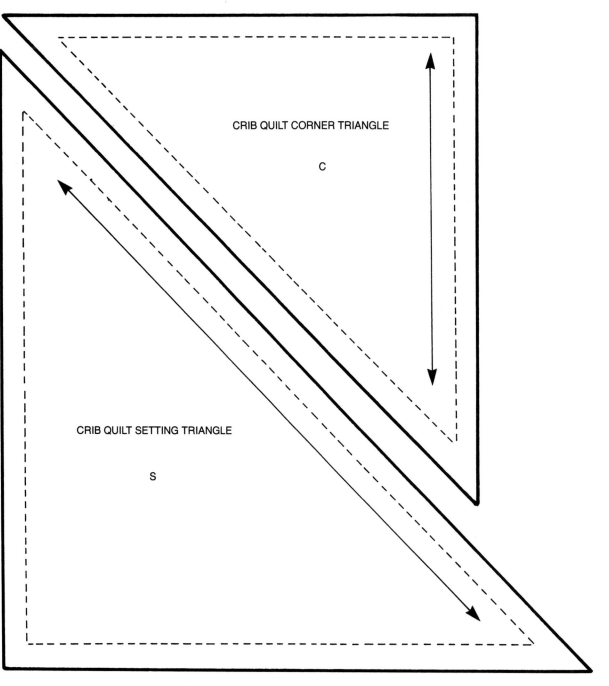

CRIB QUILT CORNER TRIANGLE

C

CRIB QUILT SETTING TRIANGLE

S

MACHINE QUILTING PATTERN FOR BORDER

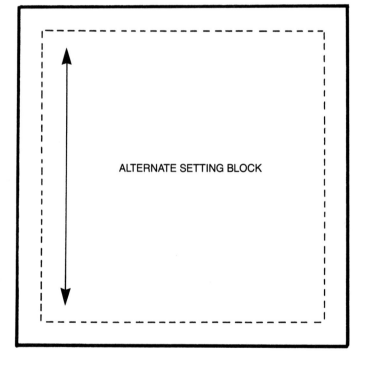

ALTERNATE SETTING BLOCK

Home for the Holidays

For many people, decorating for Christmas is the biggest, most important project of the year. Sometimes it is fun to do a theme Christmas in which all or many of the decorations follow through in one color or design theme. Country Christmas decorating usually features the collected treasures of many Christmas seasons.

In several places I have said it is your fabric selection that makes the greatest statement or tells the story when working with fabric crafts. That is probably most obvious with Christmas crafts. Let's look again at projects throughout the book, but with an eye for Christmas.

Any of the patchwork items can be done in red and green. Add a border to the Ohio Star Doll Quilt for great Christmas place mats. Seem like too much work? Fuse the patchwork instead of sewing. Several designs in the book can be interpreted as garlands for the mantel, stairway, or tree. Ornaments for the tree could include the Cascading Mittens, string quilted or plain hearts from the Hearts, Hearts, and More Hearts projects, even the Prairie Doll. In this chapter we introduce stuffed bows and fabric strip crafts to help fabricate new Christmas treasures, then revisit the bears and rabbits and dress them properly for Christmas.

SIMPLE FABRIC STRIP CRAFTS

Before you can make fabric strip crafts, you need to make fabric strips. It sounds simple, but there are a few helpful hints to follow:

- **Straight-grain strips** can be torn or cut either with scissors or with a rotary cutter. Torn strips have more character because of the irregular feathery edges, but tearing also tends to pull and distort the fabric. Test the fabric you are planning on using. Torn strips usually need to be pressed before using. That means the time you save tearing is used pressing. Straight-grain strips are the only ones that can be raveled effectively.

- **Bias strips** must be cut. It is best to have bias strips when you are wrapping round items with them and the strips need to mold or stretch accordingly—or any other time you need flexibility. Bias strips will not fray or ravel, which is both positive and negative.

How much fabric? The only items listed with each project under Materials and Notions are notions and those fabrics that require more than ¼ yard to make as shown.

Making Continuous Bias Strips

There is a well-published method of marking and cutting continuous bias with scissors. It is being shown here with a new variation that takes advantage of the rotary cutter.

Making the Parallelogram

Making the continuous bias strip always seems easier to me when I start with a square.

1. Cut the square in half diagonally (Figure 1) and lay one pair of the original opposite straight sides so they are right side up and side by side (Figure 2). This is the position they will be in after seaming.

2. Lift A and put it right side down on B as shown in Figure 3. Stitch as shown. Press the seam open to eliminate bulk in the bias strips.

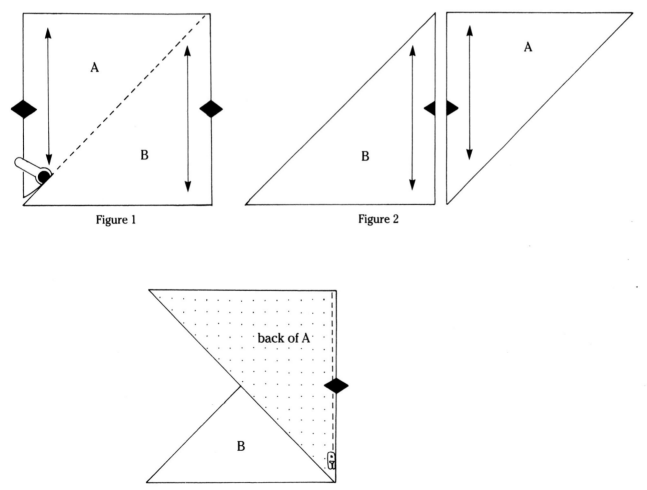

Figure 1

Figure 2

Figure 3

189

Marking and Cutting the Bias

1. *For the scissor method,* use a marker to draw lines parallel to the diagonal edge and equal to the desired bias width. Mark the entire piece of fabric.

For the rotary cutter method, mark only the first two rows. You need to cut this while it is flat, but you don't want to cut all the way across. Stop at least 1 inch from both edges. Cut all rows this way, including the two you marked.

2. Lift the bottom edge and line up the second marked line on the bottom with the first marked line on the top (Figure 4). To prevent movement while stitching, pin the edges. The marked lines will be going in opposite directions. Make sure they cross at a point as far from the edge as your seam.

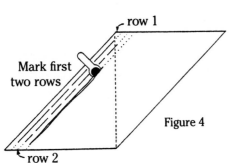
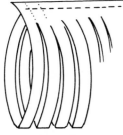

Figure 4

The method is the same for scissors and rotary cutter, except when you pick up the bottom edge of the rotary-cut piece, you have strips dangling and begging to tangle (Figure 5). Handle this piece carefully. Stitch the pinned edges together.

3. For both methods you now need to cut with scissors. Start cutting at the point where the first two marked ends were seamed. If you are using the traditional scissor method, you will be cutting around and around in one huge spiral.

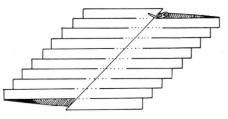

Figure 5

With the rotary cutter method, you just have to cut straight from the end of the first cut across the seam to the start of the second cut (Figure 6). Let it fall away so it doesn't get caught in the scissors. The first cut is the only one marked on both sides. From there on, you will have to eyeball. If the bias is not cutting straight along the edge, stop and redo the seam.

How Much Fabric Yields How Much Bias?

The answer to that question is a question. How wide is the bias? A 12-inch square yields approximately 4½ yards of ¾-inch-wide bias. An 18-inch square yields 9½ yards of the same width or about 13½ yards of ½-inch width.

With a little math, you can get a good idea.

1. Measure the diagonal of the square.

2. Calculate how many marks or cuts you will get across the pieced fabric (roughly the same as when it is square—that is, you can cut eighteen 1-inch strips from an 18-inch square and roughly the same from the resulting parallelogram).

3. Multiply the length of the diagonal by the number of strips.

Figure 6

FABRIC STRING BALLS

You'll especially appreciate the rotary cutter continuous method of cutting bias if you decide to make scrap balls, sometimes called string balls. These look like the delightful rolls of long strips of fabric sometimes spotted in antiques stores. My understanding is that they were prepared in anticipation of braiding projects, which would explain why wool is often found in this form. At any rate, they look great heaped in an old wooden bowl or basket. Make them in Christmas colors and mix shiny Christmas tree balls in the same bowl. There's nothing to making them. You do the cutting and let the children do the wrapping for family fun.

It is easier to make neat and orderly string balls if you start with foam ball centers. My favorite way is to use bias-cut strips and foam balls about the same size as the desired finished ball. Completely wrap the ball so it is covered twice. It will look fairly smooth and not quite real. Now take the covered ball and squeeze it to compress the foam. This makes the fabric just a little loose and more realistic, without being messy.

Alternate methods are to use torn strips and no foam balls. The torn edge is nice, but without the bias, the strips don't wrap as neatly. Without the foam ball base, it takes a lot of strips to make a ball. You can substitute a firm wad of polyester fiberfill as a center to wrap around, but it will be much less stable.

You'll see bias-wrapped foam balls as angel heads in this chapter. Another way to use fabric-wrapped foam balls is to incorporate the small wrapped foam balls into fabric necklaces or earrings. Typically, the smaller the ball, the narrower the bias strip should be.

SPOOL AND BALL AND HEART NECKLACE

This cute necklace is ideal for the creative sewer. Thread little wooden spools, alternating with fabric-wrapped foam balls on both sides of soft hearts chosen from the selection in the "Things That Look Great on Hooks and Pegs" chapter. Use two lengths of six-strand embroidery thread and a sharp-pointed, large-eyed needle to string the necklace. The two lengths give extra strength and also allow you to use a button to tie off the necklace after the last spool and before you begin knotting the floss every three to four inches.

The bottom heart is stuffed very lightly. When the next heart is appliquéd on, stitch through to the back to create extra dimension.

LARGE HEART FOR NECKLACE WITH SPOOLS

MEDIUM HEART FOR NECKLACE WITH SPOOLS

SMALL HEART FOR NECKLACE WITH SPOOLS

LARGE HEART NECKLACE

SMALL CENTER HEART

SMALLEST HEART

NOTE: The medium heart is the same as No. 5 from Basic Hearts on page 79—the dotted line here is for placement.

Double-Faced Strips

Many of the strips used in projects in this book are double-faced, a miracle we can work with the paper-backed fusibles. Some are stiffened again with fusible heavyweight interfacing.

After tearing and pressing strips, center a strip of paper-backed fusible cut to the desired finished width on the back of the strip. Fray edges until you get to the adhesive area. Then remove the paper backing and press in place on the back of another torn, pressed, frayed strip. The second strip can be matching or contrasting fabric, depending on your preference.

For stiffened strips, like those used in the Fray and Fuse Decorations, fuse a strip of fusible nonwoven craft interfacing to the second strip before completing the double-faced strips.

FRAY AND FUSE DECORATIONS

Fray and fuse strips become great holiday decorations. It is easy to think of them as Christmas tree ornaments, drawing on the memories of red and green construction paper garlands. But remember, garlands are fun for decorating doors and mantels during other holidays. Make these decorations in orange and black for Halloween, red and white for Valentine's Day, and pretty pastels for Easter. In our area, more and more people are decorating Easter trees and all of these ornaments would be appropriate. They are fun for children to help make. Starting with fabrics makes the decorations more permanent and seem more successful.

Most of the decorations are made by cutting different length strips and securing the ends together. The patterns (illustrations) included allow you to make the decorations two ways. Start with double-sided fray and fuse strips approximately ⅞ inch wide. Either cut to the measurements given and assemble matching and gluing strip ends, or just lay the edge of the strip on the drawing and cut at the end of the line. Designs shown include the simple old-fashioned garland, multiple

loop garlands, loops, hearts, combination garlands, etc. Figures 1, 2, and 3 illustrate how to weave the old-fashioned braided/woven Jack-in-the-box.

SPOOL AND BALL GARLAND

Remember the Spool and Ball and Heart Necklace? Redo it longer and in Christmas colors for the perfect Christmas tree garland. You could run it continuously, but my favorite way to make garlands is by alternating objects and spaces. Assemble four to six spool and ball pieces, then knot the perle cotton or twine mounting string every 3 to 4 inches for an equal amount of space, possibly incorporating some buttons or even a little stuffed heart.

PAPER DOLLS GARLAND

The Paper Doll Chain girls are perfect as a Christmas garland. Just cut them from double-faced fabric (fuse two layers wrong sides together, add a layer of interfacing for stiffer dolls), and connect sets of three dolls with an equal amount of twine.

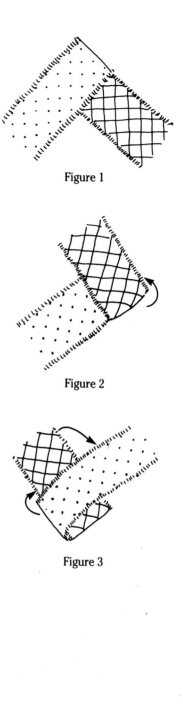

Figure 1

Figure 2

Figure 3

195

FRAY AND FUSE GARLANDS

The traditional single-loop garland shown in the photograph of garlands was made with double-faced strips approximately ⅞ inch wide and 6 inches long. Overlap the ends of one strip and glue. Put a second strip through the first ring before gluing closed. Make the garland as long as desired.

In addition to the traditional single-loop chain garland, many of the single ornaments combine beautifully to make garlands.

SMALL STRIP ANGEL

Using one fabric only—e.g., muslin—1 yard yields four to five angels.

Making the Angel Parts

1. Tear thirty fabric strips measuring ⅝ inch by 10 inches. (Tear ⅝-inch-wide strips and cut into 10-inch lengths.) Ravel a few threads off each side and press the strips. Cut a ⅜- by 24-inch bias strip of muslin to wrap the angel head.

2. To make the head, wrap the foam ball mummy style. Put a dab of glue on the foam ball and start wrapping the bias strip tightly around the ball. Pull slightly as you go, and overlap edges of strip as you rotate the wrapping. Add glue as needed to hold in place and at the end of the strip. Lay aside to dry.

Putting the Parts Together

1. Take twenty-five strips and lay them crisscross and slightly fanned. These will become the angel's body.

2. Place the other five strips with a pipe cleaner in the middle of them across the center of the body group. These will become the angel's arms.

3. With a needle and thread that matches the head color, stitch all layers together at the center several times, stitching around the pipe cleaner to hold it in position (see the diagram here).

4. Without cutting the thread, take the same needle through the center of the foam ball and out the opposite side. Reinsert the needle about ⅛ inch away from the thread and go back through the "head" and the body strips. Secure the thread.

5. Pull body strips away from the head. About 1 inch from the head, tie all strips together to make a waistline. Tie with a smaller strip of torn fabric, ribbon, or twine. Position strips as desired, to get a pleasing affect.

6. The arms are made of strips of fabric shaped with pipe cleaners. Determine the desired arm length—average is 6 to 6½ inches total, but

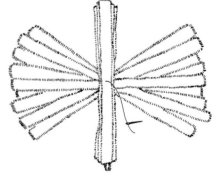

FINISHED SIZE:
Approximately 6½ inches tall

MATERIALS NEEDED:
1-inch foam ball
One pipe cleaner
Twine or tinsel for halo
Glue
Batting for wings

the length may vary if the arms are to be posed holding harps, hymn books, or other items. With small strips of fabric or narrow ribbon, tie the wrists about ½ inch from the end. Cut off excess pipe cleaner and strips. The ½ inch that extends will make a hand. Pull off a few threads at the cut end to give the same frayed edge to the fabric.

7. Make the halo very simply by gluing a circle of twine on top of the head. For a slightly more festive look, twist twine and gold tinsel stems (find them in craft stores next to wired chenille and pipe cleaners). The wire helps hold the halo in position.

8. Make wings following instructions for the Angel Bear on page 209, and attach at center back.

BLUE ANGELS DOOR WREATH

A nice variation of the muslin angels is the Blue Angels Door Wreath, a perfect example of adapting to a color-scheme-decorated Christmas. (See the photo on page 200.)

LARGE STRIP ANGEL

This angel, used as a tree topper, will be ideal for your country Christmas tree, but it could also be centered in a wreath or made over a foam cone as a table or mantel centerpiece.

1. Cut and tear fabric strips the same as for the small angel, except use these quantities and sizes.

Ten strips—1 inch by 24 inches
Ten strips—1 inch by 22 inches
Twenty-five strips—1 inch by 20 inches
     (reserve ten for the arms)
Bias strip for the head—½ inch by 43
     inches

The staggered strip lengths allow a more flowing skirt for a treetop angel. When laying strips out, stack the shortest on the bottom (they will end up on the outside of the body), then the medium strips, and then the long.

2. After the body is made, you may still want to stagger and shape the length of the strips.

3. The core in the angel shown was a straight-sided hard core that had come with kite string (the string of choice for ruffle making by zigzagging over string). It is ¾ inch across and 4 inches long. A toilet paper core is generally the right shape and length but too wide and soft. Make your own core, if necessary, by rolling cardboard to the correct dimension, then taping. The core is hidden in the middle of the strips before the waistline is tied. It will extend into the skirt also.

4. Make wings from the pattern given, following the directions given with the Bear Angel wings later in this chapter.

> **FINISHED SIZE:**
> **14½ inches tall**
>
> **MATERIALS NEEDED:**
> **⅝ yard of fabric per angel**
> **1½-inch foam ball**
> **Center core (see copy)**
> **Glue**
> **Batting for wings**
> **Twine and/or tinsel**

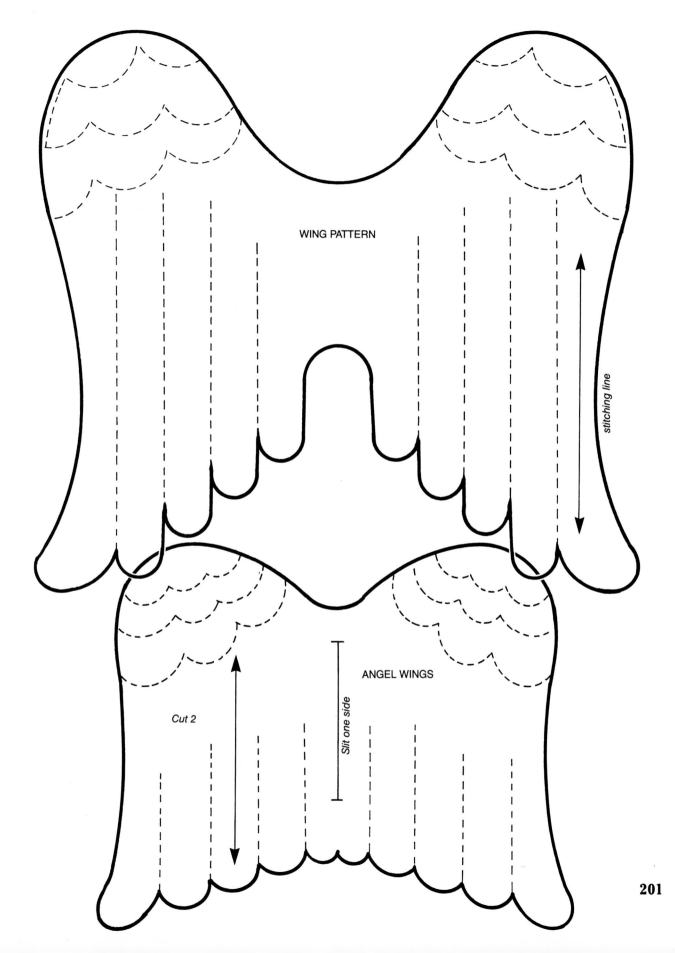

WING PATTERN

stitching line

ANGEL WINGS

Cut 2

Slit one side

STUFFED BOWS

Being able to tie your shoes is no guarantee that you can make pretty bows. However, because you can sew, you may never worry again about tying bows. Instead, make these permanently perky stuffed bows.

SMALLER SET OF THREE

These small bows can make fun jewelry pieces. Use them in necklaces or as pins, hair accessories, or shoe bows. They are also great Christmas tree ornaments, bows for small stuffed toys, or package toppers. The instructions are the same for each of the three sizes.

Making the Bow

1. Fold the square in half and seam along the long edge, leaving the seam open between the dots. Roll the fabric so that the seam is in the center back of the tube, then flatten. Sew across the ends.
2. Clip the corners and turn through the center opening. Stuff the ends lightly. Do not stuff in the middle of the rectangle.

Making the Streamer

1. Position two cut streamers right sides together. Starting about ¾ inch from the center of one edge, sew around the entire piece, stopping about ¾ inch from the center.
2. Clip at corners and angles. Turn through the openings and press. Stuff the ends of the streamers very lightly. Do not stuff the center.

Combining the Bow and Streamer

Squeeze the bow *very* tightly in the center and tie with a strong thread. Loop the middle of the streamer around the front of the bow, and tie in the back. The smaller the bow, the more it seems it simply won't tie at this point, but keep trying.

An alternate way is to tie the streamer loosely, then pull the bow section through the loop created, and then tighten.

LARGER PUFFY BOWS

This design is also given in three sizes. It can be made plain, but I prefer the heart knot option. This style bow is great for holiday wreaths, garland loops, or trim on balloon shades or tie-back curtains. The instructions are the same for all three sizes.

Making the Bow Section

1. Place two bow pieces right sides together, folded as cut. Stitch along the edge opposite the fold, leaving approximately 2½ inches unstitched in the center of the edge. With right sides still together, position the seam so that it is now in the center back and the two ends are open. Stitch across both ends.

2. Trim the corners. Turn through the center back opening and press.

3. Stuff through the center opening. Stuff both ends of the bow medium full. Do not stuff the center, where the streamers will tie.

Usually the bows are stuffed with polyester filling. If for some reason you need a very light bow, the crisp nylon net (not the soft nylon tulle) makes an effective and very lightweight stuffing. How much would you need? For the bow, a piece as wide as the bow and the full 72-inch width of the nylon net would be cut and crumpled and put in each half of the bow.

Making the Streamers

1. Cut two pieces of the streamer pattern. Put the right sides together. Stitch ¼ inch from the outside edge, leaving a 2½-inch opening along the center of one long side.

2. Clip the corners of the points and clip into the seam allowance at the center of the points. Turn inside out through the opening and press.

3. Stuff both ends of the streamers medium full. Leave the center unstuffed for about 2½ to 3½ inches.

4. Wrap the center of the streamer around the center of the bow. Squeeze tightly to make a mock knot. Tie a strong thread around the streamers to secure the knot. A plastic twist tie used on plastic bags will also work nicely. As the knot "puffs," it will hide the thread or twist tie. If necessary, pull gently on the streamer fabric above the secured area to puff the fabric artificially and cover the thread or plastic.

Heart Variation

1. Cut two fabric pieces of the matching size heart. Use the rough line-and-turn method, as the heart back will be against the bow.

2. Stuff lightly, whipstitch shut if desired, and baste in place on the bow.

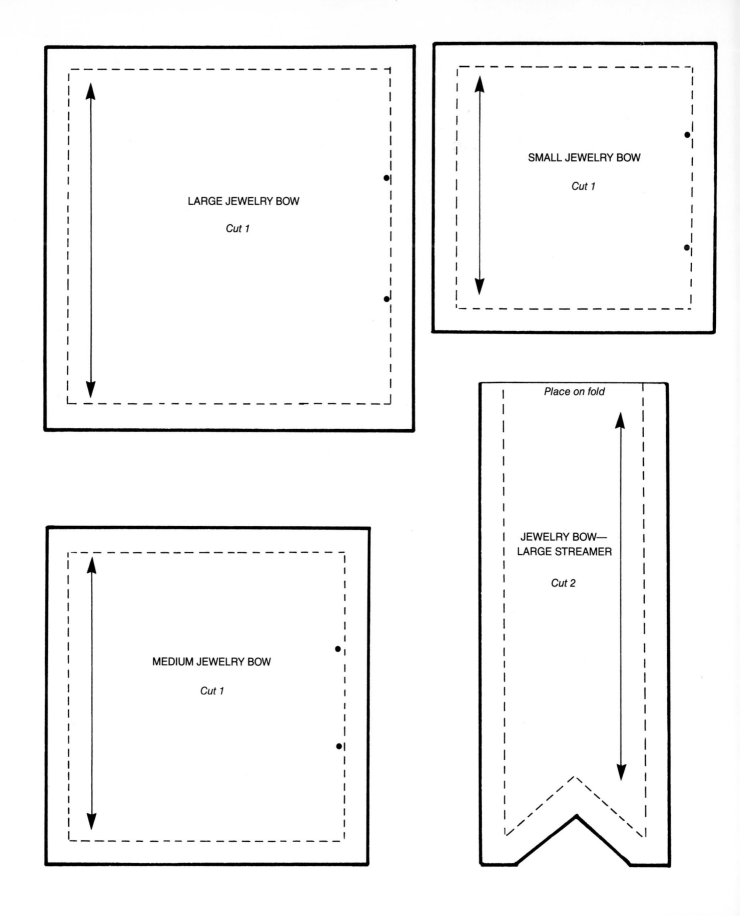

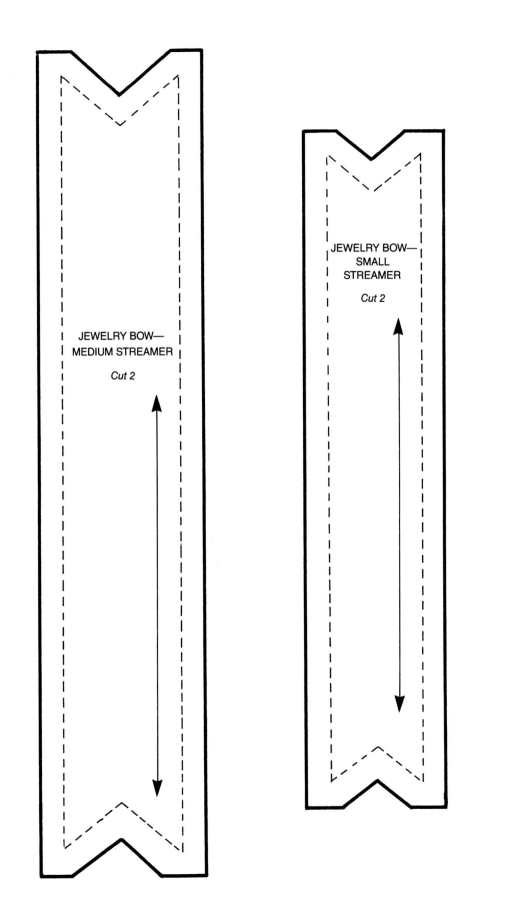

JEWELRY BOW—
MEDIUM STREAMER

Cut 2

JEWELRY BOW—
SMALL
STREAMER

Cut 2

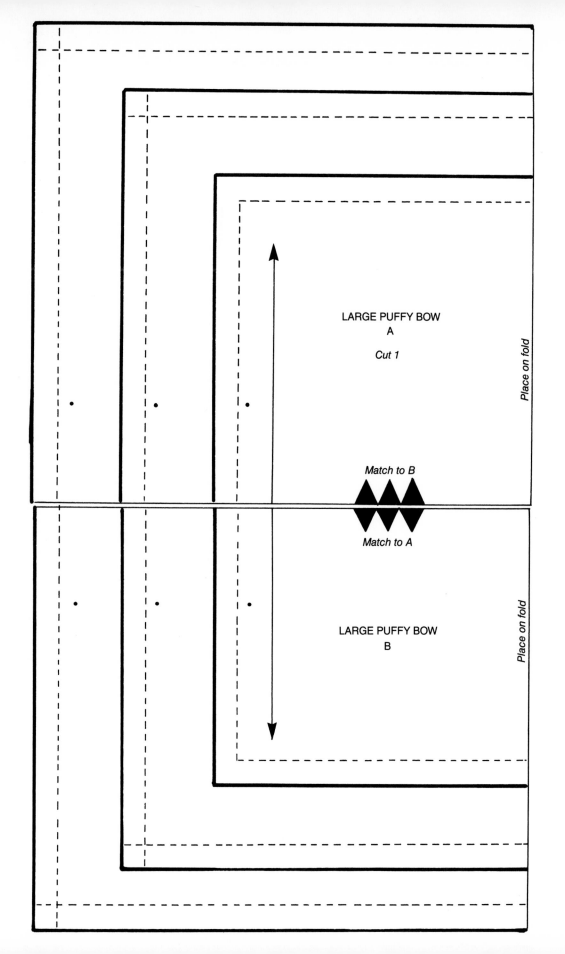

LARGE PUFFY BOW
A

Cut 1

Match to B

Match to A

LARGE PUFFY BOW
B

Place on fold

Place on fold

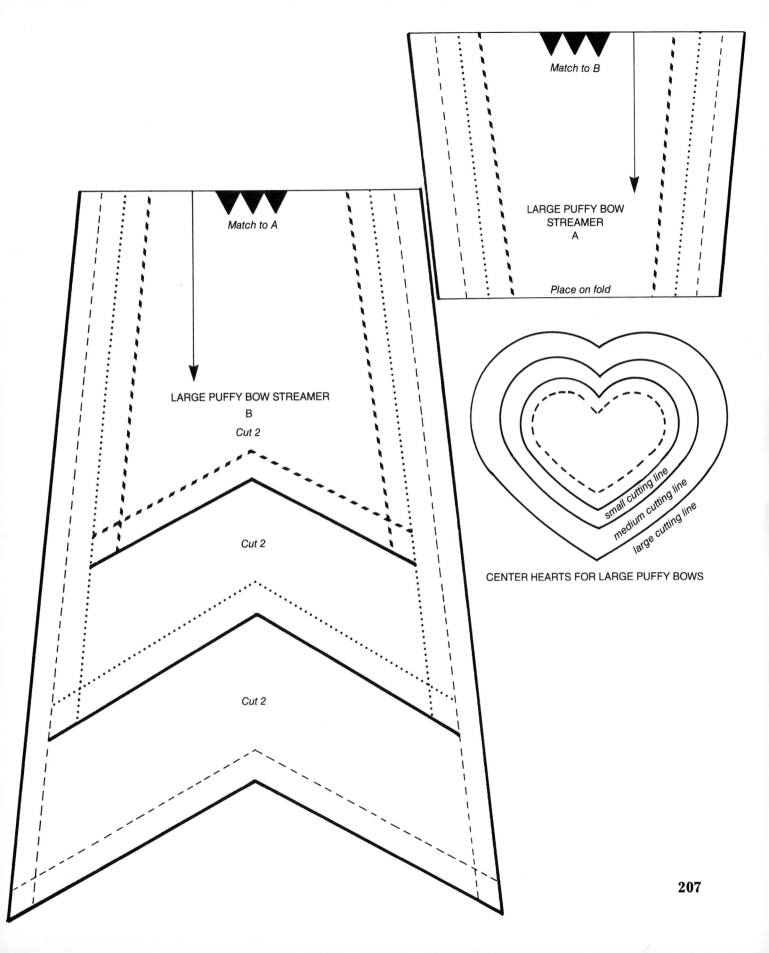

Match to B

LARGE PUFFY BOW
STREAMER
A

Place on fold

Match to A

LARGE PUFFY BOW STREAMER
B
Cut 2

Cut 2

Cut 2

small cutting line
medium cutting line
large cutting line

CENTER HEARTS FOR LARGE PUFFY BOWS

207

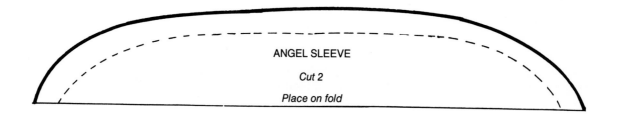

ANGEL SLEEVE

Cut 2

Place on fold

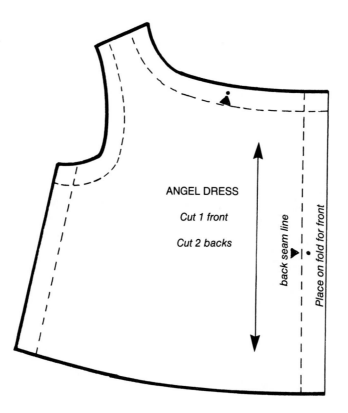

ANGEL DRESS

Cut 1 front

Cut 2 backs

back seam line

Place on fold for front

CHRISTMAS BEARS—AND A FROG

You have already been introduced to the Bear Family. Here they play different roles for Christmas. All outfits are made for the medium-size bear. (See Bear body patterns, page 151, and review pages 150 to 153 for general construction methods.)

ANGEL

This dress has different pattern pieces (page 208) but uses the same construction methods as the little girl's dress (see page 162).

The wing is made in the faux felt method. Make the cut to turn the wing right side out as shown on the pattern. It will be hidden when the wing is attached to the dress. Thinly stuff the wing to give it a little body. Sew the vertical cut closed. Machine or hand quilt the feather design. Stitch the dress to the center of the wing along the center back seam and up one side of the opening (see diagram).

To enhance your holiday angel bear, you might do the wing quilting in gold or silver thread and put a row of gold or silver French knots down the dress front.

Make a halo with the pipe cleaner, leaving the straight end long enough to attach to the back of the head or body.

NOTIONS:
Snap
White pipe cleaner

FROG ANGEL

Who or what is this Frog Angel?

Frogs, unlike bears and rabbits, aren't among the items that most people quickly associate with "country." They are, however, rural, and our frog angel seemed worth sharing. In the process of trying a body pattern variation for the bunny, I decided it wasn't necessary to put in the ears, I just needed to see the body. Wasn't I surprised when it got stuffed and turned out looking like a ridiculous frog! The features were marked in, the bear's angel dress and wings were a perfect fit, and the "frog angel" turned a mistake into a lot of fun. The frog body pattern is included. Use the same construction method as with rabbits, just leave off the ears and tail.

SANTA

Santa has lots of fringe. It is probably easier to make the fringe first for the garments and later for the beard. Tear strips the size shown and fringe in ¼ inch on each side, except for the pompon strip, which should be fringed so that there is only ⅛ inch left in the middle of the strip.

Jacket hem—9½ inches by ¾ inch
Jacket sleeves—6½ inches by ¾ inch
Jacket neck—7½ inches by ¾ inch
Hat Band—7½ inches by ¾ inch
Hat pompon—5 inches by ¾ inch

NOTIONS:
Muslin
Five snaps
8 inches of ⅜-inch black ribbon

Jacket (felt fabric—regular sewing)

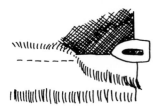

1. With right sides together, sew the two fronts to the back at the shoulder with a ⅛-inch seam. Press the seam open. Using paper-backed fusing product, fuse a front facing to the inside of each front at the center edge. Topstitch close to the edge. This will give the snaps to be positioned there more stability.

2. Cut the sleeve fringe in half crosswise. Fold and press the fringe so that the upper edge leaves about ⅛ inch of the lower fringe exposed. With the jacket laid out flat, open the fringe and place it so the lower fringe extends just beyond the cuff. Sew along the fold line. Press the upper fringe toward the outer edge (see diagram).

3. Use the same technique to attach the jacket neck fringe. Lay the fold line at the upper edge of the jacket with the short side extending off the jacket.

4. Sew the side seams and press open at the bottom.

5. Sew on the hem fringe in the same way as the cuff fringe.

6. You may want to give Santa a little more tummy via extra stuffing. If so, put the jacket on and stuff lightly so the jacket still fits. Place two snaps on the jacket, one at the neck and one at the waistband.

7. Make his belt from an 8-inch piece of ¾-inch black satin ribbon. Turn both raw ends under and fit to the bear. Sew on a snap to fasten the belt in the back.

Leggings (felt fabric—regular sewing)

1. Cut two of the leggings from felt. Cut two small reinforcement pieces from woven fabric, and fuse to the back of the leggings where the snaps will be attached.

2. Fit a legging around either leg so the jacket will cover the top and Santa's boots will cover the bottom. Mark for snap placement on the back of the leg and sew one snap on each legging.

Hat (felt fabric—regular sewing)

1. Cut out the hat and mark the placement of the ear holes. Cut the slits as marked. Fit the ears through the slits by trimming excess felt away in a personalized oval shape, so the hat fits smoothly.

2. Remove the hat from the bear and overlap the straight sides about ⅛ inch and sew together (Figure 1). Fold down the top (about 1 inch) to the side, and tack the point in place.

3. Sew a strip of the ¾-inch fringe on the lower edge of the hat in the same way you sewed on the sleeve cuff (Figure 2).

4. Hand sew a gathering thread down the center of the pompon fringe strip in ⅛-inch stitches. Pull the gathering thread up, spiraling the fringe around five or six times as you pull (Figure 3). Pull tight and take a stitch back through the center of the ball of fringe; knot the thread. (The spiraling is very important to develop a ball shape.) Stitch in place at the tip of the hat. For a good fit, fill the top of the hat with a little stuffing.

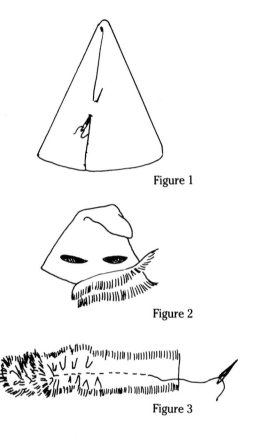

Figure 1

Figure 2

Figure 3

Boot (felt fabric—regular sewing)

Cut four pieces. Stitch each pair together ⅛ inch from the edge the long way around between the dots. Leave the front top open for ease in putting on.

Beard (fringing)

1. The beard is made by attaching five rows of 1¼-inch-wide muslin fringe—4½, 3½, 3¼, 2⅝, and 1⅝ inches long respectively—to the base fabric. These 1¼-inch strips are fringed until there is just over ⅛ inch of fabric left in the center of the strip. Starting at the bottom line on the base fabric, position the shortest row of fringe flat so that the remaining fabric is on the stitching line (see the diagram here). Stitch the fringe in place and fold the upper section down at the seam line

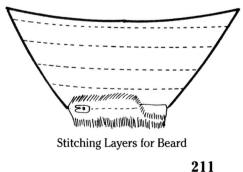

Stitching Layers for Beard

211

and press. Repeat with each row of fringe, working upward. Trim and shape the sides.

2. Center the beard under the bear's nose and pin in place. Curve the ends of the beard up so they cross the head seams just under the edge of the hat. Tack in place.

REINDEER

1. For the collar, measure a 12- by ¼-inch piece of red ribbon and tie it around the bear's neck. Mark two places on each side of the bow, ½ inch apart. Remove the ribbon and sew bells in position on the ribbon. Retie the bow.

2. Add a red pompon for the nose.

3. To make antlers, use black or brown pipe cleaners or small chenille stems. Use the diagram here to position the sections and then stitch in place between the ears. Wrap shorter pieces around the basic **U** shape to create points.

ELF

Apron (felt fabric—regular sewing)

1. Cut out the apron. Press the pocket fold up. Stitch the pockets as indicated on the pattern.

2. Attach straps as with the play apron (see page 159). Trim the center front with green felt holly leaves.

Boots (felt fabric—regular sewing)

Cut four boot shapes from felt. With right sides out, machine stitch each pair around the bottom from one side to the other, stitching a scant ⅛ inch from the edge. Put a tiny bit of stuffing in the point. Sew a little bell on each shoe point.

Hat (felt fabric—regular sewing)

This hat is designed to fit over one ear. Overlap the straight sides slightly and hand sew together into a cone shape. Place the hat over one ear on the bear's head and fold down the top so it fits snugly over the ear. Tack the fold in place. Sew a little bell on the tip of the hat.

NOTIONS:
12 inches of ¼-inch red ribbon or strip of felt
Four small bells
Red pompon
Two black or brown pipe cleaners

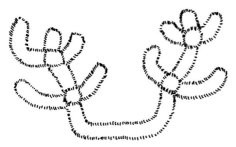

Antler Configuration

NOTIONS:
10 inches of ⅛-inch or ³⁄₁₆-inch ribbon
Three small bells

SANTA RABBIT

While it is nice to have costumes for the animals, the fabric that they are made from also can tell the story. Some of the bear clothes can easily be adjusted for the larger rabbit. It is closest in size to all the middle bear clothes. Look at the pattern markings to see how the Santa outfit was altered to fit the rabbit. Santa's hat pattern shows the slightly different cutting line for the rabbit hat, and the ear holes must be repositioned. The leggings and shoes don't fit, so they are eliminated, but who would deny that this is Santa Rabbit? The bear clothes will not fit the smaller rabbit. None of the shoe patterns will fit.

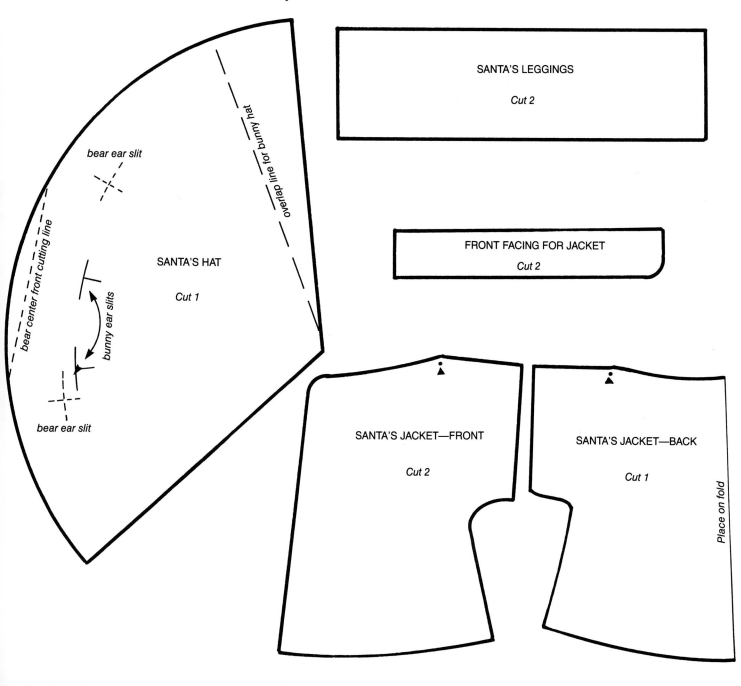

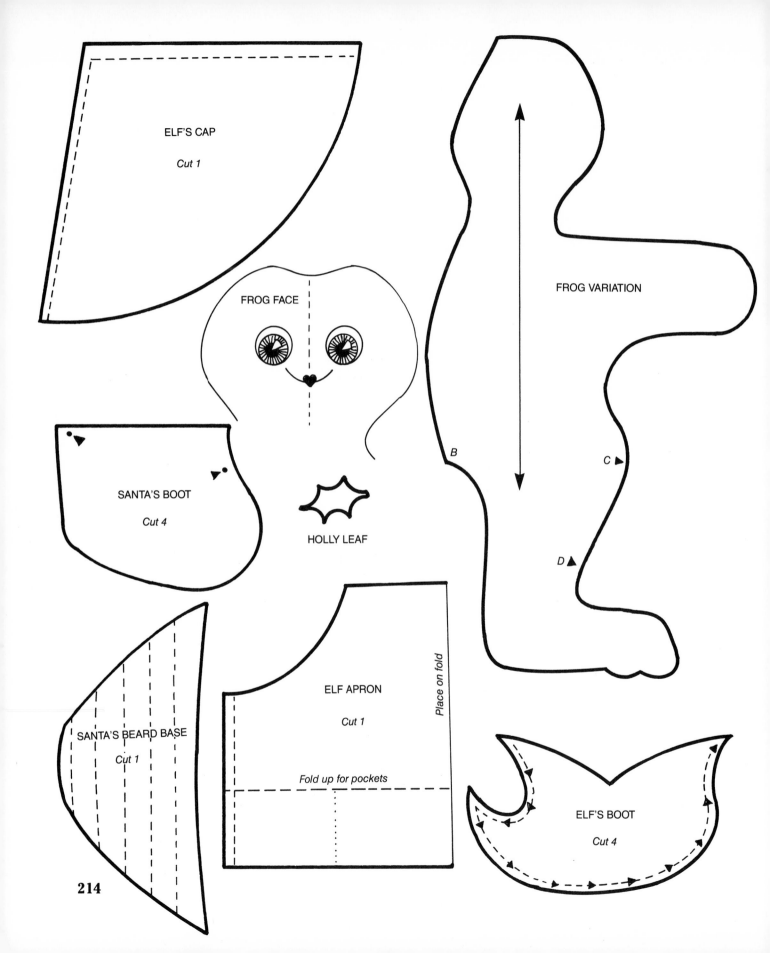

ELF'S CAP

Cut 1

FROG FACE

FROG VARIATION

B

C ▶

D ▲

SANTA'S BOOT

Cut 4

HOLLY LEAF

SANTA'S BEARD BASE

Cut 1

ELF APRON

Cut 1

Place on fold

Fold up for pockets

ELF'S BOOT

Cut 4

214

Index

All of us at Sedgewood® Press are dedicated to offering you, our customer, the best books we can create. We are particularly concerned that all of the instructions for making the projects are clear and accurate. We welcome your comments and would like to hear any suggestions you may have. Please address your correspondence to Customer Service Department, Sedgewood® Press, Meredith Corporation, 750 Third Avenue, New York, NY 10017.

For information on how you can have *Better Homes and Gardens* delivered to your door, write to: Mr. Robert Austin, P.O. Box 4536, Des Moines, IA 50336.